James Murphy

The Shan Van Vocht

the story of the United Irishmen

James Murphy

The Shan Van Vocht
the story of the United Irishmen

ISBN/EAN: 9783744731065

Printed in Europe, USA, Canada, Australia, Japan

Cover: Foto ©ninafisch / pixelio.de

More available books at **www.hansebooks.com**

THE
SHAN VAN VOCHT

A STORY OF THE UNITED IRISHMEN

BY

JAMES MURPHY

AUTHOR OF

"HUGH ROACH THE RIBBONMAN;"
"THE FORGE OF CLOHOGUE;"
ETC.

Dublin
M. H. GILL & SON LTD

Printed and Bound

in Ireland

CONTENTS.

	PAGE
CHAPTER I.—Hallowe'en	1
CHAPTER II.—The Visitor—Helena's Glove	14
CHAPTER III.—Eugene's Dagger	24
CHAPTER IV.—Forebodings ...	27
CHAPTER V.—The Listener ...	32
CHAPTER VI.—A Sudden Resolve ...	40
CHAPTER VII.—News from France ...	42
CHAPTER VIII.—A Hurried Departure	52
CHAPTER IX.—Disaster	57
CHAPTER X.—Condemned as a Spy ...	64
CHAPTER XI.—A Mysterious Warning	67
CHAPTER XII.—Suspense ...	79
CHAPTER XIII.—The Midnight Visit ...	82
CHAPTER XIV.—The Gold Ring ...	87
CHAPTER XV.—Ignominy or Death ...	93
CHAPTER XVI.—La Vengeur—The Sea Fight	99
CHAPTER XVII.—A Strange Meeting	107
CHAPTER XVIII.—In Doubt ...	111
CHAPTER XIX.—Moya's Advice ...	119
CHAPTER XX.—A Night in Old Dublin.	123
CHAPTER XXI.—Redmond's Story ...	130
CHAPTER XXII.—Midnight on the Sea	138
CHAPTER XXIII.—The Cry on the Cliffs	147

CONTENTS.

	PAGE
CHAPTER XXIV.—A Strange Discovery ...	154
CHAPTER XXV.—More Mysteries	161
CHAPTER XXVI.—The Secret Letter ...	169
CHAPTER XXVII.—Midnight Terrors ...	172
CHAPTER XXVIII.—The Sea giving up its Dead	175
CHAPTER XXIX.—The Race begun	178
CHAPTER XXX.—Again a Prisoner ...	182
CHAPTER XXXI.—The Swim for Life	190
CHAPTER XXXII.—The Pursuit	197
CHAPTER XXXIII.—Escaping	202
CHAPTER XXXIV.—In France	215
CHAPTER XXXV.—Citizen Carnot	224
CHAPTER XXXVII.—Vengeance is mine ...	237
CHAPTER XXXVIII.—The French fleet Sails	241
CHAPTER XXXIX.—The Storm	250
CHAPTER XL.—Defeat of the Expedition	255
CHAPTER XLI.—The Cliffs of Lough Swilly	274
CHAPTER XLII.—To Dublin	28
CHAPTER XLIII.—The Wedding Breakfast	289
CHAPTER XLIV.—In the Caves of Donegal	295
CHAPTER XLV.—The Escape ...	303
CHAPTER XLVI.—An Old Story re-told ...	328
CHAPTER XLVII.—The Death of Tone ...	332
CHAPTER XLVIII.—Returned	342
CHAPTER XLIX.—Conclusion	346

THE SHAN VAN VOCHT:
A STORY OF THE UNITED IRISHMEN.

CHAPTER I.
HALLOWE'EN.

THE wind howled around the old manor house with that peculiarly desolate cry the November night winds always assume; and heaped in odd corners, in angles of the house, around bases of trees, and under the door, the fallen leaves.

Similarly it roared up the chimney, carrying with it a shower of sparks whenever a log partly consumed fell from its position into the glowing fire. Now and again, in more than usually stormy bursts, it hurled small, broken branches against the window panes, giving the idea of some huge birds, storm-tossed, pecking at the window for entrance and refuge.

Within, as compared with the outside, however, the contrast was as great as it well could be. A merry group gathered around the large and glowing log-heap that blazed in the capacious fireplace—for the hands that built Seamore mansion in past days had no notion or care for the times when the use of coal would make more restricted fireplaces necessary, and accordingly built it after its present extensive fashion—and were enjoying themselves in pleasant and agreeable mood. Candles, hung in sconces around the wall, threw light on the vast flagged apartment that did duty for kitchen; but they were more or less overshadowed—perhaps I should say over-lighted—by the fire, whose stronger gleams paled their light and made the forms assembled around it throw huge and grotesque shadows on the walls.

Nor was the happy glow of the apartment made less cheerful by the flitches of bacon and ponderous hams that hung over the fireplace, benefiting largely by its smoke; nor the sense of protection and security detracted from by the heavy muskets that lay along the rack, their flint locks every now and then flashing back the light of the fire with a gleam somewhat akin to sternness.

The group that were assembled in the kitchen consisted of the servants of the house and some neighbours of both sexes that had dropped in; for the mansion, whilst splendid in appearance, was ever open, through the kindness of its owners, to the humblest of the surrounding cottiers. Indeed, as there were few of them that at one time or another, more particularly in the busy seasons, had not worked therein, or on the spreading lands surrounding and belonging to the mansion, the kitchen in which they now were was as familiar to them as their own homes.

It was Hallowe'en Eve, which perhaps was the reason why the kitchen had within its walls this night some who very rarely mingled amongst its more habitual frequenters.

In the first place, then—for *place aux dames* is a chivalric maxim always in high honour with us—there was the young mistress of the mansion, Helen Barrington, whose very presence was of itself sufficient to diffuse a sense of cheery happiness around. It would be very difficult to be near her and not feel that there was something bright and happy, as well as beautiful, in her presence. For to a form light and graceful, and a face whose sunny beauty would brighten the darkest sorrow that ever fell on men's hearts, the young hostess added a spirit as gay and joyous as could be expected from the nineteen years that had passed over her head. Indeed the beauty that attracted attention from the most careless eye seemed but the reflex of the happy spirit that dwelt within; and the deep blue of her eyes seemed at times to deepen until it melted into the light of outcoming laughter.

Nor were her accomplishments less than her beauty and light-heartedness, for the ample means which her parents possessed had enabled them to send her to the best schools then to be had in the metropolis. Unfortunately, her father and mother had both died within a few months of each other some three years before; and Helen Barrington was compelled in consequence to return home before her education was quite completed, but not until she had acquired enough of the grace of culture and education to place her above many of the daughters of the surrounding gentry whom she was accustomed to meet in society. Since then she had governed the house for her brother, a young fellow who had been for some two or three years in the army, and who had sold out and come home when the sad occurrence took place.

With Miss Barrington on this evening was, as indeed was her wont on many occasions, her cousin from the county Wexford, Kate Howard, much about the same age —a tall, dark girl, as unlike in her grave and sedate character to the former as well as could be. Although, however, possessing little of the joyous nature of her handsome cousin, there was a great deal in her serious manner that many would perhaps prefer. Without being at all a beauty, her face was attractive, and her manner was so kind and courteous and quietly loveable that few could remain long in her society without finding in it an inexpressible charm. The attractions of society in Dublin, as well as the pleasure of being with her friends, brought her many times from her home in Wexford to Seamore— which latter, we should have stated before, was situate midway between Old Dunleary and Dublin. The name is now lost, and the pleasant grounds that then surrounded the house have long since, under the builder's hands, been covered with stately terraces, but the mansion still remains—much altered and modernised, however. These were the two that, for the nonce, had taken their places among the group gathered around the fire, and listened with interest to the *shanachus* appertaining to Hallowe'en that went around. It was too early, if there were no other reasons, for the usual tricks and charms to be put in force; and meantime gossiping conversation supplied sufficient entertainment.

"And why not, Cauth—what harm would there be in it?" queried Helen Barrington, as the old housekeeper, sitting knitting in the corner, demurred to some proposition that was put forward.

"What harm would there be in it?" repeated Cauth. "Every harm, Miss Helen—every harm. It's dangerous work and ill doing meddling with these things."

"Upon my word, Grannie," said the young lady pleasantly, "I am afraid you intend to throw a shadow on all amusement to-night. What harm can there be in it?"

"If you knew as much as I do, Miss Helen, dear, you would not ask the question," said the old woman, significantly, drawing the hood of her red shawl over her head more cosily, and pursuing her knitting with greater industry.

"Well, Grannie, would you tell us why?" said the young hostess, a little put about as she saw a damper thus thrown over the joyousness of the night, for in the light and brightness of her own heart she loved to see those about her enjoying themselves. "It is not fair to frighten us in this way without reason."

"Without reason, honey! There's plenty of reasons for it, not to go farther than this very house."

"God bless us!" said Helen with some alarm—"in this house! I never heard of anything happening in this house that was strange or wonderful."

"You were too young to know of it, my dear—indeed, now that I remember it, I don't think you were born at the time. I am sure you were not; but it happened all the same."

"What was it, Grannie? Do tell us," said the young girl, as she threw a frightened glance around the vast apartment, and drew her chair nearer to that of her cousin.

"It mightn't be for your good to hear it, honey," said Cauth cautiously, "and it's better for all to take my advice than to ask for the reasons of it."

"You have awakened my curiosity now, Grannie, and I shall think the story worse than it is unless you tell it. I shall never sleep a quiet sleep in the house again unless I hear it."

"Yes, tell it, Cauth—tell it," was echoed around the circle. "It's worse to hint about an' not tell it, and so keep us in suspense about it."

HALLOWE'EN.

"I think it would be better not tell it," said the old knitter hesitatingly, "but as there's nobody here now or in the place that belongs to the story it can't do much harm, even if it don't do good. You all heard of the Morrisses of Knock Grove? There's none of 'em there this many a day, but time was when there wasn't a finer place nor a braver family in Dublin county. It's better nor twenty years—it may be twenty-three—since Rose Morris was here on a visit just as Kate Howard is now, an' for all the world of a Holly Eve night. You'd travel a long way before you could meet a sweeter or a pleasanter girl than she was; and her merry laugh is as fresh in my ears this minit as it was that night—though she is under the clay in Kilbarron graveyard this many a year. Well, nothing would do herself and your aunt—she's dead and gone, too, poor girl!—that night, but to try the trick you were talking of just now; an' so they hung out the threads of flax with gloves at the end from the drawing-room window to see who would come to take them—for whoever did would be their luck. I knew well Rose expected your father's hand, for he was not married then, would be the one to take hers. So they hung them out, and watched and watched, but no one came to take them. After waiting for an hour or two they drew them up quite disappointed, but, *agra machree*! their disappointment gave way to fright when, although they had not seen anyone, nor heard a step near the place, they found Rose's glove gone—gone!"

A chill of fear grew over Helen's susceptible heart, the roses fled from her cheek and she nestled herself still closer to the more composed and less timid form of her cousin.

"*Gone*, my dear. There was no sign of the glove, though they were quite sure there had been no one there. The poor things were terribly frightened; but there was worse in store for them, for when they sat here, just as we do now, all trembling and shuddering, telling what had happened, who opened the door but a sailor dripping with wet—every stitch on him dripping with wet—a rough, bearded man, with the remains of an old cut upon his temple, that showed itself by a long white scar that was terrible to see! He seemed the ghost of a drowned man arisen from the deep; and in a jabbering tongue, that no one could understand, he spoke to us. I'll never forget to my dying hour the fright that kem over us when we saw him enter. We thought it was the Ould Boy that had come among us. And the cry still rings in my ears that poor Rose gave, afore she fainted, when he held up in his hand—two of the fingers of which were cut off—a hand that was black and fearful to look upon—her glove!"

An uncomfortable feeling crept over the group assembled, and each one turned his or her eyes around as if fearful of the unexpected presence of some one in the apartment. More especially was this the case with Helen, whose gentle heart was more readily impressible. But it quickly subsided as Katie Howard. passing her arms around her neck, drew her over to her own chair.

"Her glove, my dear. An' though every one looked upon it as a mere chance, I know better, my dear, an' I knew that *he* was her luck. It is not all tricks that are played on Holly Eve night—and so poor Rose found it."

The old woman paused, as if her mind flew back to the dead and buried past, and as if she forgot that there were anxious hearers listening.

"Well, Cauth, and what else? Who was he anyway? Where did he come from?" asked Luke Mahon, a young fellow in the opposite angle of the fire-place.

"Where did he come from?" reiterated Cauth, as if awakening from her reverie. "He came from the sea, my dear. His vessel was wrecked in a storm out in the bay—it was a night just as wild and stormy as this—and of all the poor souls aboard, he was the only one that reached the shore. The rest went down wid the ship into the deep, deep sea—cannon, and powder, and guns, and muskets an' all; for it was a French man-o'-war, an' he was her captain."

"A Frenchman?"

"A Frenchman. That was why we could not understand what he said"

"Well, an' what happened? What became of him?" asked Luke again, as once more Cauth dropped the threads of her story, and knitted more rapidly those of the stocking now fast hastening to its conclusion.

"Ah! what happened him?" again reiterated the old housekeeper. "We had too much to do wid the fright he threw us all into, and the faint poor Rose fell into, to take heed of him; but when the poor girl was carried up into the parlour, and after some time recovered herself a little, we came back here only to find him lying senseless on the settle yonder. We were all sorry for neglecting him so long; they poured burnt brandy into his mouth and recovered him a little—but he was in brain fever, my dear, an' it was many a week before he recovered and was able to tell who he was and what had happened him. I don't know how it was, but poor Rose was so sorry for him, and compassionated him so much, that she forgot the fright he had given her, and nursed him all through his long illness."

"He recovered, Cauth?"

"He did, my dear. He recovered, sure enough, an' you'd be surprised to see what a brave, handsome fellow he turned out to be when he did. You'd never think it was the same dreadful-looking, half drowned, fainting creature that kem into the kitchen that Holly Eve night, frightening us all with his terrible appearance. Such a pleasant, gay fellow as he turned out to be—an' so handsome, only for that ugly cut across his temples, and the two fingers that were gone from his hand. An', my dear, so polite, an' so winning that when he got to speak our language—an' it wasn't long till he did—he'd coax the birds off the bushes."

"And Rose, Cauth?"

"Ah, my poor Rose! She fell in love with him—he was her luck, as I knew he would be from the minit I saw him, though no one else thought it—an' they wor married. He must have been a high-up man in his own country; for when he was able to go into the city and write to France he had money galore. But he never said much about it."

"Did they live happily, Grannie?" asked Kate Howard, for the first time breaking into the conversation with a question.

"They did, my dear. An' a finer or a handsomer couple you wouldn't see driving in Grafton Street—he with his tall figure and dark, handsome face, save where it was disfigured; an' she the picture of loveliness—for she was a dear, sweet girl—sitting beside him. But it wasn't to last long, my dear; for one day there came a messenger from abroad with a letter, or something like that, for him—an' the next day he was off, promising to be back with herself an' her little boy an' girl in the course of a few months; but he never came back, my dear—he never came back!"

"Never, Grannie?"

"No, never!" There was no word of him ever after—neither tale nor tidings—an' that's twenty long years ago now. Some said he was tried an' shot for the loss of his vessel; some said he was put in jail for not returning to France—but who'd have the heart to do that, my dears, when they knew that there wor soft white arms around him here, stronger to bind him to Ireland nor the biggest cables on board the biggest man-o'-war in France?—an' some said he was made commander of a great fleet an' was killed in a sea fight. Anyway, he never came back."

"And what became of Rose and her children?" asked Helen, the unaccustomed tears welling into her eyes.

"Ah, me! it was so pitiful! Week after week she watched for his coming, but he never came. Month after month she used to stay up at night waiting to hear his knock at the door or the wheels of his carriage grating on the sand, but he never came. Then the war broke out an' there was no chance. The look of handsomeness left her face, and the merry brightness from her eyes, an' she faded and withered away. Two years after he left—an' on a Holly Eve night, too—her sweet face lay white enough and her fretting heart calm enough—for she was dead, dead, her troubles over for ever. Poor girl!"

There was a pause of some duration as the old woman drew her shawl over her head, bent her face downwards to the firelight, and pursued her knitting. There were few of the group assembled unaffected; but the tears, unhidden, trickled down Helen's cheeks, whilst Miss Howard's eyes looked dim as the firelight fell upon them.

Brushing the tears away after a little while, the latter asked:

"And what of the children, Grannie?"

"When his mother died, the little fellow was sent to school to England. A blithe, merry boy he was, with his father's pleasant, frank ways, and his mother's bright blue eyes. He used to come here during the holidays. You might remember him, Helen asthore; but you were too young then, an' so many used to come back and forward that"——

"——I think I do," said Helen quietly. "It's like a dream to me when I was a child to remember a little boy coming here at Christmas times."

"That was he, my dear. It would be hard to forget him; for a more loveable, frank, engaging boy you could hardly set eyes upon. Your father—Lord rest his soul!—was fonder of him, I think, than he was of either yourself or Redmond. It was the pleasant times we used to have when he came here. But the time came when he didn't come. Ah, me! it was the sorrowful house that was here when we heard it."

"What happened him, Grannie?"

"No one knows—no one ever knew—except God. He disappeared from the school one day, an' nor tale nor tidings ever kem of him afterwards. Search was made for him high and low, but he never turned up. Your father went across to England and made search for him everywhere; but he could get no tidings of him. The old luck, my dear—the old luck that kem with the drowning sailor and the glove three-and-twenty years ago!"

"And what became of the girl?" asked Helen Barrington.

"The girl was a delicate child always, and, your father having a cousin an abbess in a convent in the South of France, he took her there after her brother's disappearance. And she remained there since—only once, about twelve months ago, when she came on a visit, as you will remember, Helen."

"You don't mean Alice Trainan, Grannie?" said Helen with astonishment.

"I do, indeed, my dear; she was daughter of the stranger and poor Rose, and sister to the little boy."

"Why, I never heard that before, Grannie," said Helen in great surprise. "I thought Alice was a cousin of ours."

"Your father, having taken the child under his care, and seeing the name she bore so unlucky, resolved on giving her an assumed name. And it was under that name she was always known both at the convent and amongst us here. But her real name was Alice Lefebre. Lefebre was her father's name, though your father often thought and said that too was only an assumed one."

"Well, Grannie, you astonish me. I never thought but that Alice was our cousin."

"So she was, for her mother was a distant cousin."

"Really, Grannie, that surprises me. How little I knew of her history when she was here! What a dear, sweet girl she was! How we used to make her blush at the attentions Trevor Mortimer paid her! And how sorry we were when she went away! Is it not odd we have not heard from her for the past few months? And so she was sister to that little boy."

"Poor child!" said Kate Howard. "What was thought to have happened him, Grannie?"

"The ill-fortune, my dear—the ill-fortune that comes of tempting the future, that comes of Holly Eve tricks. Some said he was drowned; some said he was stolen away to France; others said other things; but I knew, aroon, that it was the luck—the ill-luck. It swept in upon us with the storm and the rain that night long ago, when the door opened and the strange man kem in. That's the raison why, my dear, I'd never like my ould eyes to see any girl calling up her luck, good or bad, from the future, until God chooses to send it."

A pang of dread and remorse passed simultaneously through the hearts of the two girls; for just before coming from the drawingroom they had, from the window overlooking the orchard, passed down two threads of woven flax, with a glove attached to each; and the story the housekeeper had just told them had therefore startled them not a little. They would, moreover, have gone and withdrawn them immediately, but that the eerie feeling that pervaded, without exception, the company around the fire, as the result of the story they had heard, made them unwilling to face the corridors they would have to pass through on their way.

"Anyhow," thought Kate Howard with a sense of relief, "it can come to no harm even if they *are* taken. There is no one to take them but Redmond and Trevor Mortimer, for no one else can come that path; they alone have the key of the orchard."

With this consoling reflection, she gently managed to turn the conversation into cheerier channels, and in a short time the sad thoughts, that filled all present, were banished. It is not easy to retain sorrow in youthful hearts nor gloom on young faces; and under the influence of the blazing fire, and the bright firelight, the laugh soon went round as if such things as sorrow and trouble had no existence.

The wall of the orchard touched the centre of the house at right angles, and about a yard from the latter a small wicket gate opened into it, whilst at the further end of the garden a corresponding one gave egress to the meadow or shrubby land that sloped to the shore.

It was in the days of long ago, when the discoveries of the present times were undreamt of, and when no prophet had ever foretold that a machine running without horses, and with speed as that of the wind, would whirl hundreds of passengers along from Dublin to Old Dunleary. So it was that naught but meadow or whin-covered lands lay between the mansion and the sea.

A hearty burst of laughter, on the part of the company assembled, at some passing joke, was interrupted by the noise of the closing of the afore-mentioned wicket door; a step was heard; and immediately after a hand was laid on the latch.

"It is Redmond and Trevor Mortimer," thought Helen Barrington with a quick palpitation of the heart, for, in spite of her efforts at a repentant state of mind, she yet furtively hoped that the latter would pluck her glove from its pendent flaxen thread. But she was doomed to be disappointed, as a tall handsome fellow of two-and-twenty or thereabouts entered, with a pleasant smile on his face, and advanced towards the group bearing a glove in his hand! About five feet ten in height, broad shouldered, with the healthy hue on his face which plenty of outdoor exercise gives, he advanced with lithe step towards the group gathered in front of the huge fire.

"Well, young ladies," said he pleasantly, holding up the glove in his hand, "I found this suspended from your window as I came along. Whose is it? Of what lady fair and gay am I to be the chosen knight?"

"That's yours, Kate," said Helen in a gratified whisper. As Redmond had taken hers, the inevitable result was that Trevor Mortimer should take her own, and the thought came with a throb of pleasurable anticipation at her heart.

"Whose is it, ladies?" jocularly asked the young fellow again, as the two girls, half ashamed of the old housekeeper and of the manner in which they had sinned against the moral of her story, blushed and remained silent.

"Where did you leave Sir Trevor?" dexterously queried Miss Howard, to distract attention from the embarrassing question.

"Well, if you won't tell—as I see you won't—I must retain the precious souvenir to happier and more communicative times," said Redmond Barrington with a sly laugh, as he placed the glove in his pocket. "Trevor? Well, I left Trevor behind me for a few minutes; he will be here presently. Meanwhile," said he, as he drew a chair over in front of the roaring fire and beside the two girls, "it must have been something very pleasant that caused that laugh that I heard as I opened the gate. Let me participate in the pleasure of the night. Go on with the story. Who was telling it?"

"Luke was telling it; and a very droll story it was," said Helen.

"Well, Luke, go on with it. Don't let me interrupt you."

"Sorra word ov id I remember now, Masther Redmond," said Luke. "Your comin' in dhruv it altogether out of my head. I'd have to begin id all over again."

"Well, supposing you do?" said Redmond.

"I object," said his sister. "A story told twice the same night loses all its captivation. You are very selfish, Redmond, to ask such a thing."

"Well, my dear," said Redmond gaily, "I am agreeable to anything; and, as I have been the unwitting agent in spoiling your story, perhaps I may make up for it by coaxing Kate into singing one of her exquisite songs."

"If you will hand back that glove," said Kate, with a quiet smile, and a very bright look in her eye as she glanced towards him, "perhaps I might."

"It was yours, then?" he asked quickly.

"I did not say it was," she replied, with ready wit; "but, whoever owns it, I make it the condition of my singing that you give it me."

"He is a bad paymaster, my dear Miss Howard, who pays beforehand; so I shall only give it when the song is ended."

"But you promise it then?"

"Well, yes—conditionally."

"Conditionally?"

"Yes; if I like the song. Not the singing, Kate—because you sing always exquisitely—but the song—the words and air of the song. That's the bargain. Will you have it?"

"Yes; agreed."

"Well, now, select your best."

The young girl smiled; looked thoughtfully into the bright flame of the logs for a moment; and, turning her eyes on him with a look in which drollery and pleasure and affection were all combined, sang. The song was an ancient Irish melody. Her voice was rich, sweet, and musical; and the plaintiveness of the air sank deep into the hearts of the rapt audience.

She had scarcely concluded the song—rendered with a grace and sweetness exquisitely telling—when, just as the plaudits of the little group were about to be warmly given, the wicket gate was heard again to open, and a hand was again laid, after a short interval, on the latch.

"Trevor," said Redmond, shortly.

"*Your* glove, my dear," whispered the songstress into the ear of Helen Barrington, who was sitting on the same chair with her, one arm encircling her waist. An answering pressure of her hand intimated at once the young girl's assent and her delight that it was so.

The door opened as the latch was raised, and the new-comer entered.

"You did not delay long after me, Trevor—What!— Who is this?"

Redmond Barrington had spoken at first without looking around; but when he did turn to see his friend an exclamation of surprise broke from him.

Helen had arisen to make room for the welcome wanderer; but as the exclamation from her brother caused her to look around in the direction, she stood stock-still for a moment, and then, with a cry that might have been the echo of the cry of the dead and buried girl of twenty-three years ago—in which fear, surprise, mortal terror were all combined, and which made the blood run back on the hearts of the group assembled—fell senseless into the arms of her brother!

For—standing a few steps inside the door was a stranger, a gash over his temple, the white cicatrice there showing distinctly where it had healed; and in his upraised hand he held a glove—her glove!

CHAPTER II.

THE VISITOR—HELEN'S GLOVE.

It would be difficult to picture the scene of amazement and confusion that ensued at this moment, as perhaps it would be equally difficult to pourtray the surprise with which the stranger looked on the confusion his entrance had caused.

Nor was his astonishment much less than that of Redmond, who could not conceive why the simple entrance of a stranger—a by no means unusual circumstance in the hospitable mansion of Scamore—should give rise to such terrors in the mind of his sister.

Helen was quickly borne to her own room by the

females of the house, the old housekeeper muttering to herself sorrowfully the while—" her luck, *mavrone*—her luck! It's come to-night as it came three-an'-twenty years ago. Woe is me—*mavrone!* Woe is me!"

When Redmond had seen his sister safely placed in her room, and under the ministering care of the women-kind of the house, he hurried back to see the unconscious cause of the disturbance.

He was standing, with feelings of disappointment depicted on his countenance, in the spot whereon he had stood when Helen's terrified eyes rested upon him; for the remainder of the party at the fire were too surprised to bid him welcome, or even to speak to him, and, if the truth were known, were inclined to look upon his presence with almost as much repugnance as the fainting girl herself.

So he stood there stock-still, apparently undecided what to do.

But standing there, in his half-sailor, half-soldier, uniform, he certainly seemed to be one who, upon even ordinary scrutiny, was little calculated to cause terror to any gathering, much less to the breast of susceptible girlhood.

About twenty-two years of age—scarcely more—though his weather-beaten, bronzed features might make him out older, his appearance was decidedly prepossessing. To a frank, open countenance, set off by a pleasant mouth, the white teeth of which formed an agreeable contrast with the dark moustache which was beginning to shade the upper lip, was added a pair of dark-brown eyes which, notwithstanding the look of half displeasure that shadowed them, were attractive and striking. His forehead, brown with exposure, was singularly marked by the oblique cicatrice referred to, whilst under the sailor's cap he wore, with its braided band of gold, dark locks peeped out—so very dark that they almost made his forehead look marble-white by comparison. His jacket, descending but little below his hips, gave him the appearance of being much taller than he was; and, on the whole, his appearance, as we have said before, was but little calculated to create such unwonted alarm.

So, at least, Redmond Barrington thought, as, having come back again to where the stranger was standing, still with the glove between his fingers, the latter smiled and said:

"I am afraid I have unwarrantably disturbed you."

"You have disturbed us, certainly," said Redmond courteously, and smiling in response, "though I do not know why. It was certainly not your fault. Perhaps it was because I, my sister, and her friend were expecting a different visitor."

"I *have* disturbed you at any rate, and I have to apologise for it."

"I beg you not to mention it," said Redmond, who, the more he looked at the frank, attractive countenance of the stranger, the more wondered what on earth frightened his sister.

"I am not quite certain," pursued the visitor, "that it would not be becoming in me to withdraw; but perhaps it is only right that I should give a reason for my unceremonious intrusion and for the path by which I came."

Redmond had completely forgotten that the stranger had come by way of the orchard—a way never permitted to any but himself and his sister and friends—and he now bethought him of it as a very singular circumstance, and as, perhaps, in some way leading to his sister's sudden alarm.

Checking, however, any appearance of concern, he promptly said:

"You must not think of going, and indeed, I should apologise for inhospitably keeping you standing here so long. You must not take it," added he pleasantly, "as our usual way at Seamore. Come with me—the night is cold and stormy for one travelling."

So saying, he pushed open the door that led into the corridor, and proceeded up stairs to his own room, followed by the stranger.

A fire was blazing in the grate and a lamp was burning on the table. Redmond wheeled over an arm-chair to the fire opposite to the one reserved for himself, and motioned the stranger thereto. But the latter took no notice of his gesture. He was standing, cap in hand, his black hair curling over his temples, in the centre of the apartment, looking around him. Having apparently satisfied himself with his observation, he threw himself in the arm-chair.

"How well I know this room!—how well I know every article of furniture in it! Nothing altered—nothing changed!"

It was more of a soliloquy than as an opening of conversation; but it surprised Redmond not a little, and he said:

"Did you say that you knew this room?"

"Well," said the stranger.

"I do not remember ever seeing you here before."

"I was here, nevertheless," said the stranger with something like a sigh.

"Pardon me. I do not doubt your words. But it seems curious to me that you should, for you could not have been here before my time—you are not much older than I—and you certainly have not been here since, that I remember."

"I have been here, nevertheless. There is not a secret drawer in yonder oaken cabinet that I could not open in the dark. I could find, blindfolded, the door in this room that leads to the secret stairway into the cellars."

"The first time ever I knew or heard there was a secret stairway," said Redmond.

"It was a similar remembrance that prompted me to come the old familiar way by the orchard instead of——Grannie!"

Whilst he was speaking the old woman had entered the room noiselessly, and—before he was aware of it—had advanced towards him with outstretched arms. Her movements at last attracted his unsettled attention, and as soon as his eyes had alighted on her face he sprang up and in a moment she was clasped in his arms.

"Grannie! Grannie! have I seen you at last?"

"Let me go, Eugene, until I see your face once more," said Cauth, as her dim eyes suffused with tears. She turned him round, and drew back a little, the better to let the light fall on his face. If the old housekeeper's eyes were suffused with tears the stranger's were not either without visible marks of emotion.

"It's the same face, my dear—the same face. Your mother's eyes—I'd know them the world over. Oh! Eugene! Eugene! where were you these many years that you never came to Seamore?"

"I was many a place, Grannie, the wide world over; but I never was any place yet that I did not think of Seamore—never."

"How strong you have grown; or is it to my poor old eyes that you look so big?"

"I have grown, I believe, Grannie. Sixteen years is a long spell in a young fellow's life, and I suppose," said the stranger, with a furtive and awkward attempt to banish the unaccustomed dew from his eyes, "I have grown somewhat in the time."

"If your mother could only see you now, Eugene!"

The stranger turned away to the window, looked out on the garden where the orchard trees were—stripped of their leaves—standing bare and desolate, and, having recovered himself, returned to his former position.

"One of my reasons, Grannie," he said quietly, but brokenly, "in coming to Ireland, along with seeing Seamore, was to kneel once more upon her grave."

"*Aroon*, it would have been the forgotten grave this many a year," said the old woman, "but for us in Seamore."

"I think, Grannie," said Redmond, who had been a wondering listener to this conversation, "I must ask you to introduce me to this gentleman; for I protest that, familiar as he is with the place, and well as you know him, he has, I am sorry to say, passed from my memory."

"The young soon forget, my dear," said Cauth; "the old have longer memories. But, even if you forget him, you must have often heard his name. There was a little boy here once, Eugene"—

"What!" said Redmond in a burst of delight and welcome, and advancing to shake hands with the stranger, "the little boy who disappeared from the English school, and never was heard of again!"

"Until now, dear sir—until now," said the stranger, smiling at the warmth and welcome of the other's salutation. "I came," added he to the housekeeper, "expecting to see old familiar faces, and learned not half an hour ago, to my deep pain and regret, that I might never look on them again."

"That's the way of the world, my dear; the old die and the young grow up and take their places. I am the only one left."

"I can only say," said Redmond, himself not a little affected by the turn the conversation had taken, "that if they were here you would not be more welcome than you are at present."

"If I thought otherwise," said the stranger brightly, "I should scarcely have been here. But I have other inquiries, Grannie, to make."

"About Alice?" said the old woman.

"About Alice—yes," said the stranger. "You may think it odd, Grannie, that all these many years I have never come to see her any more than other dear friends in Seamore. But my life since I was taken from school in England has been cast on board ships and in distant waters, where there was no more possibility of my coming to Ireland than there was of going to Iceland. But I have never forgotten her, and her childish face was often present to me where there was nothing around but the howling sea and the hurricane sweeping the face of the waters. How is she? Where is she?"

"She is in France, and she is quite well."

"In France?" said the stranger.

"The poor dear was not strong when a child, and she was sent there. And there she remained ever since. She was here for some months, about a year ago, on a visit."

"How has she grown, Grannie?"

"Not quite so tall as Miss Helen; very pretty, with an olive paleness in her face, and an engaging, loving way with her that wins upon you at once—in that way, like her poor mother, the light of God's glory to her!"

The stranger passed his hands across his eyes and was silent for some time.

"I had expected to find her here," he said; "but that pleasure lies before me shortly, when I return to France. I am delighted to hear that she is well. Our meeting will be a strange one after so many years. But I fear," said he, addressing Redmond, "this conversation can have little interest for you—although interesting enough to Grannie and myself."

"Though all memory of you has passed out of my mind, and all recollection from my eyes, your name is familiar enough," said Redmond, "and your conversation most interesting."

"I thought, Grannie," said the stranger, with a droll look, "I should like to see whether I could climb the orchard wall as readily as I did so many years ago. Would you believe it? I knew quite readily in the dark the very crevices in the wall into which I used to place my feet. That was how I came through the orchard. And, curiously, as I came along the wind blew something in my face, and, when I put up my hand and caught it, it turned out to be a glove. This is it."

He had held the glove in his hand all the time, and now glanced at it. As also did Cauth.

Her brow darkened, and a look of pain shot across her face and eyes.

"It's Helen's glove," said she slowly, as she extended her hand for it.

He did not seem to notice the motion; but merely said, with a quiet smile:

"Miss Barrington did not know that it was an old though unremembered friend that called or she would not have been so frightened."

"Never mind that, Eugene, if you will permit me so to call you," said Redmond. "Helen is not used to such weaknesses, and I am sure the effects will soon pass off, and that in the morning she will be ready to welcome an old friend to Seamore. And, by the way, Grannie, as this is rather a cold way in which to receive a visitor, I wish you would bring us up something to celebrate the occasion."

Grannie, whose brow had again become cheerful, left to attend to the wish thus expressed, and the stranger placed the tiny glove in his breast-pocket.

She soon returned with a servant bearing some tumblers and a steaming kettle, and Redmond having produced some cigars they were prepared to pass the night pleasantly.

"Isn't it odd, Grannie," said the stranger as the housekeeper was about leaving for the purpose of seeing her young mistress, "that, many years as have passed since I was here, I could walk nearly blindfolded about the house. There was an old cabinet in the drawingroom—companion to this one here"—pointing to an oaken press fixed in the wall, and to which he had before referred—"that I remember as well as yesterday. I think I could open it this moment."

"If you could, Eugene, it's the first time it has been opened since you left. The key was lost, and the poor master that's dead and gone would not allow it to be broken."

"I think I shall not need a key for it," said Eugene, whilst a gleam of satisfaction flashed across his eyes, "and I mean to try how far my memory serves me by essaying it to-morrow."

The old woman shook her head—but whether at the impossibility of his succeeding in what he proposed, or that the mention of the cabinet brought memories of the dead and gone around her, the stranger failed to know, though he glanced at her sharply.

Leaving the two young men to their conversation, the old woman proceeded to Helen's room, where she found the startled girl fairly recovered. Notwithstanding the fright she had sustained—or perhaps by reason thereof—she was, with all a woman's curiosity, anxious to know something of the cause of it. Some of the female servants had been already describing, in language of high eulogium, the appearance of the strange visitor; and her anxiety to know something of him—an anxiety not unshared by Kate Howard—had attained a high pitch.

Cauth was, therefore, much against her will, obliged to give a detailed account of the mysterious arrival; but she concluded her narrative with the exhortation:

"An' now, Helen, honey, be led and said by me, an' take no notice of him more than of an old friend that's come on a visit for a few days. Luck nor grace don't come of Holly Eve games, an' on that account have nothing to say to him. A girl's heart is aisily turned; an' it would be a sore day if you let it change from Trevor Mortimer, who loves the very ground you walk upon."

It would have been better, perhaps, for the purposes and intentions the housekeeper had in view if she had not harped on this string or given this advice. Women are at all times bad judges of woman-nature, and the advice she gave only predisposed Helen for the result she desired to avoid. For, as one result of this exordium, Helen, with the waywardness of a girl's fancy, was now in the highest impatience to behold the handsome young foreigner who had become possessed of her glove and who had startled her so much. Trevor Mortimer seemed commonplace and unimportant by comparison with this wonderful unknown. The sad story of Rose Morris paled into non-remembrance in presence of this new sensation. It was therefore with a flutter of delightful anticipation that the two young girls—when they were left together in their room—discussed the prospects of a meeting with their new guest in the morning, and drew to themselves fancy pictures of what he was like, and what appearance he would present.

So animated and absorbing was their conversation that they failed to hear—or, if they heard, to pay attention to—a strange disturbance going on in the kitchen. It was only after a considerable time that it became evident to them that there was some clamour going on more than usual; and Kate Howard was about placing her hand on the silken bell-rope to ring to inquire, when the door opened and Cauth, cautiously closing it again, approached them and said:

"Miss Helen! don't be afeard at what I'm goin' to tell you. It's better that I should tell you than that anyone else should."

"What is it, Grannie?" asked Helen, whilst her trembling lip gave evidence of her fresh alarm at this ominous introduction.

"Trevor Mortimer has just come in."

"Well, what more—Grannie? I know there is something yet to tell."

"He has got hurt."

"Hurt—how?" screamed the two girls in unison.

"I don't kow—no one knows."

"Can he not tell?"

Before the old woman could answer, the door was hastily flung open, and Redmond entered.

"This is an awful business, Helen," he said, whilst the big drops of perspiration stood out on his brow.

"What is it, Redmond?—what has happened?" faintly asked Helen, scarcely able to articulate the words.

"He has been struck—struck with a dagger—and I am afraid he is dying," said Redmond in hurried and awe-stricken accents. "He may know your voice, Helen—will you come down?"

Perhaps it was the desire to succour, perhaps it was the fear of death to one so dear to her, that overcame all considerations of self and banished her recent weakness; whatever it was that occasioned the effort, Helen rose with firm and unfaltering steps, and hurried with her brother to the kitchen.

A woful sight met her eyes. On the settle, stretched at his full length, pillows supporting his head, apparently dead or dying, lay Sir Trevor Mortimer. The blood that poured from a wound over his left breast gave token of where the blow had been delivered. In sight of this appalling spectacle the weakness that unnerved Helen Barrington previously, vanished; and her ready hand was soon at work to remove the stained clothes and to staunch the wound. In this she received valuable assistance from the young Frenchman, whom in the confusion of the moment she scarcely thought of, but whose previous experience in the matter of wounds made him an invaluable aid at this juncture.

The morning light was breaking in through the opened windows before the wounded man gave tokens of consciousness. A doctor, who had been sent for, arrived, pronounced him not in imminent danger; and, tired Nature asserting itself, the two girls retired to rest. Redmond and his new friend, less susceptible to fatigue, having seen Sir Trevor under the doctor's care, retired to their rooms to have a cigar and discuss this unhappy and mysterious affair.

"This is a strange business," said Redmond.

"He was struck from behind—over the shoulder. The wound was downward," remarked Eugene. "Has he any enemies?"

"I never knew he had one," replied the former.

"The blow was well meant at any rate. The striker felt for his heart. His coat alone saved him."

"It was no weak hand that gave the blow."

"I should think not," said the stranger. "Weak hands do not generally go in for that sort of work."

"Well, poor fellow, I am glad his life has been spared. We shall know more in the morning or during the day, if he be able to speak."

"The doctor spoke of fever. If that supervenes it may be a long time until he is able to give any information," remarked Eugene—"although I have seen men recover from much more serious wounds in a short time. Who is he?"

Redmond proceeded to inform him, after which, having shown Eugene to his bedroom, they retired to rest.

But the old housekeeper, as she sat at the bedside of the heavily breathing sufferer, muttered from time to time. "He brought the ill luck with him, *mavrone*, as his father brought before him!"

CHAPTER III.

EUGENE'S DAGGER.

THE information which Redmond gave his friend as to the wounded man the previous night we may shortly state here.

Sir Trevor Mortimer was the son of a Scotch gentleman who held high position in the Castle of Dublin. By the death of an uncle he had recently become possessed of a large but encumbered property both in England and Ireland in his own right; but having lived so long in Dublin and become accustomed to its society, he had resolved on making it his home. He had met Helen and her brother at one of the balls in Merrion-square, and thereafter a friendship grew up between them, which gradually ripened into an engagement between himself and the young girl.

Her brother looked with approbation on the relationship that thus sprang up, and was very much pleased when this formal engagement was entered into between them.

Possessor of property and position, and moving in the best circles of Dublin society, Sir Trevor Mortimer was considered on all hands to be an excellent match for his handsome sister. For though by no means highly gifted with good looks—and, indeed, regarded by some as possessed of rather sinister expression of eyes—Sir Trevor's manners were so polished and so winning, his voice was so soft, so courteous, and deferential, that one forgot in his presence the absence of prepossessingness in his countenance, and thought only of the charm and attractiveness of his conversation. He was essentially a man fitted to make an impression on women's hearts, and no one was surprised when the engagement between himself and Helen became formally known.

The wedding was to take place some time early in the ensuing year, and was intended to be a time of great festivities at Seamore. There was no particular day fixed, but it was generally understood by Redmond himself, and Helen, that it should not be long delayed. Under the circumstances he was a constant visitor, and much of his time was spent in Seamore.

In company with Mortimer and Redmond the two girls' lives were passing very pleasantly. Occasional rides into the beautiful country surrounding the mansion, occasional yachting excursions into the bay, and occasional visits to the theatres in the city combined to make their lives pass in the happiest manner. Not the smallest cloud of sorrow came to darken the quiet homeliness and happiness of their lives—not until now, when this singular and unexpected sorrow had swooped suddenly down upon them.

This was in substance, leaving out the references to his engagement with Helen, what Redmond Barrington told the young stranger the previous night.

Who struck the blow—what spirit of ill-will or vengeance prompted it—was a profound mystery to Redmond. He turned on his bed restlessly in vain imaginings as to the cause; but he only tortured himself uselessly.

Finally he fell asleep. Curiously enough, in vague

dreamings, he in some way associated his new-found acquaintance with the deed; and he started up, once when he dreamt that he saw the arm of Eugene raised to strike his friend—only to find the former bending over him.

"You have had a disturbed sleep," said the latter.

"Oh! Is that you, Eugene?" asked Redmond, more disturbed in his waking moments than even in his dream, so surprised was he to find the visitor there. "You are risen early."

"Or, rather, late. Do you know what hour it is?"

"No."

"It is well nigh noon."

"I did not think I had slept so long. How is Mortimer?"

"Much better."

"Conscious?"

"Yes, partly so. The wound was not very deep. His thick coat probably saved him."

"I am heartily glad to hear that," said Redmond, raising himself on his elbow.

"Yes, and the oddest thing in connection with the matter is that he seems to have been struck by a dagger which I carried."

"That you carried," said Redmond, with a curious look of doubt depicted on his countenance.

"So it seems," said the other coldly, as he noticed this expression, which had all the appearance of strange distrust. "I must have dropped it when crossing the wall, I told you of last night."

"Did you see any person near at the time?"

"Well, I certainly thought I heard voices as I approached, but the shrubs might have hidden them, for I saw no sign of them when I came near."

"Was there anything particular to attract your attention?"

"Well, yes, now that I recall it. I was chiefly attracted by the sound of a girl's voice, which impressed itself upon me by the fact that it spoke in a French manner and accent."

"Of course you heard none of the words."

"Yes, I did; I remember, just as I was descending the

wall, the words, spoken apparently in anger, 'I never married you.' or 'it was a mock marriage,' or something of that kind."
" Some quarrelling folk, I suppose."
" I daresay they were."
" But Sir Trevor had no connection with them. Why should he be struck down ?"
" There you put a question which I should find it difficult to answer—or perhaps himself. Angry people often strike a blow in mistake, and an infuriated person finding my skean ready to hand might have struck a blow at a chance passer-by, mistaking him for the proper party. The words 'it was a mock marriage,' or ' I never married you,' indicated a family quarrel of which he was the innocent sufferer."
" It is very strange and unaccountable," said Redmond dubiously, as he arose and proceeded to dress himself.

CHAPTER IV.

FOREBODINGS.

THE surprises and annoyances of the previous night were succeeded by a day of rejoicing when it was found that Trevor Mortimer's wound had not been as dangerous as was anticipated.

Helen rose early and learned the good news with rapturous delight. She hurried from her own apartment to that of Redmond to bear him the glad tidings. On the way past the drawingroom door a slight movement therein attracted her attention, and, thinking it might be her brother who had already arisen, she turned aside and entered.

It was not Redmond, however; it was the stranger. He was kneeling before the little oaken cabinet already referred to, and was apparently essaying to open it. She stood for a moment undecided what to do—finally resolving to retire quietly; but the rustle of her dress caught on his ear. He turned his head, and at once stood up.

The feeling with which Helen perceived him was largely blended with something akin to distrust—if so unsuspecting a nature could possess it; but this was quickly banished by the frank, open manner in which he approached her.

"I have been trying, my dear Miss Barrington," he said, advancing towards her with outstretched hand, "whether my memory is as faithful as I thought it. I was vain enough to say to Grannie last night that I could open this cabinet after sixteen years' absence, and I was trying to see if I could make my words good. I find I cannot. But I find I am speaking without introducing myself. Permit me to say, then, that I am an old though unremembered friend, who, for the first time in many years, found occasion to visit old scenes of happiness, and availed himself of it—Eugene Lefebre."

"You are welcome to Seamore," said Helen, accepting the proffered hand with a strange and unaccountable beating at her heart, "and I have to thank you for your assistance last night in our trouble."

"I fancied you did not, in the confusion, notice me," said the stranger with a courtesy and grace which impressed her curiously. "It was not a time for introduction, so I meant to present myself to you on the first available opportunity, and I am glad it has arisen now."

"It is a long time since you were here before," said Helen in her embarrassment, not knowing what else to say.

"It is not very far from twenty years, and that is a long space in one's lifetime. I scarcely remember you as a child. I suppose you do not remember me?"

"No; I was so very young then."

"Possibly you may have heard of me. I should be sorry to think that the little boy whose young life was made so happy here should have been quite forgotten."

"You were not forgotten," said Helen, with a sligh' palpitation of the heart, as she remembered the curious story in which his name was for the first time brought under her notice.

"I am delighted to hear that," he said, with some fervour. "I am glad indeed—heartily, truly glad—that the memory of the child was not altogether lost, who once was so happy and so welcome here."

"And who is equally welcome now, though those whom he knew and who loved him are not here to receive him," said Helen, with a tremble in her voice and a changing of colour that showed how earnest were her words. He was indeed welcome to her—welcome because that it had been more than a home to him when a child, and that he was loved and beloved as one by those so dear, now sleeping in their quiet graves.

"I never had any doubt of that," he said softly, and with a tenderness that won upon her, "even when thousands of miles lay between me and Seamore. And yet I doubt if I would have come had I known that those I knew and loved were gone—that those dear to me, inexpressibly dear to me—were no longer here. I did not anticipate such changes."

The tears welled into the young girl's eyes, and her lips trembled. Her heart was too full for speaking.

"I am glad, however, now that I have come," he continued after a pause, "for it brings me into the knowledge and acquaintanceship of those that I am delighted to know and shall not soon forget."

"You were very kind to us in our trouble last night," said Helen, to whom these latter words of his brought considerable embarrassment. She felt instinctively that the conversation was growing too delicate as between a young girl and an almost stranger; and as she raised her eyes to his handsome face and kindling black eyes the feeling became stronger. Wherefore she sought to change the conversation.

"Unfortunately," said he, "my life has been cast amid scenes where sights of that class were far from uncommon, and I was possibly enabled to be of more assistance than I could be under other circumstances or than can happen again during my short stay."

"But you are not going away shortly; you are," said Helen warmly, "going to remain with us a long time. Redmond will be delighted with your presence, and," said she, smiling, "your visit has been so long delayed that it is only a good stay can make amends for it."

"It was your mother's voice spoke there, Miss Barrington," said the Frenchman smiling in response, "and I shall be happy to enjoy your hospitality in what I used to call my old home—Seamore. But," he added, as a shade of thoughtful seriousness crossed his face "my movements are not my own; and there is an old maxim 'that those that are bound must obey.'"

"But you are not bound here, Mr. Lefebre. You have no cares of business here."

"Duty follows one, dear Miss Barrington, in every quarter of the world—and if one forgot it, the French nation, whom I have the honour to serve, knows how to compel it."

"You are in the French service?"

"Yes; I merely mentioned the matter in order that it might not be forgotten. The two countries being at war does not render it the more pleasant to dwell in Ireland at present, Miss Barrington; and whilst I should not like to be a visitor here without being perfectly frank in saying this much, it would make the time here pass pleasanter that, being known, it were forgotten or left unmentioned."

"It shall not be mentioned outside this house you may depend, Mr. Lefebre," said Helen, this little tribute of confidence having the effect of putting her more at her ease with him.

"I should not have come in uniform—I just landed from a skiff on the coast outside—did I not know I came among friends, and, perhaps, there was also the vanity lurking in my breast to let the dear old friends I thought I should meet here see what the little boy they once welcomed had grown into. It was," he said with some embarrassment, "a natural feeling, and one not to be, perhaps, ashamed of."

Helen was silent; and as she looked upon him was inclined to think that if the motive was one not to be ashamed of, neither most certainly was the speaker; for, as he stood before her, he seemed to her, the very embodiment of whatever was brave, handsome, and chivalrous. She was already beginning to look upon him in the light of an old friend rather than a stranger, wholly unknown until last night.

"And as I have said so much, Miss Barrington, perhaps I may also say a little more. Whether my stay be long or short—long with your delightful invitation, or short at the call of those to whom my services are due—I would ask you to take me on trust for what I am. If anything seems to you in me or my movements strange or unusual, or—perhaps I may use the word—distrustful, always remember that what I was, when a little boy I played under yonder trees in the orchard, that I am in all respects to-day—in all essentials. The world is full of mysteries, dear Miss Barrington, whether men make them for themselves or they are made for them."

Helen listened to this statement but imperfectly conceiving its meaning. What it meant or foreboded she could not and did not try to guess, but as if by some curious incidence there flashed upon her mind the warning words:

"An' now, honey, be led and said by me, an' take no notice of him more than ov an old friend that comes on a visit for a few days. Luck nor grace don't come of Holly Eve games, an' on that account have nothing to say to him. A girl's heart is aisily changed, an' it would be the sore day if you let it turn from Trevor Mortimer, who loves the ground you walk upon."

It took some time on the previous night for Cauth to say this much, but it flashed through Helen's mind whilst the young Frenchman was saying his concluding words. Conscious that she had been inhospitably silent, and that some reply was expected from her, she said at last:

"We shall be delighted if you can prolong your stay with us, Mr. Lefebre, and shall look upon your visit as doubly pleasant because of those to whom you were once dear and welcome."

"Thanks, Miss Barrington. And now, as I have probably detained you from other matters, I shall, with your permission, pay a visit to your brother."

"I was about going there myself," said Helen; "but, as you will be a more welcome bearer of the good news, I shall resign the mission in your favour."

With which genial leave-taking she left the apartment, and proceeded to see the housekeeper. But she had scarcely parted from him than an indefinable feeling of dread and insecurity and evil forebodings sprang up in her breast, which she could not account for, and which caused a quicker pulsing at her heart.

Eugene Lefebre, when she had left, walked over to the window looking out on the orchard, and thereover on the distant seas. There was a white haze over the latter, and the horizon in consequence was limited. If he wished or expected to see anything thereon, there was nothing visible —and so, after a few minutes' observation, he left the room and proceeded to that of Redmond, who was still sound asleep.

CHAPTER V.

THE LISTENER.

The days passed delightfully at Seamore. The injured man grew rapidly convalescent. The wound rapidly healed; for though there was no mistaking the intention with which the blow was given, his thick overcoat prevented its force proving fatal.

Many were the conjectures and surmises as to who could have made the attack and the reasons therefor. But as no reason could be alleged, the guesses had no base, and resolved themselves into mere fancies. The only one thing that stood out clearly was that someone must have been close at hand when Eugene clomb the orchard wall, had seen him drop the dagger, and had waited until Trevor Mortimer came upon the scene and had stealthily struck him therewith from behind. Happily, however, the striker failed in his aim, as we have seen, and Trevor was now with great rapidity getting well.

Meantime, and awaiting his recovery, the time passed very pleasantly. Eugene doffed the uniform, much to the regret of the girls, who thought it handsome and becoming, and attired himself in civilian costume. Redmond kept a yacht, and whenever the stranger had no occasion to go into town—which latter not infrequently happened—he rigged it out, and in the November days ran out to sea or swept down the Wicklow coast. It was a very joyous company—Eugene, himself, and the two girls; and as the first-mentioned was seldom without some entertaining narrative of his adventures abroad, and found ready listeners in the others, it would be difficult to describe the sense of enjoyment with which the time sped.

Many a laugh there was at the fright which Helen sustained at the first appearance of the handsome Frenchman, in which Helen herself, blushing deeply, joined; but the incident of the glove, whether forgotten or not, was never referred to—never mentioned.

At other times Redmond saddled his horses, and the four cantered along through the beautiful scenery and the exquisite country—then wholly unbuilt upon—that lay between Seamore and the mountains; and not infrequently the city lights were glimmering before they descended the hills for their ride homewards.

"It would be delightful if this were to last always," said Helen in a burst of enthusiasm, as one evening, glowing with health and exercise, she handed over her horse to the hands of the attendants and turned with Eugene to enter the house.

"Yes, it has been a very pleasant time to me—the pleasantest ever I spent, or —" said the latter gravely, "the happiest I possibly shall ever again spend."

"You speak as if it were about terminating," said Helen quickly, whilst a sudden gravity supplanted her enthusiasm. "I hope you have no intention of leaving us?"

"If I have, you may rely on it, dear Miss Barrington, it is an intention begotten of no wish of mine, and comes of causes I cannot control."

"But there is not, is there?" said she, in undisguised anxiety, "any present prospect of your leaving. I had quite made up my mind that you would remain for the Winter with us."

"It would not be of my own motion I should fail to do so; you may certainly believe me in that," said he somewhat evasively.

"But is there any doubt of your doing so? Redmond would be so grieved to hear of it."

"And would there be no one else sorry, Miss Barrington?" asked he softly.

"Yes, all. Everyone would be sorry. Why not? What could be more delightful than the present time?"

"I am scarcely gratified by that reason," said Eugene disappointedly, and not without a touch of sadness in his manner.

"But there could be no better reason," said Helen, not failing to comprehend his remark, but desirous of evading it. "It is always sad to part with friends, and always sorrowful to see a time of enjoyment ended. Don't you think so?"

"I quite agree with you, Miss Barrington; everyone feels it more or less. But there are occasions when one is more touched by it, and for deeper reasons than because it puts an end to enjoyment. I should like to be regretted for something more than that when I am gone."

"But you are *not* going," broke in Helen earnestly. 'Say that you are not. You have quite thrown a gloom over me by even mentioning it."

"You must remember, dear Miss Barrington, that as I told you before, I am not the controller of my own actions. Fortunately it is so, as otherwise I should never succeed in tearing myself away from here. You cannot know how inexpressibly dear to me Seamore—and—and those in it—have become to me, short as has been my stay here."

There was a touch of tenderness in his words which kept Helen silent, and they walked together slowly and thoughtfully for a little while.

"I, too, should be sorry—very, very sorry. But I hope —indeed I do most truly—that you will be enabled to spend the Winter with us. Think how short you have been here. Surely you have got no commands to go?"

"I fear, even without them, it would be better for me that I should. For many reasons, which I need not enter upon at present, I think it would be better for my future happiness that I should leave soon."

"For many reasons?" said Helen, wonderingly.

"For many reasons, Miss Barrington."

"You puzzle me," said she after another slight pause. "I cannot comprehend why your stay here should interfere with your future happiness. You are dearly welcome to us for many sakes, and—I—I hope you are as happy as we thought you were, and as we would wish you to be."

"It is because I am so very happy that I dread the regret that will come to me when I am gone. Did it ever strike you, Miss Barrington—or Helen, if you will permit me to call you so——"

He paused, as he stood by a laurel tree under the window.

"Yes, Helen, certainly," she said. "We are too old friends to stand on ceremony."

"Well, Helen," said he, with a brighter tone in his words, "did it never strike you that one might remain in a place until feelings grew up in his heart he could not control; until chains of attachment and affection wound around his heart that he could not rend; until a power he could not break enthralled him, and until disappointment might poison his whole existence? It has arisen before with many; it might—nay, would—with me."

"Not here."

The words were so simply spoken that he thought at once she failed to comprehend his meaning.

"Yes, Helen, here. My own heart tells me that it is dangerous for me to remain."

"Why? Because of what—of whom?"

"Because of you."

"Of me?"

"Of you, Helen. Ever since that first night I saw you I cannot describe the feelings that possess me. Your face is before me at all times. Your eyes break in on my dreams at night; I cannot——"

"Oh! for God's sake, Eugene," said the young girl in affright, "don't speak thus. You don't know what you are speaking of. You don't know that——"

There was a rustle at the window overhead that startled her, and Redmond's cheery voice was heard saying:

"What! you here, Trevor! I am delighted to see you able to move so far. Why, you will be able to come out with us in a day or two."

"I thought I should like to leave my room and get a little fresh air at the window," said the invalid, who had been sitting there silently all the time, in reply.

"Oh, my God!" thought Helen, "he has heard it all," and with a most uncomfortable feeling flew into the house.

Eugene entered more slowly, and walked into the apartment where the two young men were. The lamps had not yet been kindled, and, save the dim light that came from the dusky evening outside, there was none other in the room.

He was, therefore, unable to see the pallor that overspread the face of the invalid, or the stormy light of anger and jealousy that shone in his eyes. There was no trace of any feeling but one of good-humour, however, when, in a few seconds afterwards, the latter said:

"Well, gentlemen, I hope you have had an agreeable ride."

"A most agreeable one," said Redmond cheerfully, "and only wanted your own presence, my dear Mortimer, to make it perfectly enjoyable."

"Many thanks. I find myself much stronger this evening."

"I am delighted to hear it. The fact is, I have been just considering since I came in whether I have not been acting a little selfishly in leaving you so much alone. But the necessity of showing Eugene old scenes which he may possibly never see again must be my excuse."

"Don't mention it," said the invalid. "I have been the unfortunate cause of trouble enough without bringing the house into additional gloom. If not with you in person I am in spirit in all your excursions."

"Whenever Mr. Mortimer comes to France," said Eugene, with frank good humour, "we shall make good to him his present deprivation."

"Your French wine shall give him back some of the strength your French dagger robbed him of," said Redmond laughingly, as he lit the lamps and handed round a box of choice cigars. "By the way, Eugene, someone has been here looking for you to-day during our absence."

"For me?"

"Yes, so they tell me. I hope he brings you no abrupt news."

"Did he leave no message?" inquired the other with quick concern.

" A letter. It is on the drawingroom chimney-piece yonder."

Eugene went for the letter, looked at it curiously, opened and read it, and after some time returned to his place. The lamp was lighting and the table was spread for dinner.

" Well, Eugene; no unpleasant news, I hope. You are looking rather serious."

" Am I ?" said Eugene brightly. " Then I shouldn't. There is nothing unpleasant in it. Merely an invitation to town to-morrow evening. But where are the ladies ?"

" Unfortunately," said the old housekeeper, " Helen has a bad headache, and Miss Howard remains to keep her company. So you will be deprived of the pleasure of their presence."

" It is very unfortunate," said Redmond pettishly— " particularly as it is the first occasion you, Sir Trevor, have been able to dine with us."

" Helen is rarely subject to headache," said Sir Trevor, " and for that reason it is all the more afflicting when it comes."

" The ride was too much for her strength to-day," said Eugene. " I am afraid I am to blame for her absence."

" It may have been something that tended to excite her nerves," remarked the baronet, with a keen glance at the young Frenchman; but the latter did not seem to notice the remark.

The dinner passed over amid many anecdotes, in which much of the then condition of things in France and Ireland was discussed, and it was late when the gentlemen retired.

When Eugene was in his room he took the letter from his pocket, looked with fresh curiosity at it, remarking to himself, " This letter has been certainly opened and re-sealed It is singular if the sender should have done such a thing in a confidential communication."

" I half expected this," he muttered, as he re-opened the letter and read aloud :—

" Come in to-morrow evening. Important news has come from France. It is more than likely you will have to go back hurriedly. Come prepared for it.—O. B."

"Bond might have taken more care with so important a communication," he soliloquised. "'Go back hurriedly.' I half expected as much from the absence of communications for the past month. There is some blunder going on, I'll be sworn. Heaven grant it may not be a serious one. And so here ends my happiness for the present. Better, perhaps, it is so. I should be madly in love if I were to remain much longer. In love! I fear I am that already."

A smile passed over his face as a beautiful form and a pair of bright blue eyes grew up before his imagination.

But the feeling was quickly replaced by more serious considerations. "These papers!" he continued—"they told me I should find them in that oaken cabinet in the drawingroom. And I have completely omitted to secure them. Shall I tell Helen? No, better not. I shall leave them there for the present. If it be necessary I should leave, they can await my return. They concern no one but myself."

With which soliloquy he retired to rest, first kneeling down—a very unusual thing with Frenchmen of the day—to say his prayers; and taking out a gold crucifix from his breast, ornamented with *fleurs de lys*, curiously engraved in filigree work, kissed it, muttering "Poor father—dear mother."

In a few moments he was asleep. Bright dreams and fair faces haunted his slumbers; and he awoke when the sun was high in the skies, with Helen Barrington's blue eyes, as he thought, beaming on him—but it was only the stray sunbeams coming in through the half-closed shutters and falling on his face.

"Redmond," said Sir Trevor to his friend, when Eugene had left, and before they proceeded to their respective rooms. "I find I shall have to go into town to-morrow."

"Into town? Why, you are not nearly strong enough for that. It would be dangerous to attempt it."

"I am strong enough, and even if it were dangerous to my health I must run the risk, for I have pressing business; but I am quite strong enough to go. What I do feel is that I may not be strong enough to return, and I dislike the idea of remaining all night in town in my present condition. Could you meet me there and we can return together?".

"I shall accompany you in," said Redmond heartily.

"No, no. I should not care to take you from your friends for the day. It would simply suit me quite as well, if you were to meet me there, say about ten or eleven o'clock at night—I shall not be ready to come sooner—and we can then return together."

"I am heartily at your service. Fix the hour and the place."

"Say eleven o'clock, and at the Eagle in Eustace-street."

"All right, I shall be there. I shall bring the carriage with me."

"I should prefer not. We shall hire one to take us home. Truth is, Redmond," said he confidentially, "I am rather ashamed to admit that my late illness has made me somewhat nervous—and cowardly if you will. It is not an agreeable character to bear before the ladies, and I should therefore take it as a favour if you would not state to anyone the reason of your coming."

"Certainly not," said Redmond. "There is no reason why I should."

"Thanks. You were always such an agreeable fellow, Redmond. This feeling I have referred to will wear off when I get more out-of-door exercise, but you can well understand one's weakness in desiring not to have it known."

"Of course. And after the illness you have had your nervousness comes natural enough. I shall not mention the reason of my going, and I shall be there at the appointed time. Your going may do you good, too, and give you strength to accompany us on our future excursions."

"It may. I am sure it will. Nothing has given me more pain than not to have been able to enjoy the pleasure of your company and Eugene's during the past few weeks."

"By the way, how do you like Eugene? He is a very agreeable fellow, is he not?"

"Yes, I think so," said Mortimer cheerfully.

"The girls like him very much—Helen particularly. If," said Redmond, "you had been able to enjoy his company frequently I am sure you would have been delighted with him, too."

"It is a pleasure yet in store for me," said Sir Trevor, with less heartiness, however, than Redmond had expected "In a few days I trust to be able to make one of your party."

"We shall all be so glad of it. Meantime you should retire to rest without further delay. This being your first night up, it may overtax your strength for your proposed city visit to-morrow."

"I daresay you are right. You will not forget the time, the place, and the secrecy."

"I shall remember all. Good night, Mortimer."

"Good night."

And they separated.

CHAPTER VI.

A SUDDEN RESOLVE.

"You slept rather late, Eugene," said Redmond, as the former entered the drawingroom.

"So I see," said Eugene gaily, "but I have an excuse in that we had so long a ride yesterday and retired so late. I hope our friend Mortimer has not suffered from the unreasonable time we kept him up."

"Mortimer!" said the other, "why Mortimer seems the strongest of the three. He has gone into the city already."

"What? Why I thought he was unable to stir from the house."

"You would not have thought so had you seen him this morning. He looks as vigorous as either of us. His recovery has been something wonderful."

"Much more than I expected. But when did he leave for town?"

"Not quite half an hour since."

"He made no mention of his intention last night."

"No. It was some sudden notion he took. Some business matter that occurred to him probably. Or perhaps, he wished to take some exercise to aid his recovering strength."

"I am surprised he should not try it with us."

"Possibly he thought his strength would not be sufficient for that."

"Well," said Eugene, "I am sorry we are deprived of his company. When is he returning?"

"Probably to-night."

"If he had waited until this afternoon I should have had the pleasure of his company."

"Are you going to town to-night?" asked Helen.

"Unfortunately I must."

"We shall have a lonely evening in that case," said she.

"If the ladies would only permit it, Eugene," said Redmond, "I should be very glad to accompany you. We shall be probably back with Mortimer."

"You would not deprive us of the company of all the gentlemen, surely, Mr. Lefebre?"

"I would not of my own, I assure you, Miss Howard," said Eugene gallantly, "for it brings myself too much pain."

"You look this moment like one who is suffering by anticipation," she said sarcastically.

Redmond laughed—as indeed did all—for the young Frenchman looked at the moment the embodiment of gaiety and enjoyment.

"But, surely, you are not going, Redmond?" said Helen. "Think how lonely we shall be."

"I shall undertake to bring him back early and safe and sound," said Eugene.

"With that undertaking I think I shall venture it," said Redmond indolently. "What time do you purpose going?"

"I shall not be due in town until after dusk. The moon rises early. We shall have a pleasant walk; the tide will be full in."

"Very well; I am at your service."

"Well, gentlemen," said Miss Howard, "it is very unkind of you. How shall we two ladies pass the time until your return?"

"And the worst of it is," broke in Helen, "they have all made up their minds to leave together."

"We must only make amends for the present by enjoying the time we have," said Redmond. "What say you, ladies, to a long drive after breakfast?"

"Of all things," said Helen.

"It is a delightful morning for one. How soft and bright and mild the air is," said Kate.

"Always providing," said Eugene, "that we shall be back in sufficient time to permit me to keep my engagement. I am sorry to have to make such a proviso; but, unfortunately, my engagement is important and must be kept."

"We must prevail on Redmond to remain with us," said Miss Howard, addressing Helen.

"I have given my word to Eugene—he only can give permission to me to withdraw it." said Redmond.

"A permission I must withhold," said Eugene earnestly, 'for I desire and need his company very much. You must remember, ladies, I am more or less a stranger in the city."

"Under these circumstances we must see that the stranger is protected," said Miss Howard, and amid much laughter they sat down to breakfast.

CHAPTER VII.

NEWS FROM FRANCE.

REDMOND and his friend proceeded on foot to the city. The night was clear and starlight; and, as the tide was full in, their walk along the sea shore, with the murmur of the waves in their ears, was very pleasant.

Arrived in the city, they separated, with an arrangement to meet at the Eagle, a famous inn that then stood in Eustace-street.

The Frenchman proceeded swiftly in the direction of the quays. Arrived at a narrow street leading off the Southern quay, he came to a public house, in the window of which a small oil lamp was burning. There was but little appearance of business in the shop, and the hostess sat knitting, in the absence of customers, behind the counter.

Lifting his hat courteously, to which salutation the good-looking landlady replied with a smile of recognition and welcome, he passed rapidly through, and, pushing a door open, ascended a narrow and lightless stairs that led upwards. When he had groped his way to the top he turned the handle of a door and entered.

A flood of light burst on his vision as he did so. The apartment which he entered was splendidly lighted, and its comfortable—nay, elegant—appearance was but little indicated by the exterior of the house or the shop. A number of gentlemen were scattered about—some seated, some standing, and some playing at billiards. Evidently they had been expecting him, for there was a general movement towards the fireplace as he entered.

"Late in coming, Eugene?" said a handsome-looking man, as he presented the new comer with his cigar case, the while the diamond ring on his finger flashed its scintillations around.

"A little later than I intended, but not too late, I hope."

"In these uncertain times it is difficult to say whether one is too early or too late," said another, whose foreign accent betrayed him as not of Irish origin.

"Why, Antoine," said Eugene quickly, "has the messenger come?"

"He is here since dusk."

"What news does he bring?"

"Excellent—but he is here to speak for himself."

At this moment a hand was laid on his shoulder, and, turning round, a young fellow, whose boyish face was round and soft as a girl's, and whose age was certainly not more than eighteen, stood before him.

"Hallo! François," said Eugene in much surprise; "is it you that have come this time?"

"Yes, *mon capitaine*," said the youth laughingly, "I thought I should come over and see what this new country is like, and how it may look with the French banners flying over it."

"Well, I certainly did not expect to see you here, François, but you are welcome to Irish soil. Any despatches?"

"Yes, here they are," said the youth, as, pressing a spring in the head of a light cane or riding whip which he carried, the top flew open, disclosing a very small cavity, from which he drew forth a slight roll of thin paper not much thicker in diameter than a quill.

"Well, François, before I read this, tell me how matters are going on in France. It is so long since I heard any news from that dear land that I am really athirst for information."

"You have not heard the great news, then?" said François, with wonderment expressed on his face.

"No; how could I, François? You are the first that could tell me since I left. You don't suppose we are in Paris?"

"I find it difficult to think I am not," said the youth gaily. "I fancy ever since I came in here that I have only to step outside to be on the boulevards again."

"Well, François," said Eugene with a grave but good-humoured nod of his head, "you will be much more fortunate than some of your predecessors or it will be some time before you tread the boulevards again."

The youth laughingly put his handkerchief to his eyes as if to mourn for the afflictions that awaited him.

"Look here, François," said Eugene, as he watched this fanciful piece of acting, "take my advice and remember that it is not playing pranks in General Clarke's office you are now. A hempen rope and a dance over the battlements of Carlisle-bridge is a vastly different thing from a saunter down the Rue des Victoires. But advice was always thrown away on you. Tell me the news. What is Bonaparte doing?"

"Doing? Carrying the French banners over Italy. You have not heard that he has carried everything before him there? The Austrians were beaten at Castiglioni last month, and Marshal Wurmser, who never saw his banners in retreat before, was barely able to save his rereguard from the sabres of the cuirassiers. So also the bayonets of the infantry, under Bonaparte himself, swept the army of

Alvinzi from his position at Arcola, and with the exception of Mantua, Italy from end to end is ours."

"He is a wonderful soldier," said Eugene.

"He is the great master of war," said the youth enthusiastically. "The army is in ecstacies over the triumphs he has won and the glories he has achieved."

"I hope they will prove glories for France," said Eugene thoughtfully.

"Of course they will. What is glorious for her army is glorious for France."

"I trust so."

"Trust! Of course they are."

"Well, François," said Eugene, laughing at the airy, enthusiastic manner of his friend, "you are a very angel of good news. And now for the despatches."

Eugene unrolled the delicate tissue of paper, and, holding it up between his eyes and the light, read the secret writing thereon with deep attention, whilst the gentlemen assembled stood silently around him.

"This is wonderful news, gentlemen," he said at last, after a pause of great expectation.

"What news does he bring? What is in the despatch?" asked half a dozen of voices at once.

"De Morand de Galles sails from Brest on the 15th instant with a French army on board, for the shores of Ireland!"

A ringing cheer went up from those assembled.

"Read it—read it!" cried a dozen enthusiastic voices.

"Here it is, gentlemen," said Eugene once more holding the paper to the light, and reading:

"'Morand de Galles will sail on the 15th December from Brest for Bantry Bay, on the Southern Irish coast. Hoche will command them.' That is all. Oh! by the way, François, you are likely to see your comrades sooner than I wotted of. Here is yet another note from De Galles, laconic enough too. 'Come back at once with bearer—by any way you can, but come. You are appointed to command a frigate.' There, gentlemen, is all the news for you. The French fleet with a French army on board, will sail for Ireland on the 15th."

"Can it be true? Is it really true?" was anxiously asked.

"It is true enough," said Eugene. "Here is Clark's signature at the end. There is no mistaking that C. The Brunswicker's sabre on the plains of Valmy did not tend to improve his handwriting."

"This is wonderful news, certainly," said the gentleman who first spoke when Eugene entered the room. A buzz of conversation immediately spread round the little party, each discussing or giving his opinion on the last despatch. "He does not say what the number of ships to be despatched is?"

"No; but the Directory are not accustomed to doing things by halves. They who sent separate armies at the same time marching on the high road to every capital in Europe are not going to send a squadron of sabres to fight England. Take my word for it, Clarke knows his business too well for that. It will be your duty, gentlemen, to see that his efforts are well seconded."

"We can readily answer for our country, can we not, Bond?" said a young gentleman who had remained silent during the communication of the message, but who, now when he did speak, was listened to with great respect and attention. "A hundred thousand men will be ready to lift the Irish banner the moment the first French cannon thunders on Irish soil. All we want is arms and ammunition, and officers to lead them."

"No doubt, my lord," said Bond, "we can promise such an array of fighting men as never yet were under the banners of France. But it seems to me that the point of destination of the fleet is, next to its sailing at all, the most important matter. The despatch mentions Bantry. Now I am inclined to think that is a mistake."

"But you remember," said Eugene, "the first night I came here we went carefully over all the possible places of disembarkation, and Bantry was mentioned as one of the most secure and ample harbours on the Irish coast."

"True," said Bond, "but I certainly do not remember —I may be mistaken—but I do not remember that it was urged as a suitable or likely place as the objective point of the French expedition. It is, in the first place, a remote position in the wildest and most thinly populated part of the whole country. For any considerable body of men to array themselves under the French colours, they would have to march immense distances. The reception, therefore, our French allies would meet would be disheartening at the outset, and that is to be avoided."

"I quite agree with Bond," said Lord Edward after a pause. "The best place assuredly for a French army to land would be in the centre of a populous district, where the cheers of an enthusiastic people would greet their disembarkation. With smart officers to drill them, one week would place an army, such as no power of England could dream of meeting, in your hands. I fear that there would be many obstacles to success if so remote a landing place as Bantry is chosen. The proper place to strike is at the heart, and that place, so far as Ireland is concerned, is—Dublin."

"You must remember that it will take some time to drill the raw levies that will flock to our standard," said Eugene, "and that you cannot drill and fight at the same time. A short breathing time after landing is for that reason necessary, and a remote district would give us that."

"You have forgotten the question of the commissariat," said Oliver Bond, whose vigorous mind grasped all the difficulties of the position at once. "The fleet are not supposed to carry more provisions with them than will last the voyage?"

"No," said Eugene, laughing; "we carry better things than provisions—plenty of bullets and powder, long muskets and bright sabres—the sort of cargo that befits a conquering nation."

"And how," asked Bond, "would you provide for your French soldiers, not to speak of the people who would flock to your standard?"

"Why the matter is very simply settled by our generals, at all times," said the Frenchman, interrupting with some haughtiness. "If our troops are in a friendly country they expect support, if in an enemy's they compel it."

"I am afraid you have mistaken the point of my question," said Oliver Bond, smiling at the other's mistake. "I did not refer so much to the manner of obtaining supplies as to the possibility of getting them at all. My impression is that the country there for many miles around would not provide, if it were all taken, as much commissariat supplies as would last an army for two days."

" Could they not march on Cork ?"

" That would be a long and weary march, and to little purpose. They would be still a long way from where they could meet an enemy or strike a telling blow. I greatly befear me"—it was Lord Edward who spoke— " your generals would get disheartened fighting, not against the enemy, but against the difficulties of the position. No ; the only place a landing can be effected with any hope of successful result must be somewhere on the Eastern seaboard. One successful battle, a march on the capital, and Ireland were free from Malin Head to Cape Clear."

" You are forgetting, gentlemen. There are two initial matters to be thought of—one is the difficulty of landing at all—the English fleet is by no means to be despised, and our admirals must try and avoid it as much as possible. A fight between a fleet prepared for an engagement and one crowded with ammunition and guns and soldiers is very unequally fought. It would be simple massacre. France does not hesitate to shed the blood of her children in the cause of freedom—whose eldest born she is—but she will not needlessly sacrifice them. The first difficulty, therefore, is the landing at all. The second is the safe anchorage for the vessels."

" You cannot carry on warfare," said Lord Edward, " with rosewater. A blow at England will in any case entail sacrifices ; and I am, for one, of opinion that between an expedition to Bantry Bay and none at all, there is not much to choose. You must further remember that it is a matter of life and death to us. We cannot hope to succeed without your aid, but to be of use to us, that aid must be effectually rendered. A failure in that respect would place us neck and heels at the feet of England for another hundred years."

This and much more was urged by other speakers, until the young Frenchman's mind was much impressed by their arguments.

"Well, gentlemen," he said at last, "you see how matters stand. The fleet will sail on the fifteenth if not otherwise counter-ordered. What would you have me do? Time is pressing, and it may be difficult, if not impossible, to alter matters thus definitely fixed."

"I think," said Lord Edward, "that it is of the very first moment that the destination should be altered, and that I take to be the opinion of all here."

"But how is it to be done?" anxiously queried Eugene.

"I see no other way for it," said Oliver Bond bluntly, "except by your proceeding immediately to France and laying our views before Hoche and the Directory."

"A message by our young friend François would not be sufficient?" suggested Eugene, whose thoughts went back to the mansion of Seamore and the friends therein.

"The matters progressing are too important," said Lord Edward gravely, after some deliberation, "to place the mission in any hands but your own. The consequences of failure are too dreadful to think of anyone of less importance undertaking it."

"Well, in any case," thought Eugene, "this appointment Clarke has bestowed on me would necessitate my departure in a few days at the very furthest." Then aloud "Well, gentlemen, I am completely at your service. When do you think I should leave?"

"At once," chimed in a number of voices. "This night."

"It will take some time to get a vessel ready."

"As for that, the boat by which this young gentleman came," said Bond, "is lying safe and sound at Dunleary, and, I have no doubt, long before daybreak will be ready to sail."

"In that case, François," said Eugene, turning to his young countryman, "you shall see the fair city of Paris sooner than you expected. I am sorry you could not see more of Ireland, but——"

"Why, I shall come back with the expedition," said the youth, with enthusiastic glee at the idea of his again seeing his beloved Paris. "We shall have a holiday march through Ireland, something like what we had through Prussia with Davoust."

"Were you there?" asked Eugene with a smile.

"Yes, I was drummer boy in the regiment of which Hoche was colonel," said the youth proudly.

"That's it you see, gentlemen," said Eugene, addressing the group around him. "It is little wonder that our French armies march to victory when the drummer boy in a few years wears the epaulettes of a sous-lieutenant."

"I hope to wear the baton of a marshal of France yet," said the youth.

"Very well, François," said Eugene, laughing. "There is nothing like aiming high, at any rate. Meantime, my young marshal, there is many a swelling wave between us and France at this moment, and if you have any traps to prepare you had better be getting ready."

"They are all in the cutter where we landed."

"So much the better. It will take the less time. And now, my lord," said he, addressing Lord Edward, "what further message may I bear across?"

"Simply this. If Hoche lands with ten thousand men on any of our Eastern seaboard counties, and with one hundred thousand stand of arms, tell him from the Irish Directory the freedom of Ireland is assured. An army such as he never led to victory will be beneath his banners within half a score days after his landing."

"Very well, my lord, that message covers everything. And now, gentlemen, as the night is growing late—it is closing on twelve o'clock—I think my young friend and myself may be taking our leave."

"If you will permit me to drive you to Dunleary—my trap is in the stables," said John Sheares—"I shall have much pleasure in doing so."

"You place me under great obligations," said Eugene.

"It is but a sorry way to entertain an ambassador," said Lord Edward laughingly, "but we shall give you a right royal welcome when the van of the French army is tramping with banners flying, through Grafton-street."

"Which may be very much sooner than you think," said Eugene, falling into the hopeful mood of the hour.

"And not sooner than they will be welcome," said Oliver Bond.

"I think, however," said William Byrne, the Wexford delegate, who until then had remained a silent listener to the conversation, " we are bidding our friends a most un-Irish adieu. You have never heard of the stirrup-cup in France, I suppose?"

"The stirrup-cup! What is that?" asked Eugene.

"Upon my word, Byrne, I should not have thought of it if you had not mentioned it," said Lord Edward with hearty good humour. "My mind was so preoccupied with the business on hands that I never once thought of it. The stirrup-cup by all means."

Champagne bottles were promptly in requisition, and as the silvery bubbles of the wine sparkled in the glasses a feeling of trust and hopefulness in the future seemed to breathe through the atmosphere of the room.

"Here's to gallant France!" said Lord Edward, as he and others clinked their glasses against those held by the two French officers. "May the light of victory never darken on her banners."

The toast was drunk with enthusiasm.

"Gentlemen, one toast from me," said Eugene, as he glanced at the young sous-lieutenant, whose face, like his own, was flushed with pleasure at the enthusiastic manner in which the toast had been received, and whose eyes were not undimmed as the hurrahs called up memories of their native land:

"The men of Ireland! may they soon be enabled to strike a blow—and a successful one—for freedom!"

This toast was not less honoured than the previous one, and a subdued hurrah, sounding most strange to unaccustomed French ears, rang through the apartment.

"I claim the right," said Oliver Bond, when the acclaim was over, " to give the final toast. It is:

" To our next meeting. May it be amid the thunder of French guns bearing the crown of victory to the Irish nation!"

Amid a cheering and laughing that was delightful to witness, the toast was drunk; and, amid hearty wishes for his safe passage to France and the success of his mission, Eugene and his friend François shook hands with the gentlemen of the Directory of United Irishmen, and in company with John Sheares, passed down the dark stairway.

Over these buoyant and joyous hearts, full of high hope and expectation, but little of the shadow of coming disappointment fell that night! Coming events, it is said, cast their shadows before; but the statement was falsified in that company. For the Fates were weaving their gloomy shrouds for unfulfilled anticipations and dead hopes even then, and unseen lips were already chaunting the dirge for many of the gallant and high-hearted gentlemen whose pulses beat with lofty and chivalrous feelings.

There were no policemen to keep watch and ward over the streets—none but the old watchmen, "the Charlies"—and so in a few moments they had passed the back way into the stables, had harnessed the horses, and were soon swiftly driving through the dimly lighted streets.

"You had better drive to the Eagle for a moment or two," said Eugene, as they passed along the quays, "there is a gentleman there for whom I promised to call."

CHAPTER VIII.

A HURRIED DEPARTURE.

"Do not delay," whispered Sheares, as he sat, closely muffled up, on the driver's seat. "There is but little time to spare. You should be well down the channel by daybreak."

"I shall not be long," said the other, as he stepped to the door of the Eagle and knocked. It was opened immediately, and he entered. He returned without delay, alone. As he passed over to the car a form hurrying quickly collided against him.

"Hallo!" called Eugene.

"Why, Mr. Lefebre, I did not expect to meet you here so late."

"I have been just looking for Redmond and failed to see him. Have you seen him, Sir Trevor?"

"I saw him—that is—I mean to say I saw him in the forenoon."

"But to-night?" asked Eugene. "Have you seen him to-night?"

"No."

"I am surprised he has not met me. I wish to see him particularly, as I leave to-night."

"To-night."

"Yes. I am going back to France. Tell Redmond how sorry I am I did not see him. Good-bye, Sir Trevor. Shall return soon. Good-bye."

They parted, and Eugene leaped upon the trap.

"It is very odd," he said, as he re-took his seat, "the gentleman has not called, although he promised to meet me here an hour ago. He must have gone by some other route. Drive quickly; we shall have another stop to make."

"Was not that Sir Trevor Mortimer you spoke to," asked Sheares.

"Yes."

"I hope you did not tell him who was with you or where you were going."

"I told him where I was going certainly," said Eugene.

"Better you had not. He is a *mauvais sujet*, that gentleman. Not worse in Ireland."

The conversation ended with this.

The importance of the subject they had been discussing, the joyous enthusiasm of the meeting, and finally the necessity for proceeding without delay on his voyage, had prevented Eugene from more than a passing thought on Seamore. But now that they were alone on the road, no conversation passing between them, the sob and sigh of the waves breaking against the shore alone in his ears, his thoughts went with wonderful yearning to the place. The memory of the days he had spent there came with strong force on his mind now that he was hurriedly leaving it. He thought of Helen—of her welcoming voice, of her winning and handsome face, of her eye so bright with pleasure and delight when she saw him, until his brain filled with dream-pictures of her, until the dark night gave forth her face to his eye, and the murmur of the restless sea her silvery laugh. Attached to her as he had become, he never felt, until now that he was leaving her, that she had become so dear—so inexpressibly dear—to him.

The dark cloud or mist—obscuring the starlight—that hung over the sea seemed to him, as he vaguely gazed at it, a barrier of gloom and disappointment that should soon separate him from her and beloved Seamore. There was, however, the silver lining to it—the happiness that awaited him when he should come back and rejoice once more in the light of her presence.

Her presence! Why, what right had he to rejoice in her presence? She had never given him, in the slightest degree, to understand that the feelings which he now felt he so strongly entertained for her were reciprocated. She was warmly friendly to him, as became her to one who was so well beloved of yore and so long absent. Her frank and pleasant nature never concealed the delight she felt in having him among them; but that was all—of love there was none. And, then, on the other hand, Trevor Mortimer! He knew well enough—he could not be long in Seamore without understanding it—that Mortimer looked upon her as one who, in the natural course of events, should in time be his wife. Redmond possibly viewed matters in the same light. And for aught he knew, for no words passed between them on the subject, Helen might be possessed with the same views.

In the midst of these thoughts the trap reached the meadow that led up to the orchard. He quickly got down, desiring them to await his return, hastily crossed the meadow, clambered over the orchard wall, as he had done on the first night of his arrival—it was the shortest way—and, lifting the latch, entered.

It was close upon one o'clock. A solitary light was burning on the kitchen table, and one of the girls was sitting up awaiting his return.

"I am sorry to have kept you up, Norah," said he, as the girl, half-asleep, raised her head from the table. "I suppose they have all retired to bed, along ago."

"Ay, these two hours and more."

"Give me a light, Norah; I want to say a word in haste to Redmond."

"Redmond!" said the girl, in sleepy surprise; "is he not with you?"

"With me?" cried Eugene, in tones in which a sense

of disappointment was manifest. Do you mean to tell me Redmond has not yet returned?"

"No," said the girl, in alarm, "he has not. He went out with you, and we thought he would have returned with you."

"So he ought, but he did not meet me at the appointed place. I suppose he remained with his friends. I am going away for a short time, Norah, and——"

"Going away," said Norah, now roused completely from her sleepiness, "an' at this hour of the night! Won't you wait until morning?"

"Unfortunately I cannot, Norah. I shall be many a mile away before morning. I wish to leave a message for your mistress, Norah. You will give it to her?"

"Yes, I'll give it," said the girl; "but what am I tell her about Redmond?"

"Redmond will likely be home in the morning," said Eugene, as he finished the letter. "He has probably stopped with his friends in the city. Give Miss Barrington this note, Norah; and now good-bye. I am sorry I cannot remain longer," he said.

"When will you return? or how long will you be away?"

"Two questions pretty difficult to answer, Norah," he said, smiling. "I don't know myself; but I shall return as soon as I can. Tell Miss Barrington so, although I have said as much in my note. Once more—good-bye!"

He held out his right hand to bid her good-bye, and with the other handed her the note, and a gold ring which he took from his finger.

She took the former and returned the latter.

"I could not take this, Mr. Lefebre," she said. "If there was anything I could do for you I would do it, and with pleasure, but I could not accept a reward. You have been too friendly and kind since you came, and——"

"It is not a reward, in the ordinary sense of the word at least, Norah," he replied, as he noticed her rejection; "it is rather a memento to remember me by. In my hurried departure it is the only gift I can make, and you must accept it—at least until we meet again. Good-bye!"

Before the girl could make further motion he was gone.

Out into the darkening night, and this time by a circuitous route, until he reached where the parties were awaiting him.

"I fear I have delayed you," he said, as he resumed his seat, "but though it was at rather an unreasonable hour, I could not leave without a parting message."

"We have not too much time to waste; the night is passing, and you would want to be well away from the seaboard by sunrise," said John Sheares, as he handed him his cigar case.

The Frenchman wrapped his cloak around him, lit his cigar, and the vehicle whirled along the road to Dunleary in silence, so far as the three travellers were concerned.

They drove swiftly over the rough, scrubby brushwood —the Dunleary common—on which the town of Kingstown now stands, and without stop or stay until they reached the shingly strand, where in a sheltered nook the Albatross was rocking to and fro in the plash of the waves.

There was a weird silence around, when they had, after tying their horses to a tree, descended the steep hillside down to the little cove where, in the dim and misty moonlight, the little barque lay vaguely on the waters like some phantom vessel. There was no light on deck, and nothing to indicate that there was anyone on board. A sharp whistle, twice repeated from the lips of François, caused the appearance of some dim figures over the bulwarks; and after another interchange of similar signals a boat put off from her side, and with muffled oars was driven rapidly shorewards.

In a few moments her keel grated on the shingle.

"Is that you, captain?" asked François.

"Yes, *mon officer*," said the skipper. "I did not expect you back. We were just getting ready to start."

"I am glad you delayed," said the youth. "I am going back with another gentleman. How is it out at sea?"

"A fine spanking breeze from the Nor'-West; just the thing to suit us," said the skipper; "but we have very little time for delay. The night is waning rapidly. Jump in."

A HURRIED DEPARTURE.

The young Frenchman jumped into the boat, whilst Eugene and Sheares waited for a moment to exchange a word or two.

A hurried intimation from the captain that the breeze was freshening concluded the discourse; and in a few moments Eugene was by the side of his companion. In a quarter of an hour or less the anchor was hauled up, the sails expanded to the wind; and, as the United Irishman—so soon to climb the steps of the scaffold—clambered up the steep sides of the cliff to where his horses were tethered, and stayed a minute on his way to look round, a phosphorescent gleam on the water—a track of white wave—showed him where the rapid keel of the cutter was clearing its way out to sea, her sails showing in phantom dimness through the white mist that gathered over the waters.

"Good luck and God speed you," was the muttered parting prayer, as he untied his horses and turned his face homewards to the city.

CHAPTER IX.

DISASTER!

THE cold grey light of the dawn came slantingly from the East, across the breast of the Irish sea, as the cutter ran down the Channel off the Wicklow coast. The tops of the Croghan mountains far above were turning into gold as the rays fell on the white mists that circled their summits and dispersed them. The long line of surf in the wake of the boat, as the growing day-beams fell on it, showed very strikingly the effect the breeze had on her filling sails.

As it grew brighter, the captain swept with his glass the rather limited horizon within view, but closed it up again, as no sign of vessel on the sea gave indication of danger.

"With this breeze at our heels and no need for tacking," he said, "we shall be in the Atlantic in a few hours."

"You don't anticipate any danger, I hope," said Eugene, who noticed his survey of the sea with some concern.

"There is always cause for fear along this coast," said the captain sententiously.

"Well, I hope not on this occasion," said Eugene. "It seems perfectly clear of sail of any kind just at present."

"A run of a few miles might change all that," said the captain.

"You seem to me," said Eugene, as he stood up from where he had been sitting, "to have some cause for dread on your mind. Is that so. Have you?"

"As I said, there is always reason to be more or less uncomfortable."

"Is there any special reason for it now?"

"A little. Not much."

"What?"

"Well, as we came along last evening I thought I saw more than usual of cruisers in the Channel. But our little barque is rigged so like an English vessel, and so unlike a French one, that they never noticed us. They might now, though, seeing us coming back so speedily."

"They are on the alert in consequence of the movements of the French fleet," said Eugene confidently; "they have more weighty thoughts and cares on their minds than looking after such small craft as we."

"I am not so sure of that," said the captain. "All is fish that comes to their net at present; and if they even do not suspect our mission they might readily overhaul us for the purpose of strengthening their crew. The press-gang is nearly as busy on sea as on shore."

"You are pretty much of a Job's comforter," said Eugene, laughing. "It would be rather an unpleasant exchange to make from that of captain, that is to be, of a three-decker, to an able seaman before the mast in an enemy's vessel."

"More unlikely things have happened," said the skipper significantly. "There are a great many seamen serving on board the English fleet who learned their duties first in Brest and Toulon.

"Well, I must say," broke in François, as he lit a cigar,

"your conversation is not of the cheeriest character. A plague on all your ships, say I. I should rather ride beside Hoche on the Champs de Mars as a simple sous-lieutenant, looking at the long lines of glistening bayonets and with the thunder of the guns shaking the earth under your feet, than walk the deck of the finest 74 that ever rode the waves."

"There you are wrong, François," said Eugene enthusiastically. "There is no sight on earth so magnificent as a stately three-decker with her acres of canvas given to the breeze, and with her long rows of shotted guns protruding from her portholes, as she bears down like a thing of life on the enemy. There is a sense of power as she rides haughtily over the waves, crushing them with contempt beneath her, that nothing on land can give. With curving lines of grace and beauty she anchors off a hostile city broadside on, and before morning leaves it a heap of smoking ruins. That is the sense of power that makes a great ship at once so attractive and so glorious."

"It may be a matter of taste, but give me the charge of a gallant regiment on the enemy. See the thunder of their rush as the earth trembles and smokes under the hooves of their horses! See the glancing row of drawn sabres speeding like lightning! The waving plumes, the flashing eyes of the horses that seem to catch from their riders something of their gallant courage and chivalry; and hear their cheer as they burst like a thunderbolt on the foe! Oh, it is magnificent!"

"Your ideas are very fine, gentlemen," said the skipper, "and I am sorry to disturb them, but just now we shall be running in the neighbourhood of strange craft. I don't quite like the way the semaphores are signalling along the coast; and if you would take my advice you would retire to the cabin and take a sleep. Your presence here might attract the attention of curious telescopes and bring inquiries upon us."

"I think your advice sensible; and, as I have not closed an eye these thirty hours, I, for one, am quite prepared to follow it," said Eugene, as he raised himself from the little deck whereon they had been reclining over a heap of sails.

"And I, too," said François. "I not only slept none last night, but very little on my way here from France. This sea-travelling does not suit me, I fancy."

"You can have a long sleep if you will," said the captain, "for I do not wish—however much I like it—your presence on deck until after the sun goes down. We shall be then well into the Atlantic."

The two young men descended to the little cabin, where the two seamen who, in conjunction with the skipper, were to work the vessel to France, were arousing themselves from their short sleep; and but partially undressing, turned into their places.

Fatigued as he was, and worn with want of rest, Eugene felt himself unable to close his eyes or woo sleep to his brain—although his young companion had scarcely lain down when he was in a sound slumber.

He thought over the events of the past few weeks at Seamore, so peaceful and happy; and, whilst he did not murmur at the sudden call that brought him away, he felt sorry that his time had not been longer there. He wondered what Helen and Miss Howard would say, when, in the morning, they read his hurried note. He could almost see now—he felt sure that about this time they would have read it—the expression of surprise that would fasten in Helen's blue eyes, and the look of disappointment that would pale her face. What would he not give to have been able to say one last hurried word to her, and tell her that, though seas might roll between them, her face would be for ever present to him, and how dearly he loved her. How dearly, indeed, he loved her he did not himself feel until now, when circumstances hurriedly separated them. His very heart went forth to her in passionate tenderness and yearning! Every glance of her blue eye brightening into a smile as she looked, every movement of her graceful form as they rode side by side, the airy grace with which she handled the tiller when the breeze sent their little yacht aflying along the Dublin coast and brought the rich tints of rosy health into her cheeks, the musical voice as she carolled softly some old lay whose cadences seems to sink into the most inmost recesses of his heart and lie there—all came up on his thoughts with great force. There was a loneliness at his heart, a sinking of his spirits, as he thought that he was going from her presence—going, without even knowing that she returned his love, or that he might ever hope she would.

One thought occurred to him to brighten the gloom that was clouding on him: he would speedily return— the fleet, of which he was a commissioned captain, would shortly spread its sails for the Irish coast; and, once there, he would soon bask in the light of her beauty again, and tell her those passionate thoughts of love that were now passing through his brain and pressing at his heart.

In the middle of these reflections he fell asleep.

The sorrow of the separation that weighed on his heart whilst awake acted on his dreams, which partook of their desponding character.

He was at Seamore again, but, somehow, incongruously as is the manner of dreams, as a prisoner. Lonely, dejected, and outcast he was, amid the gaiety and joyousness of the place. There appeared to be but scant welcome for him, and, though surprised at this, he was unable from his position to find the reason. He saw Helen occasionally passing through the orchard at a distance, in all the enchanting gracefulness of her handsome form, or on horseback cantering along, turning her bewitching eyes upon the cavalier in attendance, whom he knew with a pang even in his dream to be Trevor Mortimer. A spasm of pain, like sudden poison killing the life within him, shot through his heart as he saw the easy, careless way in which her glances of affection were received by Mortimer, as if he were so certain of them and so assured of her love that it were needless for him to take the trouble of winning it.

Suddenly the scene changed. He stood beside the pillar of a church, a looker-on at some ceremony of which, for the nonce, he could not make out the meaning. By degrees the scene became clearer—it was a wedding. The altar was draped with flowers. The candles were lighted. The forms standing before the clergyman revealed themselves into distinctness—oh, heavens!—they were Helen Barrington and Trevor Mortimer. A feeling of rage, despair, insanity, suddenly seemed to possess him and render him helpless and stunned. The torrent of passion rendered him for a moment all but unconscious, out of which vacuity he was stirred by the words falling dimly on his ear: "Wilt thou take this man for thy wedded husband?" and the answer came in Helen Barrington's voice, low and soft, "I will."

Careless of place and time and circumstances, his agonised heart cried aloud:

"I forbid it! She is mine by reason of the strong love I bear her!—mine by reason of the heart and life she has made her own!"

Undeterred by—indeed, uncaring for—the effect his conduct had produced, he was pushing frantically his way up to the altar to claim her, if not by her own will, by the strength of his right arm, when a hand rudely placed on his shoulder—awoke him!

A confused murmur of voices was in the little cabin!

The sinking rays of the sun shone dimly in through the window, darkened occasionally by the rush of the white-crested wave as it flew by; but, though this was vaguely palpable to him, so absorbed had his dreaming brain become in the imaginary pictures called up before him, that for some time his waking thoughts could not realise whether it was imagination or actuality!

He was roused into complete consciousness by a rough shake; and a harsh voice said:

"Come, come, my good fellow, get up! You cannot be so sound asleep as all that. Don't have us to awaken you with a cutlass point. It is a capital awakener, but might be a trifle injudicious now, when his Majesty wants men so badly. Get up!"

"Where am I? What is this? Who are you?" asked Eugene in half-awaked astonishment as he saw the strange uniforms crowding the cabin, and the strange faces filling the doorway. "Where am I?"

"Where are you?" said the speaker with a mocking laugh, reiterating the question. "You are at present in the cabin of the Albatross—as villainous a little craft as ever tricked his Majesty's cutters, and stole treasonous messages and traitors from Ireland to France. And if you ask who are we: I am first lieutenant of his Majesty's ship of seventy-four, hard by, on board of which I must ask you to accompany me."

"Is this true, François?" asked Eugene, still half doubting that his senses were not deceiving him.

"True—yes," said the other mechanically; and Eugene saw at once from the manner in which he spoke that they had been seized whilst yet he slept.

"I am a French officer," he said, "on active service in the Republican fleet, but at present proceeding on private business; and it is not according to the rules of war to make me prisoner."

"The greater the reason why you will be welcome to us. You will need less training," said the officer mockingly.

"This mockery is not the part of brave men to those unarmed," said Eugene, as, having dressed himself, he stood upright among them.

"Perhaps not," said the officer sneeringly, "they act otherwise in your service. A swing from the yard-arm or a fusilade on the quarter-deck is the distinguishing honour you confer in *your* service on English prisoners."

"It is false," said Eugene angrily, "French officers know how to treat a captive foe."

"So I have said," said the lieutenant with a wink at his comrades, who answered with a laugh. "They only know it too well. But we have not time to discuss the subject at present. We shall have ample time later on. Meantime, I shall thank you for any papers you possess."

"Pardon, monsieur," said Eugene haughtily, as he noticed with ill-restrained anger this disposition to jeer on the part of his captors. "You must get these as best you may. Even if I possessed them I should be sorry to yield them up. You have no right to make prisoners of men not in arms."

"Not in arms, possibly; engaged on a treasonable mission, yes. But if you do not wish to yield them up we shall make search for them otherwise. Men, take the prisoners on board the Thunderer."

The order was at once complied with; and between files of marines the five prisoners marched on deck and up the gangway that depended from the side of the huge man-of-war.

After a long and careful search into every part of the Albatross, the lieutenant and the few men that remained with him clambered on deck also; a long gun was run out from one of the portholes and depressed on the little barque. A puff of smoke, a flash of light, a sharp boom, and the Albatross, shattered from stem to stern, filled rapidly, and sank in the deep waters—her sails destined never more to fill with the freshening breeze or her keel to cleave the glistening waters.

Her voyages between France and Ireland were ended.

CHAPTER X.

CONDEMNED AS A SPY!

It was with a heart beating with conflicting emotions that Eugene found himself in the officers' quarters of the Thunderer, wherein at a large table sat the captain and a number of gentlemen resplendent with all the gorgeousness of naval uniform. If he had had time to analyse these emotions he would have found the principal one to be a vague sense of disappointment and loss and disaster. Not loss or disaster to himself—for he knew well enough that every man in warfare on sea or land must run the risk of these—they are the incidents of his profession; but for others. Simple as was the little barque in appearance that was even then making her rapid way through the deep waters to the bottom, she bore important fortunes. The future of a gallant and brave nation struggling into the light of freedom was in her keeping, and mayhap the safety of a powerful and friendly fleet. He was convinced, from all that he had heard the night before, that the only chance for success attending the great venture which France was about to make in Ireland's cause, was in making the Eastern coast their point of debarkation; and that unless the present intention of the Republican leaders were altered, sorrow would come to the cause now engaging the attention of the high-hearted men whom he had left last night—and misfortune to a French army and fleet.

Relying upon the great success with which hitherto their messages had been conveyed, he knew the Irish leaders would rely on *this* message reaching safely also, and would not send a duplicate. Indeed, except himself and François, they had no one sufficiently acquainted with French customs and ways to do the work. He shuddered as he thought of the tremendously important efforts now making in France in the wrong direction, and the impossibility at present of a warning or advising voice reaching them.

He banished, with a strong effort, these uncomfortable feelings and thoughts, as he perceived the necessity for keeping a bold and unconcerned front to the group of officers before whom he was brought. And his first thought in this new train of ideas which his position suggested was, what information as to his position and recent doings should he give his captors, or should he decline to give any at all? The query had no sooner occurred to him than he immediately answered it by mentally adopting the latter course. But the first question addressed to him showed how futile it was.

"Your name is Eugene Lefebre?" half queried, half affirmed the captain, after glancing at a paper lying on the table before him

"Yes, that is my name," said the prisoner with great surprise; for he was quite unable to comprehend how they had acquired knowledge of his name.

"First lieutenant on board the French Republican frigate, *La Vengeur*?"

"I hold that position," said Eugene, bowing.

"You have been in Ireland?"

"I have."

"State to the court here assembled the mission or business that brought you there."

"That I must decline doing."

"It is unnecessary for you to do so. It is all set out here. You were, in the first place, sent on business, on a treasonable errand, from the usurped Republican Government to stir up disaffection in Ireland, and to give countenance and aid and advice to certain traitors there Is not that so?"

"I decline to state."

"Be it so. You were further sent over to make arrangements for the possible landing of a French invading force, now or at some future time. Is not that so?"

"I decline to state," said Eugene, with some difficulty, endeavouring to keep a calm and unconcerned bearing in face of these statements. He was completely puzzled how they could have arrived at this information, considering the secrecy with which his mission had been conducted.

"It is entirely unnecessary for you to do so; I see the statements are quite correct. You see, lieutenant, how well we are served in our information. This is a question you can perhaps answer: What treatment is awarded in your nation to emissaries caught stirring up rebellion and anarchy?"

"That is a question for yourself to answer," said Eugene haughtily.

"Perhaps it is. What treatment is awarded in your nation to persons found acting as spies from the enemy's camp?"

"I am no spy," said Eugene indignantly. "The French service never sends its officers on such service."

"They do not give them that name, perhaps. We do. Well, as you prefer not to answer, I shall answer for you. If caught on land, they are shot on a trench side without trial; if on sea, they are summarily strung up from the yard-arm without investigation."

"I fear neither the one nor the other," said the prisoner proudly.

"Fear would be useless and unavailing before the inevitable. We shall, however, recognise your position and your youth by according you some time. We shall not take you as short as your nation have taken many of our brave officers—if we are strong we shall be merciful. We shall give you the night to prepare for the next world. The sentence of the court is, that you be hung from the yard-arm at gun-shot in the morning. Take the prisoner away."

It was a short and inglorious termination to a career so bright with hope and future promise. The glorious life which he had pictured to himself in the French service had vanished, as a cloud obscures a burst of sunshine of an April day.

Yet he thought not of these things as he lay upon the bunk which was the only article of furniture in the ship's prison wherein he was confined.

"I have too often faced death before," he thought to himself, as he extended his form thereon, "to fear it now, though it presents itself in an unexpected shape. I have often enough seen those bright with hope and radiant with enthusiasm go forth in the morning—and never return. There was no sorrowing over them, for they had died as became brave men, in the high and honoured remembrance of their comrades. Wherefore should I care for death? But—I should like to see Helen. I should like to see her if for one instant only, to tell her of the deep love I bore her. The only sad thing in this end of mine is that she shall never know it. The will of heaven be done."

His thoughts went over to the seashore at Seamore, to the orchard which he had passed so blithely through some weeks before, and to the rambles in the soft November sunshine through the meadows around or over the white strand. He placed his hand on his breast to assure himself that the treasured glove was there.

He placed it to his lips and kissed it.

Finally he fell asleep. The end was now come, and all anxiety and care in the future for him was terminated. Precisely as the convict—knowing the worst, and anticipating in the world nothing further—falls asleep the night before his doom comes, so the young Frenchman, without seeking it, obtained the sleep he vainly courted when in safety, and in dreamless slumbers passed the night.

CHAPTER XI.

A MYSTERIOUS WARNING!

When Helen awoke the next morning and rang the bell, instead of her maid, it was the old housekeeper, Cauth, who made her appearance, and with a letter in her hand.

"What is that?" asked Helen.

"A letter, dear."

"A letter, Grannie—from whom?"

Her words were not spoken without some alarm, as she noticed the look of trouble that was over Cauth's face.

"From Eugene Lefebre, dear."

"Eugene Lefebre! What should he send a letter for? Where is he?"

"Gone——"

"Gone!" cried Helen. "Gone where."

"I don't know. No one knows. He came late last night or towards morning, and gave this note to Norah for you."

"Does Redmond not know where he is gone to?" asked Helen tremulously, as she mechanically took the letter addressed to her.

"Redmond has not come back yet."

"Where is Sir Trevor—does he know?"

"Sir Trevor has not returned either, Helen."

"Not returned!" said Helen, with a feeling of unaccountable dread rising at her heart. "What happened, Grannie? Tell me. I am sure your are concealing something from me."

"Nothing has happened that I know of, Helen. Don't frighten yourself without cause. Redmond and Sir Trevor are sure to be well. What would happen them?"

"I don't know, Grannie, but I *am* awfully frightened. Who came with Eugene?"

"No one. He came alone. But read the letter, *aroon*. He'll tell you all in that."

Helen opened the letter with trembling hands. It contained but a few hastily written lines.

They ran:—

"Dear Miss Barrington—or dear Helen, as you have permitted me to call you—I am leaving Seamore without having time to bid you good-bye. But I shall see you again shortly. And until I do return, believe me there is not a waking moment that your dear face and pleasant Seamore shall not be in my thoughts. My heart is too full to say more. Adieu, dear Helen.—Eugene."

Helen blushed as she read the concluding lines, and felt how much warmth and love lay behind them. But the feeling of embarrassment quickly gave place to one of trouble as she folded the note.

"He does not say a word in this of where he is going, or why. Nor a word of Redmond. Could Redmond have gone with him? Nor of Trevor Mortimer."

"Why would Redmond have gone with him, Helen? What had Redmond to do with him?" asked the old woman in a more cheerful tone, as she witnessed the distress palpable in her young mistress's face. "Eugene came, my dear, as his father came before him, and it's well he went away without leaving, as his father did, sorrow behind him. I was always afraid ever since the night he came that he would bring, as his father brought, trouble and grief about the house and to the family. I thank God he is gone!"

"And you were so fond of him, Grannie!" said Helen, with tender upbraiding. "And he was so handsome and pleasant!"

"I *was* fond of him, Helen *aroon*," said the old woman, as the tears arose in her dim eyes, "and I was fond of him when his head could not reach the table—for there never was a sweeter or more engaging child; but I am fonder of others, my dear, and others that I am bound for the sake of your father and mother to love more dearly and take care of; and, therefore, I say it again, I am glad he is gone. And as to being handsome and pleasant, my dear, there never was braver or pleasanter or handsomer than his father, and see what came of it! See the sorrow and short ending he brought to a young life that never knew care until she looked upon his face."

"I wish you would not be telling me these things," said Helen, and her eyes suffusing with tears; "they bring distress to me."

"Better that distress now, my dear, than life-long sorrow and distress—the distress that knows no ending and no relief. It is sad to lose a pleasant acquaintance, and no one can say but that he brightened the house, but it is as well that he is gone. I am an old woman, Helen— my hair was grey and my form bent before you were born —and you should be said and led by me. I see the world in a different light from you. Think no more of him.

He was a wild bird of passage that but appeared and disappeared. But think of *him* that is true and tried, and will always be beside you. And now, Helen, it is time for me to go, and time for you to get up; for Redmond will be coming home shortly. I thought I'd come up with the letter myself, for Norah, the hussey, would be only putting *raimshogues* in your head."

The old woman's advice had but little effect, or rather the opposite effect to that intended; for as Helen dressed herself when Cauth had departed she had a good hearty cry to herself. The future in Seamore seemed so darkened, wanting the light of his cheery presence! and she felt at once so indignant and mortified and sorry at his abrupt departure without even seeing her! At times her indignation grew so strong that she resolved to think of him no more, as one not worthy of their welcome and their kindness; but the next moment she found herself dwelling on some pleasant incident in their daily lives—on some graceful and marked attention he had paid her—some little trifling event that his innate taste and chivalry had turned into an occasion to give her pleasure.

Helen would have laughed joyously if Kate Howard had hinted whilst Eugene was there, that she seemed to be more attracted by his attentions than by the warmer devotion of Trevor Mortimer. It was so absurd! But now that he was gone it seemed to her as if all the light and grace and beauty had departed from Seamore, and there was nothing but dulness and desolation left. The remembrance of the fact that if the gay sailor had gone, Trevor Mortimer still remained, hardly seemed to abate in the least the sense of loneliness she felt.

"Why, Helen, what's amiss?" asked Miss Howard, as she entered her friend's room and saw the signs of tears in her eyes.

"Read this," said the latter, presenting the letter.

"How absurd!" was the unsentimental remark of the other. "What a mysterious way he has of coming and going. He first terrifies us by his strange appearance, and then worries us by his equally strange disappearance."

"Is that all you care for the departure of a friend, Kate?" said Helen indignantly, her friend's practical way of viewing the matter grating very harshly on her tenderer nature—" one, too, whom we may never see again."

" Have you never had a friend leave you before, Helen?" asked Miss Howard.

" Of course. Why should you ask the question?"

" Because in that case, Helen, if you did not grieve so much in that parting—and I am sure you did not—there must be something more than usual in the circumstances of this. And yet the idea of your being in love with him, my dear! It could not be."

" I have never said so," said Helen, blushing, " but even if I did, what would there be extraordinary in it?"

" Everything, Helen, my dear—everything. But as you have said you are not, and as I am sure you are not, let us not talk more of it. Come to breakfast. I am sorry, too, he is gone, he was so cheerful and agreeable; but we did not expect him to remain always—did we, my dear? And to tell you the truth, Helen, he was always a little too mysterious for my taste. You remember the alarm he created the first night by his sudden and unexpected coming?"

" The fault was on my side for being so easily frightened," said Helen, rather more inclined to stand up for her late guest now that every one seemed against him, " and not on his for coming."

" True, Helen, but it was a little startling, was it not? And you remember that matter of the glove."

" I had almost forgotten that," said Helen with a slight recurrence of her old alarm.

" Well, I am glad you remember it now, and I don't think you should regret his absence," said her friend, noticing with satisfaction the change in her manner. " Depend upon it, Helen, he is one of these gay foreigners who delight in winning girls' affections for the triumph of the thing, and who make themselves agreeable because it pleases themselves to do so, more than because it pleases others."

Helen said nothing, but, having completed her toilet, descended to the breakfast room with her companion. The mention of the glove, which had previously escaped her thoughts, gave them a new complexion—and a distressing one—but of this she said nothing. It was of a very different character, however, from what Miss Howard inferred.

They had, indeed, sufficient in the conjectures as to what delayed Redmond—who did not turn up at breakfast—to wholly change the subject of discourse. He very rarely remained a night away from the roof, and never at all without previously acquainting them of his intention so to do, and his doing so in this instance gave rise to many conjectures.

Kate was stronger minded, as we have said, than the young lady of the mansion, and, therefore, to arouse the latter's attention from what she considered her morbid fears, suggested a ride before dinner, by which time Redmond would have returned. To this Helen assented.

The day shone, for a November one bright and bracing. The ground was hard and dry, and the sides of the hills in the distance looked starred with rubies and amethyst in the clear rays of the morning sun. The sea was still and calm along the sands, though farther out the freshening breeze off the land sent the vessels within view sweeping merrily along.

"I think we shall ride along the coast to-day," said Helen, after they had cantered for some time in silence. "It seems pleasanter than inland. What do you think, Kate?"

"I think, dear, as we have the day before us, and you need some change, we shall ride inland."

Helen agreed and they turned their horses' heads towards the mountains, where, on the hills over-looking the Dublin coast, they spent an enjoyable hour. The little fishing village of Bray, with its cluster of thatched cottages, embowered in woods, stood to their right, whilst the sea coast thence to Dublin—now almost a continuation of the city and studded with mansions—lay in unbroken solitude. To their left the city, lying close together as befitted one of the "walled towns of the Pale," centered upon the Liffey; for the splendid and stately townships of Rathmines, Rathgar, and Pembroke were then undreamt of, and the districts they now occupy were covered with gardens and orchards.

A quick ride brought them back within sight of Seamore.
"As we did not take the sea route in the morning," said Helen, "suppose we do so now. The tide will be in, and once we get out of this scrub a canter along it will be very pleasant."

"As you please," said her companion assentingly. She was glad to see that the paleness of her friend's face, arising from the news of the morning, had given place to a rosy look of enjoyment. "The sea is really pleasant to-day. Let us canter along this bypath here, and have a gallop over the meadows. I am glad you are enjoying the ride——Oh, Moya! is that you?"

The address was delivered to an old crone who had arisen from a seat by a bush on the narrow pathway, and whose sudden appearance had caused the horses to swerve violently.

"Why, you have frightened the horses, Moya," said Helen. "What brings you out so late? You cannot expect to meet anyone to tell fortunes to at this hour?"

"And why not, acushla?" said the old woman, leaning on her staff and peering curiously at them both from under her disengaged hand. "Why not? Is there anywan in the world, gentle or simple, that wouldn't like to hear what's comin to them with the winds of heaven and the flow of the sea day after day? Is there anywan humankind to whom the year that's comin' won't bring changed fortunes that they might be wishin' to hear?"

"If there be not, Moya," said Helen, laughing, "there must a great deal of simple people in the world."

"Maybe ay and maybe no," said the old woman, with a peculiar significance. "There are many that think themselves fortunate an' happy when from parts unknown the very waves are carrying and the wind of heaven hastening to 'em sorrow and trouble they know little of and dream little of. And there are others that cry salt tears over misfortunes that if they only knew about as I do they would look upon as brightest blessings."

"Well, Moya, I was always an unbeliever; I am afraid I shall remain so."

"Avoch, an' it's many is the sore day people had for that same thing," said the old woman, "an' many a wan hastened the wearin' ov their shroud for want ov listenin' to Moya's advice. An' maybe it's yourself that's havin' the sore heart—if you'd only let on, Helen Barrington—for what you 'ud rejoice at if you only knew it as well as I do."

"What's that you say, Moya?" asked Helen, but faintly catching up the meaning of the old woman's words. She had been letting her horse go forward, and the motion prevented her hearing them exactly. She now reined back the animal and gazed on the old woman's face with wonderment.

"What's that you said, Moya?"

"What I've said is said," said the old crone mysteriously and with apparent indignation, "an' you'd have saved yourself many hours of sorrow an' woe if you had hearkened to Moya's advice when she offered it to you."

"You are speaking in riddles, Moya," said the young girl, grievously disturbed. "What *do* you mean? What are you talking about?"

But Moya, leaning on her crutch, had hobbled into a sheep track that led to her cabin by the seashore, and, as they well knew from her habits and character, was quite unlikely to come back again to them.

There was nothing for it but to proceed on their journey homewards, which somehow they did with but little of the elasticity and enjoyment of heart they possessed when they had first been startled by her appearance.
must be some dreadful meaning behind her words. She "What in the world does she mean, Kate? There has made me feel dreadfully alarmed."

"What does she mean, Helen dear?" reiterated Kate, who herself felt but little at ease. "Nothing. Have we not heard her rhapsodies dozens of times before?"

"Yes, I know. But she seems to have more meaning in what she says now. I know she has by the way she looked and spoke."

"What meaning would she have? You surely do not believe in her powers of fortune-telling?"

"No; but she has such wonderful acquaintance with everything and everybody that I am sure she is predicting some misfortune."

"Predicting, Helen?"

"Well, no; but she certainly knows of it somehow. Could you remember what she said? I cannot remember a word of it, she so alarmed me."

"I was not paying attention enough to remember—nor indeed is it worth while," said Miss Howard brightly. "I remember, however, that she said something about people sorrowing over troubles which may not turn out troubles after all, but blessings—which, indeed, is perfectly true, though old Moya said it. But the mists are rising, dear, and the dusk is gathering. Let us go quicker."

"I hope Redmond has returned. I hope she augured no evil to him," said Helen, whose heart was but little rejoiced by her companion's words,

"Why should she augur evil to him or you? You have never done her harm. You have always been friends with her."

"She was always made welcome whenever she came—when father and mother were there—which was seldom, I don't know why. But I know well they always more or less dreaded her. I don't know why, either."

"But they never offended her?"

"No. They were always kind to her as to others."

"And Redmond and you the same?"

"Yes."

"Then, Helen, she would have a blacker heart than most of her kind to croak evil to you or of you. But she has done neither, you will find. She has been only airing some of her crazy follies. Come quicker, dear."

The remainder of the ride was performed in silence, for the dusk was falling and the white mists arising from the sea were still further darkening the landscape. The scrubby ground they were travelling over was not pleasant in the dusk.

Arrived at Seamore, Helen dismounted, threw the bridle to one of the men, and, gathering her riding dress in one hand, walked gravely towards the hall-door, up the steps, and into the hall.

"Cauth—Grannie!" she said, in a burst of anxiety. But a look at the old servitor's face, with the signs of anxiety also thereon, caused her to recoil, and the question died unspoken on her lips.

"Redmond has not returned, Grannie?" she said as soon as she recovered her speech, interpreting the look upon the other's face.

"There is no cause for alarm in that, Helen dear," said the housekeeper; but her assurance came on unheeding ears. Indeed her looks belied them.

"O Grannie! Grannie! I know something has happened him, for he would not remain away without telling us. Could he have gone with Eugene? I feel an unaccountable dread of something having happened him."

"What would happen him *aroon?* Men are not accustomed to go astray. There is many a thing to keep men away for a day or two when they meet friends. He may have met some of his cousins and gone to Kildare for a day's shooting."

"So he might, Grannie," said the young girl, much relieved all at once by this suggestion, which she knew to be a very likely one. "I hadn't thought of that."

He had not infrequently before driven down with his friends to their place in the country from Dublin; but then it was mostly by appointment. Still it was not unlikely—quite the contrary, it was very likely—that having met them accidentally he had taken the notion and driven down with them. Helen felt quite rejoiced, and the weary load of forebodings that pressed at her heart since morning was greatly lightened.

"But I'll tell you who has returned," said the housekeeper.

"Not Eugene!" said Miss Howard, who had rejoined her friend.

"And why not Eugene?" laughingly queried and interrupted Helen, whose spirits gradually rose to their accustomed lightness in the warmth and protection of home. "Who is it, Grannie?"

"Trevor Mortimer."

"Trevor Mortimer," said Helen, with a voice of pleasure, but in which there was also a tinge of disappointment, for, in spite of herself, she was hoping that it really might be Eugene. "I did not expect him."

"And he is not the less welcome for that, I trust," said the gentleman in question, coming forward. He had been standing in the shadow of one of the pillars of the spacious hall, an unseen and unobserved listener to the conversation that had passed.

"No, indeed, Sir Trevor—the pleasure is only the greater for that. But how strong you are looking! You have quite recovered."

"Quite. And I am none the less improved for seeing yourself and Miss Howard again. But I am sorry to hear that our friend has left. I had hoped to have the pleasure of seeing both gentlemen again this evening."

"Mr. Eugene Lefebre has disappeared nearly as mysteriously as he came," said Miss Howard, as she warmly welcomed the new comer, "and that was mysteriously enough in all conscience."

"How good it was of you to visit us when the others had deserted us," said Helen. "I don't know what we should have done by ourselves this evening. Do you, Kate?"

"Sir Trevor is always true to his trust—perhaps I should say, true to his tryst. He is most chivalrous in his disinterested championship of forlorn ladies," said Miss Howard with malicious good nature, which not a little embarrassed Kate.

"I am sorry trysts are not for such as I," said Mortimer, joining, with easy self possession in the raillery. "I am too matter-of-fact and unromantic for that."

"What a good natured soul!" said Miss Howard, taking him by the arm with charming familiarity. "One always knows where to find *you*—don't they?"

"I trust my friends always will—and my enemies too," said he, not a little proudly.

"If such a dear fellow could have enemies—a sheer impossibility, I take it," she said.

"I am afraid this," said he, pointing to where the wound over his breast was, "showed the impossibility was very possible indeed. It was bad enough—don't you think so?"

"Your heart?" said she, maliciously mistaking his reference. "I did not think it was so bad as that. I gave you credit for one that was large, open, and chivalrous."

"It was large and open enough," said Mortimer, pretending not to hear her earlier words, "but as to being chivalrous, I fear it lacked something of that high quality."

"Touching dinner, Grannie," interrupted Helen, who had been an amused listener to this bit of repartee, "if this pair would descend from their high world of compliments and entertain the idea, I should be glad of it. I shall not object to it, whoever else does."

"After a ride of some fourteen miles—it was that, was it not, Helen, dear?—I don't think I shall have any scruple against it, either."

"If Sir Trevor would only do us the favour to——" suggested Helen.

"No entreaties necessary, my dear Miss Barrington. I came a very long journey myself to-day, intending to dine with my absent friends, but I do not see that I shall sorrow much for their absence under the circumstances!"

"Well, Grannie?"

"It is ready at any moment, and can be served at once."

The ancient housekeeper, as was her wont since the death of Helen's parents, presided at the table—a position her long standing and the affection entertained for her by Helen and Redmond, readily accorded her. The former took her place at the lower end; and, with Sir Trevor at one side and Kate Howard at the other, a very pleasant and agreeable entertainment was entered upon.

The ruddy glare of the fire—not at all unpleasant in the lowering darkness of a November night—and the brilliant light from the chandelier overhead—for it was long preceding the era of gas—coupled with the musical laughter of the girls' lips, made it a scene of rare happiness and enjoyment.

For the time there was no shadow of care or misfortune. If ill bodements were near, they must have stowed themselves away in the shadows thrown by the burning logs and so hidden themselves, for they did not otherwise dim the scene; and no thought of the fate of him who slept in the Thunderer, 74 line-of-battle ship—with death on the yardarm at sunrise for the pale watcher over his slumbers —came to them; nor thought of him also unaccountably absent—and *not* gone to Kildare.

Verily Moya was not far astray when she said—"There are many who think themselves fortunate when, from parts unknown, the very waves are bearing and the very winds hastening sorrow and trouble to them they little know of and little dream of."

CHAPTER XII.

SUSPENSE.

THE wonder and anguish of the girls grew and grew as a day passed over, a second day, and a third day, without Redmond's turning up.

Each successive day diminished the belief, that Helen entertained, of his having gone to the country.

On the fourth day, early in the morning, Mortimer undertook to ride down to the place in Kildare to look for him, being actuated thereto, as he said, by the agony of suspense which had grown up in Helen's breast. Inquiries had been made about Redmond in Dublin, but at none of the places where he had been accustomed to call had he put in an appearance.

At one place only had he been seen—at the Eagle in Eustace-street. There was no one with him there answering at all to the description of Eugene. Friends and acquaintances he had among the members of Parliament assembled in Dublin, and who were wont to spend an evening at this great resort of country gentlemen; but the most minute inquiries among these failed to acquire a knowledge of his coming or going. In the numbers of young gentlemen who were accustomed to come to the metropolis—the great centre of attraction at that time in Ireland, the tendency to go to London not having then taken hold of the Irish people—and who spent their gay time between the theatres and fashionable resorts, it would be out of the question to pay attention to anyone in particular, or, indeed, to single him out from among the crowds of wealthy young *habitues.*

Helen's heart was overwhelmed with suspense; but when

Mortimer returned from Kildare, in company with one of her cousins, with the news that he had not been there, her anguish and agony knew no bounds. Indeed, the friends in the country were not less surprised than she was, and, thus in their anxiety, had despatched one of their people to come to Seamore and see what way matters stood.

At a little family council that evening in Seamore it was determined—and Mortimer undertook—to put the authorities at the Castle in motion concerning him.

Various surmises were entertained as to where he had gone, but the only tangible one—the only one that was not based on the airiest conjectures—was that which set him down as having departed on some secret errand with Eugene. Were it not for this, and this alone, Helen's heart would fairly have broken with the feeling of dread and uncertainty and suspense which filled it.

At times she buoyed herself up with the hope that this was the case. But when she came to examine the matter her heart again sank into seas of woe. He had never departed that night, had he been with Eugene, without acquainting her of his intention. No inducement would have led him to leave her in such uncertainty. And then, again, was not Eugene alone when he came? In his letter there was not a breathed word about Redmond— nothing that could give even the most unreliable colour to the belief that they had departed together.

The terror of being alone—of losing the only one guide that she had in the world—was driving poor Helen into a state of agony that was indescribable.

What had become of Redmond? That was the question that unceasingly passed through her thoughts. Had he been secretly conveyed away or imprisoned—or, oh, merciful heavens! had he been drowned or murdered?

There was more in the latter idea than might be thought. In those remote days—though not quite a hundred years ago—Dublin was but scantily lighted. The quay walls had not been built—or were but partially built. The stalwart array of policemen, who now guard the streets whilst its inmates are sleeping, had for their predecessors the old infirm "Charlies"—not unlike the celebrated watchmen of Limerick—who generally managed to hide themselves when an outburst in the dark street, not at all infrequent, indicated a murderous brawl.

All these things smote in a vague way on her tortured mind.

Meanwhile, in some way, Moay's strange talk on the evening of their ride home occurred to her, and, taking fast hold of her thoughts, became associated with her fears and her terrors.

As she sat at the table absently listening to the subdued conversation around her, she suddenly fixed on a resolution. She would go and see Moya—see her that very night. *She* would throw some light—Helen felt sure she would—on the mysteries that were surrounding her. Helen always, though laughingly joking at the old woman's dazed prophecies, had yet, like an impressionable girl, a furtive belief in them. Her half-belief was now changing into an entire one. The old crone's mysterious hints on that evening evidently had reference to the present troubles. What if she could throw light on the present mysteries? What if she could tell where Redmond was, or what had become of him? More unlikely things had happened.

Helen's resolution was taken. She would that night proceed to the hut by the seaside, and see the old woman and interview her. It was an unusual thing for a girl in her position to do, but the circumstances were unusual, and Redmond's fate—nay, perhaps his life—hung in the balance.

That night, when Mortimer had proceeded to town to prosecute searches and set the authorities in motion, and when Kate Howard had retired in disconsolate sorrow to her room, Helen, drying her burning tears and wrapping herself in her cloak, let herself out noiselessly, and, opening the wicket doors that gave ingress and egress to the orchard, passed across the scrubby sheepwalks that led in the direction of the old woman's hut.

G

CHAPTER XIII.

THE MIDNIGHT VISIT.

Helen Barrington knew very well that she was sure to find the old fortune teller up. Often, when driving with her father and brother on their way from the theatre late, she had wondered to see the light burning in the old woman's window. Redmond, out with his yacht at night at sea, had often remarked when coming home, the uncanny look her solitary candle or rushlight in the dim darkness had. He always said it looked like an omen of evil. The fishermen, coming in at or before daybreak of Winter-nights, used to say when they saw it, "Old Moya's reading the cards yet," or, "It must be the devil that's keeping company with Moya, else she wouldn't be up so late."

All—as Helen thought of them—assuring enough as to the chances of finding her up, but far from assuring in other respects.

In truth, the farther she left her home behind her, and the nearer she came to the old crone's den, the more her heart failed her. She was in a tremble of terror, yet she bravely kept on. Unheeding the coarse whins, whose long ragged arms now and then sent a new shiver of fear over her—so like ghosts did they seem to her—she pursued her way with trembling courage, wishing to see the light in Moya's window, and yet fearing to see it. And when at last it did become visible—like the bale-fire of some evil genius—her courage seemed suddenly to give way, her knees bent under her, thick mists seemed to rise before her eyes, and she felt as if she were about to swoon.

She made an effort to bless herself with the little gold cross that hung suspended over her breast, and recovered courage.

"It is for Redmond—for poor Redmond's safety," she said to herself to strengthen her beating heart, and once more moved forward along the sheep-track so fearfully sentinelled on either side by the ghost-like waving arms of the rugged whins. Her hands were scratched and torn with them, and her face smarted under the pain they inflicted when they re-bent as she passed; but, unheeding either, she breathlessly hurried along—hurried to give herself no time for thinking or faintheartedness.

She was running a race with her fears, and at any moment they might overtake her and beat down her resolution!

She dropped upon her knees as she came in sight of the half-closed door of the hut, through which a faint light shone. It seemed to her now as if something unholy and wrong was the object of her mission. She tried to offer up a prayer as well as her disconnected thoughts would allow her, and bent her head in fervency of the words that placed her under the protection of the Queen of Sorrows.

She raised her head and was about standing up when a cry rose to her lips—but died thereon. For passing out through the opened door, and between her and the light, came a form that she recognised in a moment. She could hardly be mistaken. It was that of Trevor Mortimer! Her eyes had lighted upon it for a moment in the brief space whilst the form was passing from the light into the thick darkness beyond it—for a moment merely—but she felt sure it was he.

"What could have brought him there?" she thought in wonderment so excessive that it banished her previous fears. "What had brought him there? He had set out from Seamore with the intention of going to the city direct. Did he know Moya, and if so how and why? Or had he been possessed by the thoughts that actuated herself, and, believing in the old fortune-teller's powers, had come to test them in Redmond's behoof? There was nothing more likely. It was what a kindly, thoughtful, high-spirited man would do in the interests of his friend."

Helen's heart rose within her, and, with less trepidation than she had yet shown or felt, she moved forward to the door—opened it gently, and entered.

The fortune-teller was sitting on a low boss or straw seat in front of the fire that burned on the hearth. The room was full of smoke, and through the haze Helen could see her but dimly, as she crouched rather than sat, with her head bent down upon her knees.

"Moya!"

She called softly, for her motion entering was so noiseless, that her light footfall disturbed not the attention of the old hag. Nor did her name, now called.

"Moya!"

This time the strange voice struck on the old woman's ear. She started up in alarm, startled by the unexpected call; and as she did so a quantity of coin that she had evidently been counting, fell to the ground with a jingling noise.

"Who's that? Who's there?" she cried fiercely, as raising her bent form, she turned her bleared eyes in the direction of the visitor.

"It is I, Moya—Helen Barrington," said the latter deprecatingly.

"An' what brings you here this hour ov the night, Helen Barrington?" shrieked the hag still wrathfully.

"I came to talk with you, Moya—good Moya," said Helen pleadingly. "I want your advice."

"Advice!" jibed the hag. "Advice! Helen Barrington, that always laughed at Moya's advice, comes now in the dark hours of the night to seek it!"

"I am in trouble, Moya—in great trouble—and—and I think you would help me. If you can, Moya—for the love of heaven!—do."

The old woman stared at the slender form of the young girl, standing on the floor before her, for some time without speaking.

"Sit down!" she said at last, motioning her to a seat somewhat similar to the one she had arisen from herself, but higher.

Her words were so almost menacing that the young girl, though instinctively disliking to sit in the smoking cabin, was fain to do so.

"What trouble are you in?"

"Moya, Redmond went into the city with a friend——"

"Ay, the Frenchman! I know. A good companion he had," said the woman sneeringly.

"Did you know him, Moya?" asked Helen, the train of her thoughts entirely disconcerted by this remark.

"Did I know him?" hissed the hag. "Did I know his father before him? Ay, and others had cause to know him. Bad; seed and breed—all bad."

"Not Eugene, Moya. Good Moya! not Eugene, I hope."

"Not Eugene!" repeated in mocking terms the fortune-teller. "Not Eugene! not Eugene, with his hands red with blood!"

"With blood!" cried Helen, her indignation for the moment getting the better of her fears. "You are mistaken, Moya, his hand and his heart were as innocent as my own."

"Do you tell me that in my own cabin? Do you tell me, who watched him skulking around here night after night until he found opportunity to strike a favoured rival the coward's blow that would have been a murderer's but that his hand failed him, and heart too, at the last minit. Didn't I see him strike the blow? Didn't I see him creep along, the knife in his hand, until——"

"Moya! Moya! for the love of the Blessed Virgin, who are you talking about? Who are you speaking of?" cried Helen, whose thoughts ran at once on Redmond.

"Who am I talking about? Who were you talking about? Your Frenchman. Who else? Didn't I see him follow him——"

"Follow whom, Moya?" asked Helen faintly, her heart in her throat.

"Who? Sir Trevor Mortimer. Follow him—as the ferret glides behind the rabbit—until he got near enough to strike him, an' it wasn't the fault of his black heart but of his weak arm that he did not creep into your house that night a murderer in deed as well as in intention."

"Moya," said the girl with an intention of rising to her feet, but her knees refused to lend their aid—"Moya, you must have been mistaken. He could not do such a thing. It is utterly impossible."

"Impossible! Whose knife was found—whose dagger did it? Tell me that!"

"It was his—but he lost it, and somebody who found it made use of it, and with it struck the blow."

"Somebody who found it!" she cried exultingly. "Poor deceived girl! You were harbouring a monster in your house. Where is he now?"

"I don't know, Moya; he went away suddenly."

"To be sure he did, because *he* knew *I* knew who struck the blow. And because I knew other things as well. Who went with him?"

"Redmond went into the city with him, Moya, and——"

"And where is *he* now?"

"I don't know, Moya," said the afflicted girl, bursting into a flood of tears, hot with the agony and fears that were twining themselves, like serpents, around her heart—around her heart as if they would crush the life thereout. "He never came back since that night. It was of him I came to speak to you?"

"You don't know where *he* is. Maybe I know."

"Oh, Moya, if you do, for the love of the good God that sees and knows all things, tell me! Tell me, for the life is scarcely in me with fear, and terror, and suspense! Oh, Moya, if there was ever anyone that was dear to you, for their remembrance and sake—tell me."

She placed her hands entreatingly on the woman's shoulder, and, bending over to her, her head came much closer than before. Wherefore, when the old fortune-teller turned her eyes up to her entreating face, they seemed to Helen like the flashing eyes of a wild beast: and she withdrew her hands and head in dire affright.

"Where is he? Where would he be, d'ye think? Helen Barrington, when you threw off the old love that you knew and trusted, and that loved you dearly, an' took up with the one that crept out of the sea and kem into your house, no one knew how but me, you brought trouble an' sorra on yourself, an' you brought ruin on your brother. Redmond Barrington is in the mud of Dublin Bay—dead an' drowned, an' food for the eels—an' 'twas the Frenchman done it!—There!"

The cry that burst from Helen's lips might fairly have made her father's bones stir in the grave for the suffering of his daughter, or have brought his shrouded form to her rescue—so terrible, so intense, was the agony it bore to the listening night. She made one or two unconscious efforts to rise, but failed; and, in doing so, fell fainting on her knees on the floor.

Moya was not unstartled by this occurrence, but she was still more startled when a step was heard on the threshold, a form strode into the apartment, and a cheery voice said: "Well, old Moya! what's all the row? Frightening someone with your fortune-telling—eh? Merciful Providence! What is this? Is this Miss Helen Barrington? God protect us! what could have brought her to your den?"

CHAPTER XIV.

THE GOLD RING.

WHEN Helen left her apartment under the belief that the household was safe in bed, she erred grievously. They were not all gone to rest, for two lingered by the kitchen fire long after the others had departed, and these two were Norah and Luke Mahon. The former was generally last to retire, and the latter, referred to incidentally in a former chapter, contrived also to remain up under the pretence of looking after the horses in the stable, but really to enjoy a *tête-à-tête* by the kitchen fire with his good-looking fellow servant. It was very agreeable, Luke thought—and we are not quite sure that Norah didn't agree with him— to hold converse in the pleasant gloom of the fire-light and in the glow of the smouldering ashes on the hearth turning grey and white in their waning.

"Luke," said Norah confidentially, "isn't it very odd about Redmond. Where could he have gone?"

"It's that that's surprisin' to myself every hour in the day," said Luke, taking Norah's right hand in his own. "I can't under the sun imagine what could have become ov him."

"He never would remain absent this length of time of his own accord."

"That he wouldn't," said Luke.

"The young mistress is in great distress about him."

"An' no wonder," thoughtfully assented Luke.

"I was in hopes he might have gone to Kildare, but now you see he hasn't, an' Miss Helen will break her heart over it—God help her! He couldn't have been—been killed—could he?"

Norah's voice sank to a whisper and her hand trembled in his as she put the dreadful question.

"I don't think so, Norah. He wasn't the sort ov fellow to get into a row or brawl, an' even if he did there was no one he need turn his back upon. There wor very few abler young fellows than Redmond, or more likely to hold his own if anything of the kind took place."

"Unless he was set upon," said Norah.

"Who would set upon him? He hadn't an enemy in the world that I know ov. You know yourself he had everyone's good word."

"But why doesn't he come back?" inquired Norah, her anxious heart much relieved by this cheerful statement.

"Who could tell?"

"Or where is he staying?"

"I'd just give a good year's earning to know."

"D'ye think, Luke, that he could have gone—d'ye think it's possible—he'd have gone an'—got married?"

"Got married?" said Luke in a burst of amazement, which was immediately followed by subdued laughter. "I really think," said he, during an interval in his cacchination, "that the womenkind never under any circumstances have marriage out ov their heads for any one half hour in the day."

And another hearty burst of laughter followed this declaration.

"You've a great deal of impudence, so you have," said Norah indignantly, and endeavouring to withdraw her hand from where it was safely locked in his. "It's just like the way wid the whole of you. When you are not bringin' sorrow and trouble on unfortunate women with your scapegracin' and your comin's and your goin's, you're insultin' 'em with your laughin' and your jokes. Let go my hand—let go my hand, I say!"

Her companion was not disposed to comply with this indignant request; on the contrary, having made, as he said, his sides "sore with the laughin'," he took hold of her hand, previously locked in his left with his right, and placing the former around her waist, drew her over to him, and, bending down his head, was about—in the best humoured way in the world—to kiss her lips.

Norah's offended dignity not being disposed to allow her hand to remain in his, at least until he apologised for his quite unnecessary remark, was still less disposed to allow of this familiarity—which she prevented by a pretty sharp slap on his cheek with her left hand.

To prevent a recurrence of this defence, Luke caught her left hand also; but in a moment his fun and good humour changed into seriousness, and he bent the captive hand downwards where the smouldering logs still waningly flickered and burned.

"Norah," he said gravely, "what's this?"

"What's what?" said Norah, quickly impressed by the sudden change in his manner.

"This ring—this gold ring?" said he.

"What's that to you what it is? It's a ring—that's all," said Norah, with a saucy defiance, but with a beating at her heart that was not pleasant.

"I see it's a ring, Norah," said he with great gravity, "and a gold one, too. Where did you get it?"

"Just wherever I pleased."

"Norah! you must tell me where you got that ring?"

"I won't then," said Norah, turning up her handsome face angrily. "What is it to you where I got it?"

"It's everything to me, Norah," said he, coldly but earnestly, "it's everything to me that *I* didn't give it to you."

"I'd like to see you offerin' me the like!" said Norah, with womanly wilfulness, the while her heart throbbed and the tears stood ready to burst forth.

"Well, Norah," said he, releasing his hold on her hand and letting it go with indifference, "all I can say is: it's what you oughtn't to have on your hand, an' what I didn't ever expect to see on wan ov your fingers until I gave it to you. It was time enough for you to wear it when I did."

The fact was that Norah, from the moment Eugene had given it to her until this evening, had kept it safely in her pocket, but on this unlucky afternoon had taken the opportunity of putting it on her finger, when she was all alone, with a flutter of vanity, just to see how a ring would look on her. Unluckily, also, she had forgotten to take it off; and this gave rise to the sudden *contretemps* we have just seen.

If the matter had not arisen so suddenly, Norah would have had no hesitation in telling when and how the present had been made her; but in the spur of the moment the opportunity was lost, and his quickly developed suspicion destroyed, for the present at any rate, any chance of a bridge of gold for the purpose.

There was no retreating, and nothing remained but to act still more haughtily on the defensive.

"I wonder who told you, Luke Mahon, that I ever wanted a ring from *you?* I'd have you to know, then," said Norah, rising and smoothing down the folds of her dress with a most bewitching movement—" I'd have you to know, then, that if you took that notion into your head it was a very foolish one, and the sooner you banish it the better. There now!—A ring, indeed."

And smoothing back the masses of dark hair, that had somehow fallen over her forehead, back into their places, and without one look at her discomfited sweetheart, Norah left the kitchen and proceeded in the dark to her room, which was under her young mistress's, and which lay at the back of the wall into which the great chimney was built. This wall was, indeed, the dividing part of the mansion—the sleeping-rooms of the family, and the drawing-rooms, study, and parlour being separated by it from the apartments in which the servants slept—all except that of Norah.

If Cauth had been to the fore at this untoward ending of their conversation, and had seen the quarrel the Frenchman's present had given rise to, she might well say that he brought ill-luck with him. Here were two simple and loving hearts, between whom he had been the unconscious means of introducing unhappiness. In truth, it seemed as if her words in his regard were perfectly correct, and that his coming to Seamore had brought with it, and left behind, sorrow and trouble.

Luke, left alone, and with very sombre reflections in his head, did what most people would do under the circumstances—he raked the white ashes off the slumbering embers, lit his pipe, and began thinking.

His thoughts were not of a bright order, nor were they cast in a cheerful mood; nevertheless, thinking of any kind being very unusual, and, in consequence, very fatiguing to him, he presently fell into a sort of disconsolate doze, and was soon fast asleep.

From this he was aroused by a smart shake and a whisper in his ear:

"Luke!—Luke, I say! Will you waken, you *big owmadhawn*? Is it sleepin' you are, an' you wantin' so badly? Waken, I say! D'ye hear me?"

"What—Norah? Is that you? What's amiss?" asked Luke loudly, startled in this summary fashion out of his sleep. "What's amiss?"

"Hold your tongue, an' speak easier," whispered Norah vehemently—not noticing, or caring to notice, the somewhat contradictory character of her command.

"Why, what in the world is amiss?" asked he again, considerably startled by the breathless manner in which she addressed him. "Is there anything wrong?"

"Everything is wrong—an' you sittin' asleep here. Did anyone ever see the like?"

"Why, what is it Norah? How did I know that I should keep awake?" queried Luke, in most ludicrous distress. "Why don't you tell me? Is the house afire?"

"Did anyone ever hear the like of that?" asked the distracted girl. "Is the house afire?"

"You'll set me mad, Norah—that's what you'll do. Why don't you tell me what's gone wrong?"

"Didn't I tell you afore? An' you sittin' there—doin' nothing only talkin'! The young mistress is gone!"

"The young mistress gone!" almost shouted Luke as he jumped to his feet. "Is it Miss Helen?"

"Yes—yes—yes!" said Norah, putting her hand on his mouth to prevent his speaking too loudly.

"Where is she gone?"

"I don't know. She's gone across the Rath—through the scrub—and towards the sea."

"For what?"

"I don't know, but she's gone. God knows for what—only I think she's distracted. You must go after her, Luke, an' watch her, an' see that no harm come to her. The life will lave me with fright."

"That I will," said Luke promptly. "Will I be able to overtake her?"

"To be sure you will. Hurry, man alive! an' don't be wastin' time. Across the Rath, Luke, she went—an' if you take the byepath to the low strand you'll get in view of her; an' don't come within sight of my two eyes evermore if you don't see that no harm comes to her, an' bring the poor girl back safe and sound."

Luke didn't want to hear more, nor did he scarcely wait—or perhaps if he did it was little more than wait—for the encouraging kiss which Norah, in her thankfulness to him for his alertness, bestowed upon him, but hurried through the door and was quickly in the Rath through which Helen was said to have gone. Having passed this, he hurried in the direction indicated until he reached the shore. The tall whins shut out his view previously, but having arrived on the strand, the horizon, so far as it was not limited by the darkness, was clear. But there was no one in sight! No moving form, as far as his vision reached, disturbed the silence of the place, nor interrupted his solitude.

He ran up and down swiftly on the low margin of grass that bordered the strand in order that the grating of his feet on the gravel should not prevent sounds or cries falling on his ears. But in vain. There was no one around. No figure disturbed the calm of the night; no voice or cry reached his ears—nothing but the sound of the waves, beating softly and placidly, falling on the strand.

The bead-drops stood on his forehead, partly with the exercise but more because of the excitement and anxiety he was in.

"Where did Helen go? Why was she walking anywhere at this hour of the night? Could Norah have been mistaken?"

These were the thoughts that coursed through Luke's mind as he stood on a projecting rock above the scrub bushes and looked around and listened.

There was no one in view. No sound came on his ear. Only a distant light, faintly glimmering, attracted his attention.

He knew the light well. It was the one that so constantly burned in old Moya's cabin. Without any fixed purpose, other than there was nothing to be done else, he turned his steps in that direction, and entered the cabin just as Helen, shocked by the utterances of the old crone, had fallen on the floor.

CHAPTER XV.

IGNOMINY OR DEATH.

EUGENE woke from his slumbers as the first beams of the morning, glinting along the sea, came in through the port-hole that gave light and air to his prison. The motion of the vessel, the creaking of chains and rattling of cannon balls as they grated against one another, gave evidence enough to his ears that the ship was under weigh. The rush of the white-crested waves apast the port-hole proved it to his eye.

He marvelled much that they should have weighed anchor with his execution so near. It was quite unusual, at any rate in the French service, for executions to take place on a vessel proceeding on her course. A floating anchor was generally dropped, and the vessel stayed in her course on such occasions.

Whilst he was revolving these thoughts in his head the door opened, and a footstep sounded on the floor of his cabin.

The prisoner jumped at once to the conclusion that it was his acquaintance, the lieutenant, coming to make the announcement of his doom to him.

He turned his head around, but curiously enough, it was not the expected face upon which his eyes fell. Instead of the officer whom he anticipated, a gentleman, well dressed and in civilian attire, stood before him—one evidently, too, from his fresh face and unweather-beaten appearance, not long on board or at sea.

Noticing the curious look that grew on Eugene's face, he said:

"It's clear, M. Lefebre, I am not the person you expected to see."

"No," said Eugene.

"Well, I trust I shall be a more acceptable visitor."

"I trust so. I shall have no objection to your being so."

The stranger's manner was so affable and agreeable that Eugene was disposed to respond to the advances he made.

"It will certainly not be my fault if I do not."

"Nor mine either, I should fancy," Eugene said.

"I am glad to see that you are in such cheerful mood. I hope you have slept well, M. Lefebre?"

"Yes, quite well," said the prisoner.

"Notwithstanding your sentence?"

"Notwithstanding my sentence."

"Don't you think, M. Lieutenant, that it is a pity one so young as you should die so unhonoured a death?" said the visitor, somewhat abruptly, taking his seat on a projecting beam.

"I don't see that I have any very great choice in the matter," said the prisoner.

"Well, I should think you have."

"How?"

"There is no difficulty in the matter. You have been in Ireland on business of which we have cognizance."

The visitor paused, as if seeking for suitable words wherein to express his ideas.

"Yes. Well?"

"You must have intimate knowledge of the designs of the conspirators. Information of that nature would be invaluable to England just at present, and ours is a nation that rewards with unstinted and lavish hand those who do her service. In this case it would be an essential service, indeed."

He paused again, as if with some embarrassment. Eugene glanced through the port-holes, and on the wide sea over whose surface the rising sun was now spreading a mantle of rosy light. The eastern sky was red with the bright effulgence of morning, and, higher in the horizon, the fleecy white clouds were edged with crimson as its rays just tipped them.

For the moment Eugene thought of Helen Barrington, and the bewitching tints that occasionally crimsoned the delicate whiteness of her cheeks. His eye turning on his visitor, however, brought his wandering attention speedily back to the present.

"Ours is a nation that rewards," pursued the visitor, "with unsparing generosity those who do her service. Do you understand me?"

"I think I do," said Eugene quietly.

"There are men high in command in your armies and your fleets who can bear evidence to this. You understand?"

"I am afraid I do not," said the prisoner, whose face promptly darkened with a red purple flush, not unnoticed by his visitor.

"Well, I cannot enter into further particulars nor pursue this matter further than to say that there *are*," said the other guardedly, "Now, it can be of the least possible consequence to you, personally, what course things take in Ireland. For a brave officer, young, and in a brilliant service, what possible advantage can you hold out to yourself by aiding a half-savage country like Ireland, with a miserable, ignorant, and degraded population? Is it worth sacrificing your life in such an ignominious cause?"

"I think I said before," said Eugene, again smiling—but this time at the awkward manner in which the other sought to cloak and at the same time reveal his object, "that I have no choice in the matter. Your officers have doomed me—me an officer in the French fleet—to death at the yard-arm. It is they, not I, should fear it—because of the consequences for them. It is not the British fleet alone who hold prisoners of war."

"You are to remember—I say it with all courtesy—that you are *not* a prisoner in the ordinary acceptation of the term. You are and have been—I say it again with all the respect due to your position in the French service and to your present position as a prisoner—more in the character of a traitor and a spy——"

"What!—do you use these words to me?" said Eugene fiercely, leaping up from his resting place.

"Well, we shall not quarrel about words. It is in that light, however, we look on it. We do not hold that you can look upon yourself in the character of a prisoner of war. But, waiving all that, the question stands thus—Are you prepared, for the sake of an ignorant, semi-savage populace like the Irish, whose futile attempts at insurrection might as well be essayed by a nation of red Indians, to throw away your life and the bright prospects that await you, or are you rather prepared to act the part of a brave and sensible man by courting the advantages which are now held out to you?"

"What are they? Service under your flag?" suggested Eugene, with a half perceptible sneer.

"No; there would be many disadvantages in that. We could probably neither offer, nor *you* accept, such a proposal?"

"What then?—for I am quite at a loss to understand your meaning."

"It is this. Information as to the present intentions and resources of what some are pleased to call the revolutionary army of Ireland, their prospects and their leaders, would be highly valuable at this moment—not that we do not already know it, but confirmation at your hands of what we *do* know would be regarded as quite as valuable as if it came to us for the first time."

"You want me to give you this information?"

"Yes."

"And your reward for that?"

"Your life, in the first instance. A draft on a Hamburgh bank for any amount you choose to mention, payable in the Bank of France at sight and signed by a Hamburg banker, in the second. No trace of how you obtained, or from whom you obtained, the draft can ever be by any means discovered. We shall place you on board an English cutter which we shall contrive shall be captured by one of your vessels, and you can readily reach France without detection and without suspicion."

"What if I were," said Eugene, turning his eyes fully on his visitor, "to give you false information—unreliable information?"

"We shall trust to your honour as a French officer for that."

"To my honour as a French officer?" cried he, rising from his seat. "And is it one who bears that title—that honoured dignity—you dare to offer the shameful and degrading proposition you have now made me? Do you think that the humblest officer bearing the uniform of France would sink so low as to accept all the gold your country could offer as the price of his own degradation? No. I can readily meet death—I have met it often before unshrinkingly—this," said he, pointing to the cicatrice across his forehead, " bears witness to that—it was on no carpet-tournament that was earned, but amid the smoke and thunder of battle, where gallant men contended for victory with their lives—I met death there fairly face to face—and often before and since—but the proudest death a man can die is that wherein unnoticed and unhonoured he gives his life for the sake of a gallant though downtrodden people. If I had a thousand lives I should give them in the cause. Not all the wealth that England boasts of could tempt me. Tempt!—the very idea is dishonouring!—to breathe a word that could endanger the brightening fortunes of her people! I have known them to love them. I have learned to respect their high spirit and their undaunted bravery, and it was the highest hope of my life to die fighting for their freedom. Go! The threat of death at the yard-arm was a tribute of high respect compared with your insulting offer."

" There are those higher in your service than ever you can hope to obtain who would not, and have not, despised such a one," said the visitor cynically.

" I disbelieve it. I should mourn the day, when the flag of France covered such a scoundrel."

" Harsh words, monsieur. Were you to live long enough you would see the truth of my words; and see it in the disastrous ending of your boasted armament. I tell you, if all the strength of France were put forward in your vaunted expedition there are those within it who would neutralise it—and not the subordinates either. You see we know all. We need no information, though I would gladly have saved your life at the price of what is really worthless to us, because it is in our possession at present."

Eugene turned on his heel to the port-hole, the only parting word he said being, " Go."

" You will think better of it."

Eugene made no answer.

"If you should—I shall be here for a week—send for me. My name is Castlereagh—Lord Castlereagh. All Ireland knows me."

Eugene did not hear his concluding words. A chill of deadly cold was at his heart.

Could it be possible the words were true? Could it be possible that there were within the French ranks, high up in command, scoundrels who would sell their country for British gold. His heart spurned the idea. And yet there was something in the words of the visitor which showed that in this instance, at any rate, he knew what he was speaking of, and spoke truth. It is always so easy when one really speaks the truth to see it: one may mistake the false for the true, but the truth for falsehood—never. It bears its own distinctive characters never to be mistaken.

He stood there gazing vacantly at the growing day brightening the face of the waters, wholly unconscious of what he was looking at, a dull sense of pain and dread, and humiliation weighing on his heart like a foreboding of unaccountable evil—evil not to himself, but to France and to the cause of Ireland, with which he inseparably linked Seamore.

How long he stood there he knew not, until a voice behind him aroused him. It was the cook bringing him his breakfast.

It was only then he remembered—and, remembering, wondered at it—that the hour for his execution had long passed without his once thinking of it. In presence of the unseen danger threatening France and the expedition and Ireland, all considerations of self had completely vanished —quite as much as if he were non-existent, or a third party who had no connection with himself.

CHAPTER XVI.

LA VENGEUR—THE SEA FIGHT.

WHATEVER change came over the counsels of the officers on board the Thunderer, or whether it were merely a threat to extort information from him, the death sentence was not executed. Nor was he afterwards visited by the gentleman whose discussion with him was narrated in our last chapter.

Neither, however, was he allowed the freedom of the ship. For some inscrutable reasons known only to his captors, he was kept closely confined to his prison. Sunset succeeded sunrise, and night succeeded day, with ceaseless regularity, but still he remained a prisoner. Occasionally the ship fell into company with others, when they dropped floating anchor for some time, and an exchange of news or of men took place, and a general intercommunication between the officers of the different vessels. At other times the vessel pursued her own way unaccompanied. This much was apparent to Eugene as he looked through the thick glass of the side light. She appeared to him to be on some sort of sentinel duty, for, although for days nothing but the wide waste of waters encompassed them, at others his quick, experienced eye detected the mountains of the seaboard lying like blue clouds dimly on the distant horizon.

All this time Eugene wondered what had become of François and the crew of the Albatross—whether they were still on board, or whether they had been transferred to other vessels. Also, he marvelled what had become of the expedition. Had it sailed, and, if so, what port in Ireland was its destination? What was its measure of success?

If it had sailed he knew well it must have escaped the watchfulness of the British Fleet. There were no signs of a conflict on the vessels they had come across. The torn sides, the smashed bulwarks, the broken masts, the ragged rigging and sails that showed the terrible effects of a fight at sea, were absent from them.

All he could do was to wish it success when it did sail, and to breathe a hope that victory might light upon the banners of France when once they were unfurled on Irish soil.

The which thinking always brought his thoughts back to Seamore. In the loneliness and isolation of his position his mind kept constantly revolving about Helen, until his dreams at night as well as his reveries by day were haunted by the loveliness of her presence. Her bright and laughing eyes beamed in on his sleeping brain through the darkness of his cell, and her slender, graceful form seemed at times to fashion itself out of the rolling wave that rose, curled upwards, and swept by. He might, in a more active life, mayhap, have forgotten her, or she might have retained but a weak hold on his thoughts; but here, with nought to do but think of her, her face stamped itself on his heart almost as if it had been seared by burning brand!

Knowing the danger of dwelling too constantly on one idea, he essayed to think of other things that might attract his imagination. Of the earlier days of his life in the French Naval School, of his first voyages in *La Vengeur*, of his transports when he first donned the gold epaulets of an officer—in vain! Every train of thought of the kind brought him insensibly back to Seamore, and every boyish dream of glory and renown, by some curious metaphysical combination, brought before him Helen Barrington's winsome face, the deep blue of her eyes, or the wavy masses of brown hair above her white forehead.

"I shall go mad if I am longer left here," was his despairing thought as one night he lay down to rest—much disturbed by the fact that his remembrance of the first gun which he had seen fired in conflict served only to bring to his mind her silvery laugh.

"What an association of ideas!" he said. "None but one whose brain was giving way would have yielded to it."

He resolved within himself to detach his thoughts in the future from her—else the love he bore her should certainly get the better of his reason. In the midst of his devising plans for this purpose he fell asleep.

Only, however, to dream of her again! He was walking with herself and Miss Howard on the meadow banks that lay on the sides of Seamore, and Helen had leant on his arm to cross a stile that intervened between them and the shore.

The touch of her hand on his shoulder awoke him!

Was it that, or the rougher hand of the captain of the watch, who stood above him with a lighted candle? or was it her silvery voice that was in his ear, but the tones of the midnight visitor as he said gruffly and hurriedly:

"Get up!—come on deck!"

The illusion vanished at once.

"On deck?"—iterated Eugene, wide-a-wake on the instant. "Why? What for?"

"Ask no questions—but come!"

There was no ignoring the haste of the visitor; still less was there chance of mistaking the unusual import of his words.

Whatever was the cause, it was immediately palpable to Eugene that there was pressing need for obedience on his part. So, dressing immediately, he followed the retreating lantern as rapidly as he could.

Long before he got on deck his sense of hearing and seeing told him that something unusual was on foot. Lights glimmered everywhere on the 'tween decks. Sailors hauled at long ropes that worked the guns, and ran them out through the opened portholes. Otherwise, they were busy with rammer running home the charges of powder, and roundshot and grape. Ammunition was being rapidly passed from hand to hand; and the calls of the officers, the hurried exclamations of the men, the clinking of the irons, the cleansing of cutlasses, the flitting of lamps from place to place in the vast interior of the vessel, and the stamping and tread of feet overhead, made it a very pandemonium.

"They are preparing for action," thought Eugene, as, hurrying along, his eye took in the preparations. "There is an enemy in sight. Heaven grant there may. It will be a friend to me."

Along the 'tween decks; stumbling over cannon balls,

tripping over ropes, and anon knocking his head against the low, whitewashed beams that supported the next upper deck; then up a ladder, then another, and, finally climbing the companion ladder, he followed his leader—until he found himself on deck.

It was a singular sensation for him: to feel the cool breeze once more on his forehead, to see the deep vault of the sky with here and there a star peeping out through the darkness, and to hear in unbroken freshness the rush of the waves as they swept past the vessel. It seemed as if a new life had been given to him, and the blood came in unwonted flow, coursing through his veins and throbbing at his temples.

It was all the difference between bondage and freedom.

He had not long to experience these sensations undisturbed.

"Follow me," said his guide sharply, as Eugene stopped for a moment to witness the scene so fresh and so delightful to him.

A few moments brought him to the quarter-deck, whereon the captain and some of the officers were gazing with their night-glasses across the bulwarks.

So intent were they on the operation that they did not notice the approach of Eugene.

"This is the French prisoner," said the guide, touching the captain on the shoulder.

"Ah, so it is," said the latter, turning round. "Is your sight good?"

"As good," said Eugene, somewhat amused at the oddity of the question, and at the abrupt manner in which it was put, "as one's eyes can be who has seen but——"

"Take this glass in your hand, and tell me what vessel that is yonder."

Eugene mechanically took the glass, and, adjusting it, swept the horizon in the direction indicated. For some time he failed to detect the object he sought, but suddenly his eyes caught it, and his heart stood suddenly still.

For, coming along, her prow obliquely towards them—her white sails reflecting the lights that shone on her decks and glared from her mid-masts, was a French man-of-war. Lights streamed from her opened portholes—

three long tiers of lights—that made her seem like a floating palace whose windows were all alight for ball-room festivities. The moving forms, vaguely showing on her deck in the dimness, proved that the hands on board her were busy at work.

"Can you make her out?" asked the captain as Eugene steadily surveyed her.

"Yes."

"Is she French or Spanish?"

"French," said Eugene, with difficulty concealing his exultation, as the prospect of probable deliverance sent the chilled blood again bounding in ecstacies from his heart.

"Do you know her?"

"I think I do."

"What is her name?"

"*La Vengeur.*"

"How do you know?"

"She is my old vessel."

"What does she carry?"

"A few 74-pounders—the rest smaller," said Eugene, anxious to minimise the fighting qualities of the stately vessel that, like a thing of light and beauty careered over the waves, lest the captain of the Thunderer should seek to evade the challenge which she seemed prepared to offer, and so render his chance of escape hopeless.

"How does she work in a half-gale? For unless I am much mistaken there is one not far off."

"Answers to her helm badly, and her lower tier of guns cannot be worked with a heavy sea on," said Eugene readily, the while he thought to himself. "I hope they will rely on my honour for this one time."

"Humph! I thought as much," said the captain. "She seems bent on challenging us. Don't you think so?"

"I certainly do," said Eugene, with his glass still steadily levelled at the stately foe. "If she has not changed captains since I knew her, she is not likely to turn her stern on any ship that walks the water. And, by heaven!" cried he, as a red light flashed from her poop, so lurid that for the moment it completely extinguished the others and threw a purple glare upon her acres of sails, "there comes her challenge!"

In the excitement of the moment he was about to "hurrah," but fortunately checked himself, as the dull boom of a cannon came slowly rumbling over the breast of the waters.

The shot fell short, for the vessel was still a long way distant. At any rate, in the dark space that lay between the Thunderer and her it was impossible to say what became of it.

But still out against the dark background of sky and water the foe came gallantly on!

It was a stirring sight—the three-master alight with her many lamps, alone in the black darkness around; her long tiers of port-holes gleaming above the blackness of the waters; her sails filled with the freshening breeze; and the white surf surging up and around her cleaving prow!

"They have mistaken the distance," said the captain of the Thunderer coolly, as he took the glass once more into his hand, and gazed at the stranger. "She is coming pretty quickly forward. She will go back less quickly. She is one of the vessels of the Irish expedition returning, and wants to show some sign of work after their fruitless efforts."

"Has the expedition then sailed?" asked Eugene, with beating heart, as this slight piece of information fell on his ears.

But there was no answer. The captain closed up his glass, and proceeded to give orders to his officers, who set off to their various commands in the ship.

"I suppose," said he curtly to Eugene, "as you are a non-combatant you would prefer being more or less in safety below."

"I should prefer being here," said the other, in whom the hope of escape was strong. "I am not unaccustomed to such scenes."

"We can scarcely permit that. You would be quite out of place here. Besides there is no use in throwing away your life for no purpose and to no end."

"I may be of service in assisting the wounded," said Eugene, to whom the thought suddenly occurred.

"Quite so. I hadn't thought of that. You may remain on deck—but not here. There will be less danger elsewhere."

These last words were spoken in a much more friendly manner. Eugene took them as a hint to leave, and accordingly left the quarter-deck, and took his place at the bulwarks between two cannon that stood ready shotted —their gunners beside them with the lighted torches in their hands. Here, in comparative darkness, he watched with intense interest the advancing Frenchman.

Had the ship actually touched an Irish port? Where were her companions, and what had become of the division of the French army it carried? What story did *La Vengeur* bear back from Ireland to France? What would he not give at this moment to know? Who could tell but a few moments might put him possession of the information his heart was athirst for.

Meanwhile the freshening breeze grew up, as if the captain's prophecy about the forthcoming gale were in course of fulfilment, and, under its influence, the Frenchman came tearing along, throwing up a cloud of silver spray above her bows.

As she came nearer he could notice that some of her sails were being reefed.

He looked around to see what arrangements were being made near him.

The men were standing silently at their guns, everything in readiness; the lighted torches, hissing and flaring, alone breaking the silence of the night. Every eye was fixed on the approaching vessel, and every ear awaited the sound of the captain's trumpet to train the guns on the foe!

It was a moment of wonderful suspense; and the groups of silent men around the guns at intervals along the spacious deck, seemed to call up the idea of a phantom war-vessel careering over the seas in the blackness of night.

It was the stillness preceding the storm.

And what a storm!

He had scarcely turned his head around again after these short reflections when he was surprised to see, within a few furlongs, the long tiers of *La Vengeur* rising high over the water, her lighted portholes partly obscured by her protruding guns.

She was clearing the Thunderer, broadside on.

He had scarcely time to wonder at the speed with which she had come, when along her deck and from her sides ran a line of red light, that made the black darkness behind blacker still!

A tremendous boom, a concussion of the air—and the Thunderer fairly reeled and staggered in the water as the round shot struck her sides, burying themselves in her strong timbers or passing into the interior! A shower of splinters flew around him, indicating where a shot had struck the bulwarks, knocking it into matchwood. In a moment the *La Vengeur* was surrounded by a cloud of white smoke that evolved from her portholes and hung over her deck.

The trumpet call from the captain of the Thunderer at once answered this message! The flying splinters had not descended on the deck from their flight through the air when it resounded through the vessel.

In a moment the silent forms around the guns were in motion. In the twinkling of an eye the men at the ropes had hauled the guns into position to bear, had them trained on the enemy, and almost simultaneously the torches were applied.

A roar of thunder burst from under his feet and from the sides of the vessel; the sudden, sharp blaze of furious light made Eugene's eyes, so long accustomed to the dim obscurity of his cabin, close; the vessel reeled with the rebound of the guns; and a shower of roundshot had penetrated the cloud of smoke that wrapped up *La Vengeur*, doing what damage it might—most mighty damage for aught they knew!

The Frenchmen had not let their hands rest, but whilst their sailors tacked round to bring their vessel to leeward of the Thunderer, the gunners had loaded again, and just as she went round the stern of the latter a second broadside poured into her, and a swarm of grape swept the whole length of the deck, doing great execution. It fairly mowed down the gunners at their guns!

LA VENGEUR—THE SEA FIGHT. 107

Eugene felt a sharp pain at his side, pretty much as if he had got a smart lash of a whip.

He saw the French vessel bear round on the other side, so close that he could see the gunners on her deck stripped to the waist working the guns; could see where the line of red fire again ran along the decks; could hear the storm of sound that seemed to burst in his own vessel from under his feet; and tried to run to the other side of the vessel to watch the conflict there. His foot trod on something slippery and he fell; he felt his side wet, and became dimly conscious that he had been wounded and in his excitement had not noticed it; and, with a vague wonder whether he had been mortally wounded, he felt his strength fading from him and the light passing from his eyes.

He was dimly conscious that the conflict was becoming closer and fiercer, and, with a cry of "Boarding-nets up!" in his ears, grew unconscious!

CHAPTER XVII.

A STRANGE MEETING.

It was pitch dark when Eugene awoke again. As far as he could see, he was in the same cabin in which he had previously been confined. But it was thick blackness around him. He could only imagine where he was by the position of the window, which gave no light now, but showed merely that the darkness outside was of a different colour from that inside. So at least it seemed to him.

The vessel was pitching and tossing terrifically; a furious wind was blowing; a hurricane seemed to be sweeping the breast of the sea; and the ship appeared to be tumbling about rudderless—now ascending on the crest of an enormous wave, and again sinking on her side as if she were going to the bottom. The heavy waves, striking her with the force of hundreds of tons, seemed to make her stagger, more than sail, through the sea. All this appeared to him dimly, and as if more in a dream than otherwise

But he was too ill and weak to take further note of it. He was vaguely conscious that he was lashed to his hammock, and with this feeling of safety palpable to his languid perceptions, passed back into his former state of sleep or unconsciousness.

He was aroused again by the sound of voices in his ears. The gale had moderated and the ship seemed to be striving more easily through the water.

"Do you think he will recover?"

"I should think so. His weakness arises chiefly from loss of blood."

"Where is he wounded?"

"A grape shot passed through his side, and a splinter of wood or something of that kind has given him a contused wound on the forehead, bursting an old cicatrice —which makes it the more difficult to cure."

"A former wound?"

"Yes, a sword-cut or sweep of a cutlass in some engagement. What is he?"

"A prisoner—one of those French officers that are in the habit of passing in spite of all we can do between Ireland and France. *He* was over in connection with the late expedition."

"You are not particularly anxious about his recovery in that case?"

"Quite the contrary, I am. There is good metal in the fellow, for he refused his life at our hands, which we offered him on condition of his giving information about these confounded Irishmen, and he volunteered to stay on deck during the fight, and aid the wounded."

"That is a good deal in his favour."

"There is something more, however; we have received a message from the Admiralty to send him ashore as soon as he is able after we return to Plymouth to refit. He is to be sent on board the hulks as a prisoner—exchange being refused. There is some importance attached to his safe-keeping by the people at headquarters—why, I don't know."

"When do you purpose to return?"

"We must cruise up and down within easy sail of the harbour for some weeks—if we can keep afloat so long—

there being no vessel to relieve us. All the ships are busy watching the French and Spanish coasts, and we must keep guard here if we do not go to the bottom, which is likely enough in our present disabled and short-handed condition."

"It will be some time before he can be removed," said the doctor—for it was he and the captain who had held the conversation—as he took the hand of the apparent sleeper, whose closed eyes and white, bloodless face indicated a state of coma. "It will take weeks before he can be moved, without danger, from where he lies."

"But there is no doubt of his ultimate recovery?"

"No, I should think not. He has youth and strength on his side. And his wound, though severe, is only dangerous from the consequent loss of blood."

"I would be sorry anything should happen him. Apart from the courage and high spirit of the lad, the headquarters people are so interested in him that I should wish you to pay him particular attention. He is, I fancy, of high importance in France—some great family or some connection of one of the Directory—and our people want to keep him as a hostage or something of that kind."

"I shall pay special attention to him, you may depend, captain."

"Do. I shall take it as a favour."

"It will be necessary to place some person in attendance upon him. Have you anyone you could spare for the purpose?"

"I fancy some of the men newly pressed—and who are not for the present of much service—might be utilised for the purpose. I shall speak of the matter to the lieutenant."

"Have you none of those who were taken with him?"

"No, they have been sent into other vessels as ablebodied seamen. Our men are running scarce, and we must, wherever we can, force prisoners into our service at sea, as we may not do so on land."

"He will need special care, for, although his wound is not dangerous—or, at least, not likely to prove fatal—he is weak through loss of blood. Have you none of his countrymen who could be put in charge of him? These Irish understand one another better than strangers. He might not receive the attention he needs at the hand of our people."

"No doubt. I shall make inquiries when I go on deck. Meantime I suppose we can do no more now."

"No; I don't see that we can."

They moved away, and Eugene was left alone. His mind was too weak for much thinking; but in his semi-comatose state there was one idea vaguely palpable to his mind—palpable, mainly, because of the danger and terror which surrounded and accompanied it.

The hulks! This was the name that carried terror to his heart. He well knew what imprisonment therein meant. He had known young officers, brave, buoyant, and light-hearted before being taken prisoners and confined therein, and he had seen them, after a year, return—old men; every feature in their faces, every muscle in their bodies, changed by the dreadful hardships they had endured; their black hair changed to grey, their erect forms bowed and decrepid, the light and brightness gone out of their eyes as the gaiety and buoyancy had departed from their hearts. Frenchmen shuddered at the idea of these prison-hells, and Eugene almost incapable of thinking though he was, dreaded the fate in store for him.

Death by the foeman's hand at the yard-arm, death by the sweeping grape of his friendly countrymen, death by the sinking of the vessel in which he was confined—any death at all—would have been preferable to this new outlook. With a prayer for relief from this destiny, more fervent than had passed his lips for a long time previously, Eugene again fell into a doze.

He was awakened again by a fumbling at his door, and a step on the floor thereafter. He was too weak and indolent to raise his eyes, and too indifferent to care who it was. Some person with food which he could not eat, or, perhaps, coming to make inquiries.

The new-comer, however, advanced over to him and laid his hand on his breast.

"Are you awake? Here is a glass of brandy for you, my poor fellow! It will strenghten you. And from your bandaged head I have no doubt you need it. Awake! It is not everyone on board the Thunderer that gets so valuable a present, I can tell you."

Eugene awoke and turned his eyes on the speaker.

His misty dreaming had in some way turned to Seamore. He was speaking with Helen Barrington, and her voice was in his ears as he awoke. But when he turned his dim and dull eyes on the stranger a new brightness and energy shot from them, and an exclamation of mingled gladness and astonishment burst from his lips!

The attendant for a time stood still with equal astonishment; a look of recognition grew also into his eyes. In the surprise, which well nigh paralysed him, he let the glass and its precious contents fall. Unheeding of which, however, he pushed the bandage with one hand from the forehead of the invalid, hastily as if doubting even yet the evidence of his senses, and cried:

"In the name of all that is wonderful and astonishing, is it here I find you, Eugene? For Heaven's sake, speak! and say if it is really you I see!"

But Eugene was unable to speak. His emotions, combined with his weak state, were too much for him; and in the effort to raise himself on his elbow to grasp the other's hand, he fell back once more on his wooden couch.

CHAPTER XVIII.

IN DOUBT.

It was a long time before Helen had recovered from the illness into which she was thrown by the information given her by Moya. For many weeks she hovered on the confines of life and death. Finally the former, aided by her youth and strength, triumphed, and she was at last on the fair road to recovery. Trevor Mortimer, as soon as she was able to move about, took herself and Miss Howard on short journeys when the days were fine; and his presence, together with the air of the Dublin mountains and the fresh breeze from the sea, by imperceptible degress began to bring the roses once more back to her cheeks.

On these occasions her mind was withdrawn from the

incident that preceded her illness; but when left alone she invariably recurred to her visit to the old fortune-teller and the extraordinary information she had learned thereat. At times she was inclined to trust it implicitly; at others she rebelled against the possibility of its being true.

"Could Eugene, so generous, so frank, so brave to all seeming and appearance, conceal under so fair an exterior such malignant intentions? It was impossible. Even if he did, why should he bear enmity to Redmond? They had had no quarrel. There was nothing to explain it—there was no motive to be even suggested. But, then, again, what had become of Redmond? He went away in Eugene's company—why had he not returned? That he should have voluntarily gone away without acquainting anyone in Seamore and have remained away, was wholly out of the question."

These considerations landed Helen once more in a sea of suspense and doubt perfectly agonising.

It was whilst sitting one evening, thus calling up surmises *pro* and *con*, that Sir Trevor Mortimer was announced. He was immediately admitted.

"I am sorry to hear, dear Helen, that you are about leaving."

"It was only yesterday I made up my mind to accept Kate's invitation to Inch for a few months. I feel as if I should never get well here. I feel a load of trouble constantly on my heart—and Kate advises me it is only change of scene that can remove it. Everything reminds me so of poor Redmond. The only thing that reconciles me to the present is the hope that some day he may come back. I am sure he will. Don't you think he will?"

"I should be, my dear Helen," he said with gentle kindness, "delighted to be able to answer in the way you would wish. But I feel I should be only aiding to keep you in the state of suspense that is so injurious to you, and stating what I do not believe, if I were to say so."

"You do not believe——" said Helen with a shudder.

"I believe it would be the wisest thing for you to accept the inevitable, my dear Helen. It was an ill night that brought strangers to Seamore—ill for you, and very near being worse than ill for me."

"It could not be true what old Moya told me. You surely do not believe that?" asked the young girl earnestly.

"I have not heard what she said, dear Helen, so I cannot speak as to its probability or possibility."

"She said—if I remember her words aright, but I was so greatly frightened that I should not be surprised if I did not—that it was his hand that struck you at the orchard gate. Surely that could not be the case?"

"I am reluctant to believe it, but the circumstances force me to do so."

"Circumstances?"

"Yes. Firstly, it was his knife that was used. That there is no question of, and that proves nearly everything."

"What motive could he have? Would it not be absurd to think that he, an utter stranger, should on the occasion of his first visit since his childhood to Seamore, strike one whom he had never seen before, with intent to kill him—for I believe there can be no doubt it was with that intent the blow was struck."

"Very little doubt, indeed," said Trevor Mortimer, and, as he spoke, his eyes sank in deep reflection, and, for the moment, unconscious of even her presence, shone with a gleam of frightful hatred and ferocity. So malignant was the unconscious exhibition of vindictiveness—the evolvement of the feelings that actuated him for the moment—that Helen shrank from him in terror.

He noticed the movement, and, at once withdrawing himself from his reverie, knew what occasioned it, and apologised.

"You must pardon me, dear Helen," he said, "if feelings of indignation stir up within me at the remembrance of that cowardly and treacherous attempt on my life. I would fain forget it—if I cannot well forgive it—but your words bring the remembrance of it fresh before me. As to motive for it—there was the knowledge with him that you and I, dear Helen, stood on terms closer than mere friendship. The knowledge that I was blessed with the affection of one of the best and sweetest, as well as the loveliest of her sex——"

He made a movement as if to take hold of her hand and kiss it, but there was a palpable feeling of embarrassment on her part which stayed him.

"As I have learned since," said he, after an awkward pause, "he was no stranger to all this. He had been seen skulking—I believe that is the proper word to use—about the neighbourhood some days before he introduced himself here. He came over from France, an adventurer, with the intention of seeking the hand and the wealth of the heiress of Seamore; and, finding me in his way—for he had made himself acquainted with all that related to the place—he, creeping behind me with the murderer's stealthy step, did not scruple to remove me out of his path with the blow that his hand was too weak effectually to give."

"How did you learn this?" asked Helen faintly, shocked beyond measure at his words.

"From one who by accident saw him—from one who by the merest chance saw the blow struck."

"When did you learn this?"

"Almost the first day I was able to go out."

"Why did you not tell this before, Trevor?"

"Dear Miss Barrington—forgive me, dear Helen—why should I disturb the peacefulness and enjoyment of Seamore by a public disclosure and scandal of this character? Why should I bring public attention and trouble on a quiet home, and disturb the sanctity and sacredness of its privacy by having the eye of the law drawn to it? If I did not mention it—as I now believe I should have done—it was because the comfort and peace of mind of those at Seamore were dearer to me than my own life."

He spoke with such warmth and eloquence, and there was such tenderness and care for her in his words, that the girl's heart was touched, and the tears of warm affection welled into her eyes.

"I did indeed intend," he continued, "some day to make Redmond the confidant of my secret, but the occasion or the opportunity did not arise. It was only on the eve of the fatal—of the disappearance, I mean—of your brother that I had finally made up my mind at all hazards, to inform him."

"It perhaps would be well if you had," said Helen, her tears of affection rapidly changing into those of bitter sorrow. "But do you really think that Redmond will not return?"

"The fact of his disappearing so mysteriously—and what I have already told you—leads me to infer the worst. I fear it would be only keeping you in useless suspense, dear Helen, if I were to say otherwise. I would to heaven I could."

Helen wept silently for some time. The world seemed reversed to her; it seemed as if there were no reliance or trust to be placed anywhere, and that the fairest seeming and appearances only covered what was false, treacherous, and untrue.

"Turning from these matters, which only distress you to no purpose and to no good, dear Helen, will you forgive me if I refer to what concerns us both, and what is and has been pressing closest to my heart?"

He paused, either waiting for her to speak or to give himself time the better to express what he was about to say; but if the former he paused in vain, for Helen still wept in silence.

"We have been pledged to one another now, Helen, for twelve months. There is nothing, I would hope, since to change or alter our engagement. You are left alone—with the deepest sorrow I say it—in the world friendless and desolate. The past cannot be changed. Would it not, therefore, be better that our marriage, dear Helen, should take place as soon as possible, and that you should no longer be left without a protector? My happiness is in your hands, and my fate hangs upon your words."

"It would not, I think, be befitting," she said quietly, drying her tears the while, "that I should be married, with Redmond's fate still unknown. It is very kind and thoughtful of you, dear Trevor, to think of me in my loneliness and desolation; but I think it would be but treating him—on my part, that is—unkindly to not wait at least until we have a better chance of hearing from him. Besides, I am not at all strong at present, and need some rest before entering on new cares and new duties. When I return from Inch I shall be better prepared to talk over it."

"How long do you purpose remaining there, Helen? Your wish is law to me, as it shall ever be; but I need not tell you how anxiously I shall await the termination of the time that shall enable you to say 'yes' to me."

"Kate presses me to consent to remain with her until May. We are only bringing Luke and Norah with us. Cauth and the remainder of the servants will remain at Seamore."

"May is a long time to wait for, Helen. Could you not name an earlier day?"

"No, I don't think so, Trevor. Not at present, at least, for I have promised Kate. But I may change my mind in the meantime. Redmond—poor fellow!—may yet return, for something tells me that he will; and how delightful it would be if he did, and we three were once more together!"

"It is rather disappointing to me, Helen dearest, but I am content to wait my happiness at your hands. I shall have opportunities of seeing you, however—it would be a desolate time for me if I could not—for there is an estate of mine in Wexford which I have never yet visited, but which your presence there will give me an opportunity of seeing, as it will be to me the happy occasion and means of seeing you."

"It will be a source of infinite pleasure to us," said Helen gracefully and warmly, "if we should have you for a neighbour. It will be perfectly delightful, and I trust you will come there as soon as possible. Inch, Kate tells me, is by the sea, in the neighbourhood of old castles and ruined abbeys, and it would be extremely pleasant to have your company when visiting them. I sadly need some change, for I feel very desolate and lonely here."

"I shall make arrangements this very evening, Helen darling," he said, rising to take his leave and holding her hand in his; "and I trust that long before the time you mention your mind will change, and that you will come back to Seamore with a lighter and more joyous heart."

He took his leave with a courteous and chivalrous tenderness which quite won upon Helen. He was so thoughtful, so tender, so considerate, so ready to subordinate his own ideas to her wishes! She felt happy, and her heart rose to think that there was one true man in the world—one on whom a girl's heart might rest with implicit reliance and trust.

When he had gone, Cauth entered the drawingroom with Norah to light the lamps, for the evening was closing. When the latter had left she took her place by Helen's side at the fire and took her hand in hers, as was her wont when Helen was a child.

"Helen, dear, you are looking better this evening."

"I feel better, Grannie."

"Sir Trevor Mortimer remained a long time, darling. What did he say to you?"

"What do you mean, Grannie?"

"Did he," said the old housekeeper, pressing Helen's hand with affection and anxiety, "did he ask you to marry him?"

"He did, Grannie."

"And what did you say, my pet?"

"I told him I could not at present—not at any rate until after I come back from Inch in May. Don't you think I was right, Grannie."

The old woman shook her head disappointedly.

"You don't seem pleased, Grannie—why?" asked the girl, noticing the motion.

"He told me he would ask you to do so now, my dear, and I hoped you would have said 'yes.' You are all alone here now, Helen *aroon*, and the sooner you have someone to take care of you and Seamore the better. A girl's heart is sometimes foolish—and folly and misfortune go hand in hand together. I am an old woman, my dear, and I have seen a great many things that have made me wiser than you. And I have seen, *aroon*, how near you were to losing your heart to that young fellow that came to us and went so suddenly, and what an escape you had."

"Grannie," said Helen, recurring quickly to what Sir Trevor Mortimer had said, and what Moya had previously stated, "You don't believe Eugene was as bad as it is said? You don't believe he would act the part of an assassin?"

"No, my pet. God forbid! But there are people—families—I have known them in my time—many besides his—that bring always ill-luck and misfortune with them wherever they come or wherever they go. He is one of them. His father was so before him. And from the night he turned up with your glove in his hand, and——"

"Oh, Grannie! Grannie!" cried Helen, trembling, as the remembrance of her alarm on that night came freshly on her mind, "don't mention that! For the love of Heaven, don't mention that!"

"Very well, honey, I won't; but I am glad he is gone Dearly as I loved him when a little boy, for his own winning ways and his sweet mother's sake, I am glad he is gone—for more and more trouble would have come if he had not. It comes with his very presence. Misfortune stands at his right hand, whether he wills it or not."

"Don't speak any more of it, Grannie. His very name alarms me."

"Better that than worse—as it was near being and easily might be. But I am glad that you did not put off Sir Trevor Mortimer too long. There's many a slip between the cup and the lip, honey; and you might wait long before you could meet one as true, as loving, and as worthy of you as he."

Helen thought so too; and Kate Howard coming in at the moment, she kissed the old confidant for her kindness and affectionate interest, who then left.

The two girls proceeded to discuss the manner and means of their journey to Wexford—no inconsiderable journey in these days—with the which we have nothing to do.

But if Helen had been able to listen to a conversation in which she was deeply concerned, then occurring not very far from Seamore, her dreams instead of being, as they were, full of pleasure and of a roseate hue, would have been crowded with terrors to which those she had yet experienced would have been but trifling.

CHAPTER XIX.

MOYA'S ADVICE.

SIR TREVOR MORTIMER left Seamore and Helen's presence with a sense of deep mortification. He had come strongly under the belief and impression that, in the lonely and isolated circumstances in which she found herself, the young girl would have gladly accepted his proposal. Everything tended to convince him thereof.

There was, firstly, the conviction, which he had taken care, by chance hints, to impress upon her, of the treacherous conduct of Eugene, which, remaining uncontradicted, was certain to poison her mind against him, assuming that she did entertain any affection for him. There was, secondly, the fate of Redmond, in itself quite sufficient to make her fly for shelter and succour to one able and willing to shield her from further harm and danger. And there was, thirdly, their long engagement and intimacy which he had done nothing to weaken, and which only the French officer's arrival had in any degree estranged.

But he had found his calculations set at naught. The weakness of his *fiancee* was too strong for him, and he was now left with all the uncertainties attaching to a prolonged delay. He was, therefore, in no pleasant humour returning into the city.

On his way, however, he bethought himself of Moya's cabin, and partly retraced his steps. Passing along an unfrequented track through the tall whins, he arrived at the fortune-teller's cabin, and with very little ceremony, entered.

"Back so soon?" said the old woman, glancing at his angry features.

"Yes, and I might have been back earlier for all the success I had."

"Indeed," said she, half sneeringly.

"I find you have not done me much good, Moya," he said, his ill-temper in no wise lessened by her curt remarks.

"I did you good enough if you only knew how to make use of it. Did you ask her?"

"I did."

"An' she refused you?"

"No, but what was as bad—or, perhaps, worse—she postponed it until May. She is going, as you told me, to Wexford, and would not entertain the idea until she comes back."

"Well, an' what would you have?"

"Something other than that, Moya. It is a long time, and many things may happen before then."

"What?"

"Why, you know them yourself as well as I do. *He* may return, for instance, and his return would work disaster. You know it would. And then, Alice."

"Ay, what of her?" inquired the old woman keenly.

"*She* may turn up at any moment. The terror she felt at first for the attempt on my life will grow less and less by degrees. And though she has hidden herself away since, the devil may prompt her to put in an appearance at any moment."

"Could you not——"

"No, Moya; I could not. The publicity of the thing would in itself be ruin to me. How could I prosecute her without exposing myself? And if nobody even would believe her, how could I face Helen Barrington again with my statements to the public contradicted by—myself?"

"I did not mean prosecuting her," said the old hag, bending her face down to blow the dry bushes she had placed on the fire-place into a blaze.

"You did not mean prosecuting her?" said Mortimer, with a sudden change in his manner, and a lowering of his voice. "What did you mean? Not to——"

"And supposing I did?" said she cautiously, glancing at his face with a look of keenness, as the light of the now burning whins fell on it—" an' supposin' I did? Would there be anything worse in that than you have already done? Isn't it the aisiest way out of the trouble?"

"You are not serious in this, Moya—are you?"

He spoke in a whisper, and took his seat on the straw seat beside her, the better to converse without the risk of speaking loudly.

"What other way is there out of id? Didn't she try to do the same by you?"

"She did, Moya; but it was in the heat of temper and madness. This would be in cold blood."

"You are getting very tender-hearted," sneered the old woman. "You should give up Helen Barrington, an' stick to *her*. She is your lawful wife."

"For heaven's sake, stop that, Moya," said Trevor in affright, every symptom of anger disappearing from his face as he deprecated the jeering demeanour of the fortune-teller. "It is your advice I want, and I require it now of all times in the world."

"I have given you advice," grimly retorted the old woman, "an' you won't take it."

"What do you advise, Moya?"

"I have said it afore, an' I won't say it again."

"And you really mean that?"

"If I didn't would I say it?"

"It's impossible, Moya—impossible. It couldn't be done—I couldn't do it."

"If you don't you'll never see yourself the owner of Seamore, nor the husband ov its owner. You'll never put a weddin' ring on her finger. Let her but wance come afore Miss Helen with that story, an' your chances are gone as much as if you wor beside Redmond Barrington in the mud ov Dublin Bay. It's not harder to do it nor it was to strike *him* down."

"Hush! Moya. Walls have ears."

"*I* don't care for them—if they had ears twenty times over."

"I don't know about that, Moya," said Mortimer significantly. "We are both in the same boat as far as that and other things are concerned. What affects me affects you. But this is not the time to speak of this. I have been very good to you, Moya, and I am not going to be worse now than I was. See here!"

He took from his pocket a purse and emptied the contents into her lap. The grey eyes of the withered hag glistened as the golden coin jingled in her apron.

"You see, Moya, I know how to reward faithful services. And I shall reward them yet more liberally. Now, Moya, if I were to take your advice——"

He paused.

"Go on," muttered the fortune-teller.

"See here, Moya," said he after a pause—"here's how the matter stands. I am going down to Grey Abbey. You know the place—you have not forgotten it long as you have been away from it?"

The hag nodded.

"The place is ruined and abandoned, as you know, for years. I shall get it fitted up at once to live in. I must be near Helen. I cannot live away from her. For good or for evil, I must be in her presence. It is not alone that I love her—it is that I dread when away from her that some inkling of the truth may come to her in my absence and ruin me."

He paused again, more in deep reflection than from any remark or reply he expected from her.

"When I am gone there, Moya," he continued, "*she* may turn up—nay, she *will* come from her hiding place. She may come to you. If she does, Moya, could you not tell her that I have forgotten and forgiven all; that I am anxious to see her; that I am willing to receive her in Grey Abbey, where she will be welcomed as my wife? You can come with her, Moya; come in secrecy, and no one will be the wiser. What do you think of that, Moya?"

"An'—in Grey Abbey?" whisperingly queried the old woman, an evil expression lending an additional repugnance to her puckered features.

"It is near the sea side, Moya. It is a lonely and forgotten place. Let the future speak for itself."

"It'll be done. I'll bring her."

Sir Trevor Mortimer stood up from his seat, all irresolution gone from him. He had cast aside in the brief conversation whatever remained of goodness—and it was not much—in his heart. There was ruin around him, and in his desperation he resolved on the worst.

No human form should stand between him and his resolve to win and wed the heiress of Seamore.

CHAPTER XX.

A NIGHT IN OLD DUBLIN.

LEAVING the cottage of the fortune-teller, Sir Trevor Mortimer proceeded with rapid strides along the path over which he had an hour before retraced his steps, until he came into the outskirts of the city. Then he proceeded in a more leisurely manner until he reached College-green. He was turning his steps towards Eustace-street when a hand was laid upon his arm.

He turned round.

A girl's form, dressed in a long cloak, and with the hood thereof descending over her head and partly shading her face—as was the fashion in those days—stood beside him. Without seeing her face, he guessed, not without a sudden spasm of alarm, who she was. When she threw back the hood, thereby disclosing a face that, as seen by the light of the lamp overhead, must once have been one of singular beauty, though now sadly marked by pain and sorrow, his guesses were changed into certainty.

"Alice!"

"You did not expect to see me here?"

"No Alice," said he, his surprise changing into warmth of manner. "How could I—from the way we last parted? But I am glad to see you—very, very glad."

"Very glad!" said the girl, wholly taken aback by this unexpected display of friendliness and affection.

"Ay, Alice, delighted. I forgive you everything—if, indeed, it is not I who have a right to expect forgiveness."

"Do you remember how we parted?"

"I only remember it to forget it. It was only your love for me that prompted what you did. It was affection and not hatred that urged your hand. I am a changed man, Alice, and during my recovery I often thought of the wrong I had done you, and resolved to make atonement."

"If I could only believe that, Trevor," said the girl, bursting into tears. "Oh! how I have sorrowed over the unhappy act since, and how eagerly I longed for and learned the news of your recovery! But I was mad at the time and did not know what I was doing. I was, indeed. Your words had made me desperate, and——"

"Do not refer to them now, Alice darling," he said, placing his hand on her shoulder with a touch of affection that made her form vibrate, so unusual and unexpected was any symptom of kindness from him. "It was all my fault. But I have learned better since. Will you walk along with me?—it is so odd-looking to remain standing here."

Drawing the hood of her cloak once more over her head and face, the slender form of the girl moved beside him—moved closer to him—as if hungering—panting—for the love once hers but long since denied her.

"As I told you, Alice darling," he continued, as they proceeded along, "I am a changed man. I have had too much time for bitter reflection during the period of my recovery. I have had time to think of the wrong I had done you in refusing you your proper title and position. I am now anxious to make atonement."

"Trevor!"

She placed her arm in his in the excess of her joy and love. A paradise seemed to have opened suddenly to her. All the dried up streams of love and affection burst forth again, and welling up, filled her heart with a frenzy of delight and rejoicing.

"Yes, Alice," and he pressed her tiny hand to his side, "you shall have no reason in the future to regret the past. I shall publicly acknowledge you as my wife. I should have done it long ago; but it is not yet too late."

"Oh! Trevor," said the weeping girl—weeping in the excess of her joy at his returned love—"if you but knew the terror, the burning despair, that fell upon me when that evening at Seamore you spoke of our marriage being but a mock marriage performed by a mock clergyman, you would feel how——"

"That is all over and past, Alice. Let us forget what is gone by and only think of the future. We have both erred, and we have both been punished. Listen for a moment, Alice."

She gave his arm a gentle hug, for her heart was too full of unexpected happiness to speak. They had reached the entrance to Eustace-street, and forebore to pass further in the direction of the gleaming lights that showed where the golden youth of Dublin were enjoying themselves at the famous hostelry.

"I am going to reside for some time at a place of mine in Wexford, Alice. I shall have it ready for you to come there in a few weeks. There I shall be ready to acknowledge you as my wife, and after a short time we can return to Dublin. It is better that it should be broken in this way to my friends than all at once and suddenly here. Promise me that you will come."

"I shall go anywhere all over the world with you," said the girl with a burst of affection which might have won upon the most callous heart, "to the ends of the earth—only acknowledge me as your own."

"That I shall do, Alice dear. And as you may not know how or when to come—for I shall be busy getting the place ready for your reception—call to Moya; she will come with you at the proper time."

"Moya!" said the girl with an evident shudder of repugnance. "Do not, Trevor dear—do not ask me to call on her. I fear her, and—and—I dislike her."

"I do not wonder at it, my gentle girl. She is not one with whom I should like you to associate—but in this case she is the only one to whom I can with safety and with secrecy entrust you. Conquer for this one time your dislike, Alice darling, for my sake—for my sake!"

"Whatever you wish, Trevor, I shall do—God knows I shall. I showed that long ago by leaving France to marry you, and by keeping away since from Seamore because you wished it."

"I know you did, Alice. I did not then value your love and constancy, and the sacrifices you had made for me, but I do now. Trust me, Alice, and the future will be brighter with happiness than it seemed of late it could ever be."

"And all the past will be forgotten?"

"Quite, Alice. Even though your hand was raised against me, I know well it was the outpourings of your love—turned astray by my seeming coldness—that prompted it. I said so before; I now say it again."

The girl sobbed in her excess of joy.

"But, Alice, remember—not a word of this to anyone. I need not ask you not to present yourself at Scamore, or make yourself known there, until I shall introduce you as my wife. I know I can trust you to do this. You have yielded to my wishes before in the matter. I am sure you will do so now also. Will you not?"

"I will."

The delighted girl, fluttering with renewed hope and love, readily acceded to his wishes, and gave the required promise. All the old feelings of dread and desperation melted away under the influence of his honeyed words, and with a kiss on her upturned lips from him they parted —he to enter the renowned hostelry in Eustace-street, she to whither she had come.

Once inside the hotel he called for a measure of brandy, and tossing off a tumblerful or two, proceeded to the billiard-room. The events of the evening, his conversation with Moya, the terrible resolution half formed in her cabin, and the subsequent interview with the subject of that conversation, had stirred a vague feeling of alarm and terror in him—whatever remained in him of conscience was prompting him with a thousand uneasy feelings, to drown which he plunged into the gay company assembled.

The billiard room was ablaze with lights, and full of company; so also the rooms leading off it, devoted to the lesser games of whist and cards. It was a time of much and heavy gambling in the city. Country gentlemen coming up to attend to their Parliamentary duties in College-green indulged in it largely, and many a fine estate changed hands of a night over the card-table, and many a heavy rental depended upon a lucky cannon or fortunate fluke on the billiard board. Broad acres of Southern and Western counties were charged with mortgages in the morning for losses sustained over night— never to be redeemed until the Incumbered Estates Court in after years wiped them out, and concurrently swept the estates out of the hands of the unfortunate heirs. Fifty years after, the reckless squandering in the Eagle gambling rooms were to be atoned for in the beggary and ruin of the oldest and proudest names in the annals of the land.

No shadows of coming evil threw a pall over the gay halls of the hotel nor over its high-spirited frequenters, as Sir Trevor Mortimer entered the rooms; and, amid the smoke of perfumed Havannas and the clinking of glasses, the clicking of ivory balls fell on his ears. The tables, however, were all occupied; and, too excited to enter into conversation, and too restless to remain an unoccupied spectator, he turned aside into one of the rooms.

"Hallo! Mortimer," said one of a party of three sitting at a table on which were some decanters and tumblers, "you have come in good time. You are the very man we want. Will you take a hand?"

"I have no objection, my lord," said Mortimer, as he threw himself into the vacant chair and filled the tumbler that stood before him. "What do you play for?"

"For very little, unfortunately," said Lord Kingston. "Waterford is trying his hand at some new stroke off the cushion, and bets are running so heavy on it that we can find no one to indulge in a quiet game here."

"I wondered what the excitement was about," said Mortimer carelessly, as if his thoughts had run very little on the matter, which, indeed, was the case. "I suppose there is something heavy on the affair."

"Beauchamp Bagnall stands to win or lose twenty thousand on it."

"Backing Waterford, eh?"

"I believe so."

"Then he stands to lose, I fancy. Waterford is a duffer."

"Bagnall can readily afford it," said his lordship with supreme indifference, as he shuffled the perfumed pack of cards he held in his hands. "These Carlow acres are fertile and rich, and will bear many a mortgage deed on their broad backs."

"They will get sufficient to bear if he loses as he did last night," said Mortimer curtly. "But I see you are impatient, my lord. How shall we play, and for what?"

"As you are sitting opposite me, what say you to being my partner?"

"I have not the slightest objection if these gentlemen have not."

"It is too much trouble to change seats," said Sir Laurence Parsons. "I am prepared to take Sir George as my partner. Have you any objection, Ponsonby?"

"None whatever," said Sir George Ponsonby.

"Well then, gentlemen, it is agreed," said Lord Kingston, "that we play as we are. Now, what shall it be for?"

"Say fifties," said Sir Laurence Parsons.

"Say hundreds," said his lordship. "What say you, Mortimer? You gentlemen of the Government have not to depend upon the vicissitudes of the season for your long purses like us poor rent-roll owners."

"I go in for fifties, my lord. Until the Opposition allows the strings of the public purse to open a little more widely, we poor public servants must practise strict economy."

"Egad! I wish I could practise a similar economy," said Parsons, laughing. "Mortimer lost some thousands the night before last, and calls that economy."

"The long minority of the heirs of Seamore will recoup him for all," said Lord Kingston, as he shuffled the cards. "The funds at disposal there must now be something enormous."

"And none now to come in for them but the bright-eyed Miss Helen. Egad! Mortimer, you are a lucky fellow! Here's the health of the handsome heiress!" said Parsons, as he clinked his glass against that of the others.

"By Jove! it is enough," said Sir George Ponsonby, as he set his tumbler again on the table, "to make a fellow get rid of his present wife by hook or crook, to get a chance of the heiress and her hundred thousand. Eh, Mortimer? —Heavens! what's amiss?"

Mortimer had but placed the tumbler to his lips when the baronet spoke; his hand trembled; the tumbler fell with a crash, and its contents were dashed over the table. Heedless of the confusion he created, he fixed his eyes, with a sharp inquiring glance, on the speaker.

"What on earth has frightened you, Mortimer?" inquired the baronet. "Your face is as white as if you had seen a ghost. Hoot! man, I have no intention of getting rid of Lady Ponsonby and competing with you for the hand of the fair heiress."

"It was a sudden spasm—I am somewhat subject to them of late," said Mortimer, reassured by the placid, unconscious face of the speaker, and, judging therefrom that no intentional meaning lurked behind his words. "It is only so much precious liquor spilled," as he wiped the table with his handkerchief. "I hope, my lord, the cards have received no injury."

"No; fortunately, I held them in my hands. Fill another tumbler and let us proceed with the game."

"*You* cut, Ponsonby," said Lord Kingston.

"Here goes, my lord," said Ponsonby gaily, as he shared the counters around, ten to each.

The game went on; but towards morning, when the sunbeams were beginning to share with the lamps the work of lighting the room, Sir Trevor Mortimer rose from his seat a loser of over five thousand pounds.

"This has been rather a bad night for us, Mortimer," said his lordship, as he glanced at the pale face of the other, whose losses had now completely sobered him. He had been drinking rather heavily during the night, but the run of luck against him had had the not unusual result of doing away with its effects.

"It is all the fortunes of war, my lord—reverses must come to individuals as to nations."

"By Jove, it is well that you can take it so easily," said his lordship, as he sat down and wrote a cheque for the amount of his losses. "For me it is another pull at the walls of Kingston Castle. It is well to belong to the governing body in Ireland."

"I am sorry, if it is, that I cannot follow your lordship's example. Ponsonby will have to take my note of hand for the amount for a month or two. This has been rather a larger pull than I came prepared to meet."

With more or less of grace the baronet accepted the bill in lieu of cash, and Mortimer, bidding them a careless good morning, passed out of the house.

There was a sense of rage and dismay lurking about his heart, as he strode through the yet noiseless streets on his way to his quarters in the Castle, that palpably showed itself in his maddened eyes and white face.

"This has been an unlucky week," he said, "and this the worst night of all. This means ruin if I do not meet the bill I have just passed. And where shall the money come from? Where? Heaven knows. Helen Barrington must marry me—*must*, there is no other word for it."

With a muttered malediction which boded but little good to anyone that stood in his way in his intentions with regard to his marriage, he reached home, threw himself on the sofa; and, owing to the fact of his having been up all night and the quantity of potations he had taken, was soon sunk in a semi-drunken slumber.

CHAPTER XXI.

REDMOND'S STORY.

"Why, Eugene," said the new attendant, "Wake, man! Rouse yourself! What's amiss with you? Why don't you speak? Don't you know me?"

"I think I do, Redmond, though I can hardly believe the evidence of my senses," said Eugene when he had recovered the power of speaking. "Where did you come from? What brought you here?"

"It would be a long story to tell, and when I think over it myself I can hardly believe it. But if my presence is a wonder to you, yours is still more so to me. When did you leave Seamore, and why?—And of all places in the world to find you here!—But I see you are too weak for much conversation. Wait a moment till I shall bring you something to strengthen you."

He departed, and soon returned with a bottle and a tumbler in his hand.

"You are evidently a person of some importance here, Eugene, for orders have been given that your treatment shall be of the best. Take this, You will find it do you much good. There! that's better."

Eugene took a little of the liquor which was handed

him, and found himself a good deal refreshed and strengthened thereby.

"That's what we poor fellows before the mast do not often get," said his companion pleasantly.

"Before the mast!" said Eugene, with perplexed surprise.

"Yes Eugene, that's about the position I now find myself in."

"Redmond," said the prisoner, "this world latterly has become full of unexpected incidents to me, but this is the most unexpected of all. Sit down and tell me all about it. I feel myself still scarcely able to believe that it is you are here, and that I am not suffering under some of the illusions of my illness."

"You may readily believe it, then, Eugene. A very unpleasant thing for myself, I assure you."

"And how did it come about?"

"Well, Eugene, a few words will tell you as well as if I spent a month in the narration. You remember the night we went into Dublin together from Seamore."

"Yes, perfectly. It was on that night I left."

"You too?"

"Yes; but don't heed me for the present. Go on with your story."

"Well, that night I had an appointment with a friend—a mutual friend I should say, perhaps—Trevor Mortimer."

"Yes."

"He asked me to meet him that night at the Eagle in Eustace-street—that he had urgent occasion for my presence on business of importance—and to keep the matter secret. This of course I readily assented to, and did meet him, as appointed. He told me the business on which he required me had been postponed, and we stopped together for some time; not there, but in another hotel in Dame-street. We had some wine, and I cannot to this hour know how it was that my head became so confused and my feet so unsteady, considering the very limited quantity I had taken. But so it was; I felt that all ordinary perception was gone from me, and that I could scarcely balance myself on my feet. Mortimer wondered at it too, and suggested that we should walk along the quays, where the clear cold air of the river might restore me. That much I remember clearly, but very little more. I have a vague remembrance of seeing the river, with the lights flashing thereon—of wondering how confusedly the houses adjoining it seemed to cluster around me. I remember vaguely a sudden blow on the head, which struck me to the ground, and I found myself, in a few moments after, falling with a splashing shock into the river. I remember nothing thereafter until I found myself in a vessel at sea."

"Where was Mortimer?"

"I have not the slightest remembrance of his company after I left the hotel. None. He may have been with me, or he may not. Probably the latter, because on thinking over the matter since, I have come to the conclusion that after I had been struck I was lifted and flung over the wall into the river. If Mortimer had been there he would not have permitted that."

"It is a very extraordinary story."

"So it is. You have it now just as I know it myself."

"Who could have struck you?"

"I have not the slightest conception—nor could any amount of thinking give me the least clue."

"You had no quarrel with any one—no enemy?"

"I had no quarrel with anyone, and no enemy in the world that I knew of. If I had he must have been a very causeless one."

"It was clearly an attempt to murder you."

"I can see no other intention there could be. They went—whoever they were that did it—in the most certain way to effect their purpose. It is very extraordinary, is it not? considering the mysterious attempt that had been made on Mortimer himself previously. Who could have done it?"

"It *is* very extraordinary," said Eugene slowly—"very What makes it the more so in my mind is that Mortimer, whom I saw later on that night, said he had not seen you."

"Not seen me! You must be under a mistake, Eugene —or have forgotten his words."

"I may not remember the exact words, Redmond, but," said Eugene, slowly and thoughtfully, "he certainly gave me, in some way, undoubtedly to understand that he had not seen you. I was anxious about you, inasmuch as I wished to see you before leaving Seamore."

"That brings me to the point I was anxious about. Why did you leave Seamore, and how did you come to be here?"

Eugene told him in a few words, the circumstances of which the reader is already aware.

"Your story is nearly as strange as my own," said Redmond, when he had ended. "Is it not a wonderful circumstance that we should meet here again—here of all places on earth? One never knows what is in store for him, they say, but he should have been gifted with a wonderful amount of prophecy who could have foretold that, when last we parted, we should meet again under these circumstances."

"It was God sent you here, Redmond. Sit closer to me. I have something to say to you that none but your own ears must hear," whispered Eugene cautiously.

Redmond moved nearer to him, and in whispers Eugene conveyed to him the purport of the conversation he had heard passing between the doctor and the captain whilst they believed him still in a state of unconsciousness.

"This is a dreadful fate in store for you, my poor Eugene," said Redmond, with much alarm.

"It is," assented the latter. "If I am once placed in an English prison, I feel certain I shall never come out of it alive. Judging from the French officers I have seen liberated after confinement of a year or two, I verily believe that it would be better not. For they were complete wrecks—ruined alike in body and mind."

"What do you propose doing?"

Eugene lifted himself with difficulty on his elbow and whispered into the other's ear—"Escaping."

Redmond started.

"It is impossible," he said, after an alarmed pause. "And, even if possible, to attempt it would certainly end in your recapture or death."

"Not the former, certainly; the latter, very possibly or probably. But even that would be infinitely preferable to imprisonment in the hulks. But we shall talk over it again. I am not at present strong enough to make any attempt—even an attempt to get out of bed, or even raise myself."

"You have had a sad time of it, my poor fellow," said Redmond compassionately, as he glanced at the pallid face and weakened form of his friend. "Better fall into the hands of the press-gang, even as I did, than run the perils you have run. Fortunate fellow, Mortimer, to have escaped them."

"Do you know, Redmond," said Eugene, after a period of silence in which both were sunk in thoughtfulness, "I have some doubts about Mortimer's doings in this whole business?"

"You have?"

"I really have. Has it never occurred to yourself that his conduct on that night is somewhat inexplicable?"

"You have struck on a thought that has often arisen in my own mind. But I have always banished it with the reflection—what motive could he have? None."

"I can't speak as to his motives," said Eugene, "but the fact that a little drink had such an unusually stupefying influence suggests to me——"

"That it was drugged," said Redmond, seeing that the prisoner hesitated.

"Something of that kind," assented Eugene very thoughtfully. "Then surely, having induced you to walk on the quays, he should and could have taken better care of you."

"Unless he, too, was attacked and overpowered. I have often thought of that."

"I am afraid you must banish that thought from your head. You must remember I saw him afterwards."

"By Jove, yes! I had forgotten that," said Redmond with sudden revulsion of feeling. "You are quite certain it was afterwards you saw him?"

"There can be no doubt of it, from what you say," said Eugene slowly. "But that is not all. I am inclined to think that some of my misfortunes are attributable to him. You remember the evening on which we came into Dublin, and on which a letter had come for me?"

"Yes, quite clearly."

"That letter was opened before I got it. It was in the drawingroom, and he was there, as you may remember, before I entered. It struck me at the time as curious; but the incident, with the other pressing matters that followed, was banished from my head. I now remember it anew, and, in the light of what you have told me, it crops up in my mind with fresh suspicions."

"What interest would he have in your letter?"

"That I can only vaguely guess at."

"What was the subject of it?"

"Why it somewhat incautiously hinted the fact of a messenger having hurriedly come across from France, and the tenor of his message was that I should leave Ireland at once—that night if possible—which I accordingly did. It was a matter of wonderment to me how surely we were seized on our passage before we were twenty-four hours at sea."

"Who did the letter come from?"

"It came from the secretary of the United Irishmen in Dublin.——You will forgive me, Redmond, for not having told you this before, but my chief business to Ireland—independently of seeing old friends at Seamore—was to carry out on the part of France the arrangements to aid the Irish revolutionary party. I could not have told you this without violating the order of secrecy I had received."

"This seems to me to be nearly as strange as the rest of the news I have heard," said Redmond, with amazement on his countenance.

"That is so, however," said Eugene anxiously, as he saw the unpleasant expression depicted on his friend's face, and grew afraid his statement might cause injurious doubts to arise in his breast, "but you must remember, Redmond, I had pledged my word of honour as a French officer to reveal no word of my mission. I was therefore under the unpleasant dilemma of accepting your friendship and hospitality whilst concealing my true character, or of leaving Seamore and residing elsewhere, which latter I should have done with regret—for those in Seamore were very dear to me."

He spoke with no small emotion, which was not unnoticed by Redmond, who said:

"As possibly you may be aware, Eugene, I sympathise but little with the views held by that body; but, after all, I do not see that you should be the less welcome to Seamore because of any political views or sympathies you may hold. Nor, indeed, now that I think over it, was there any reason why you should have stated your business openly. It only concerned yourself. What did concern us was—that you were welcome to us and that your stay made the place very delightful to us. We shall not speak of that matter again. And as you are, I can see, exhausted with so much talking, I fancy we shall postpone all further mention of the subject until I come to-morrow—which I shall do early, unless I am prevented. Your words have made me as anxious as yourself to leave this. I am in grave doubts, after our conversation, as to how matters may be with Helen at Seamore; but we shall talk over matters to-morrow, if possible, in regard to it."

They parted—Redmond to return to his duties in the vessel in quality of his newly acquired position as pressed seaman, and Eugene to rest himself and try to sleep.

But sleep was far from his eyes.

Curiously enough, both were occupied by the one thought. It was Helen's position at Seamore.

The strangeness of the circumstances attending Redmond's finding himself one of the crew of the Thunderer, and the new and unaccustomed duties he had to perform, prevented his being able to think connectedly about her previously. He had, indeed, often felt pained and worried when he thought of the uneasiness she must have experienced at his unexplained absence—a circumstance which the strict rules of the service, forbidding pressed seamen from communicating with their friends, prevented any possibility of avoiding. But now Eugene's words awakened suspicions perfectly distracting in themselves and ceaselessly harrying his mind. What could have been Mortimer's object if these suspicions were true—and they were not without a reasonable amount of foundation—he who had so long been his friend and intimate? Moreover, he was Helen's acknowledged suitor, and this circumstance (which for some reason not quite clear to himself, Redmond felt reluctant to mention to Eugene) made any treachery on his part the more strange and unaccountable. But, on the other hand, where had he been the moment when the unseen hand had struck himself down, and murderous hands had thrown him into the water? Could Mortimer himself have done the——

But no; the suspicion was ungenerous and unjust Mortimer could never have known of it.

With all these considerations balancing in his mind, he felt an unaccountable dread of misfortune happening to Helen, and a growing desire to get back—come what would—to Seamore.

He tossed restlessly in his hammock, thinking how this could be accomplished, but vainly. He could form no idea of how it could be effected. Escape seemed impossible.

Eugene was similarly occupied. He, too, was full of anxiety to get to Seamore. He felt strongly convinced of Mortimer's treachery, and was full of fear that in the absence of her brother he might prevail on the unbefriended girl to marry him. The very thought that this could be the case—that she was lost to him for ever—was perfectly maddening. Even while they were thus wafting about on the sea his rival's wiles might be taking effect!

Finally, and as the result of these maddening conjectures, he made up his mind. He would at all risks make his escape or die in the attempt. Better that than live in suspense as to how she fared. To think of spending years in prison without hearing of or seeing her, or learning how she was!

Years!—the very word sounded like an eternity to him!

CHAPTER XXII.

MIDNIGHT ON THE SEA.

REDMOND did not turn up next day. A strange hand came instead. Why the change was made Eugene could not learn.

And so, to his infinite surprise, it continued for many torturing days and nights.

But one evening, some weeks after, he was quite surprised to see the welcome face of his friend again at the entrance to his prison-chamber.

"Redmond!" cried Eugene, delightedly.

"Hush!" said his friend, placing his finger on his lip.

Eugene looked at him and quickly recognised that there was something secret and important in his manner and bearing.

"We are now at anchor," said Redmond hurriedly.

"Yes. I know—but where?"

"Off the Wexford coast. Listen! We must contrive to escape to-night."

"To-night."

"Yes. I cannot stand it any longer. I am tortured with anxieties about Helen and Seamore. Ever since we were last speaking, the desire to get back has grown on me more and more. I cannot sleep without unhappy dreams about both. I am in constant trouble about it. Come weal or woe, I shall escape—or try to—to-night."

"And I shall join you."

"Do you think you would be able?" asked Redmond, with intense anxiety.

"I have been nursing my strength for this occasion. If the idea of escaping has been growing upon you, it has grown with ten-fold power and strength upon me. I am ready."

"Then we shall try at midnight."

"But how?—Redmond, be careful!"

"Look here, Eugene. This port-hole," pointing to one which became visible to Eugene's eyes through the opened door—"this port-hole shall be left open. Under it rocks a small boat—you understand?—We may not be heard, or, if heard, they may take it as one of the boats going ashore. Will you be able to make the attempt?"

"Trust me, I shall," was the confident reply of the prisoner, who felt already the strength mounting in his heart, and the blood coursing with fresh vigour in his veins, as he thought of escape and freedom.

"Not a sound, until then; but keep awake and vigilant," and, closing the door softly, Redmond reascended on deck.

The minutes seemed hours and the hours years as Eugene lay with palpitating heart awaiting the next coming of his friend.

How long the dusk seemed falling! How long until complete darkness had descended! How eagerly he listened to every distant footfall, to every creaking noise in the huge ship, in expectation of the summons!

As he waited and waited in anxious expectancy, how wearily and slowly the hours appeared to drag themselves along! It seemed to him at last as if it must be near daylight and that Redmond's heart had failed him, or that unknown circumstances had compelled him to abandon the attempt—when suddenly, the sound of a muffled step fell on his ear, and the door slowly opened.

"Eugene!"

The whisper fell on his excited attention and hearing with the distinctness of a trumpet sound.

"Yes; I'm ready—Redmond—I'm ready."

He felt almost as if his whisper could be heard on deck.

"Slip off your boots and follow me."

The words were scarcely out of his mouth when Eugene, complying with the order, stood beside him.

They moved towards the open port-hole.

As they did so, Eugene moved against a cutlass that some negligent hand had laid over the trunnion of a gun. It fell, and the echoes on their startled ears seemed to ring with the force of a broadside.

They paused a moment until the echoes had died away and until they satisfied themselves that no attention had been created thereby.

"For the love of heaven, Eugene, be careful!" whispered Redmond, laying his hand on the other's shoulder. "I shall go first. I know better the way, and where the boat lies."

He crept cautiously through the port-hole, head foremost.

How long the operation seemed to Eugene watching behind And what a throb of rejoicing came to his heart as he saw him cling to a rope outside and disappear!

He immediately prepared to follow his friend's example. He had got his head through far enough to see the dark waste of waters around and the indistinct form of his companion standing on the poop of the boat beneath.

A voice in command suddenly rang out on the deck above.

For a moment he feared they had been discovered, and drew back instinctively.

It was only the command of the officer relieving the second watch. Eugene knew that this would be a time of more or less confusion on deck, and therefore favourable to their attempt.

He crept out once more, laid hold on the rope that depended from the side of the ship, and with a quickness and agility begotten of his experience on board the French fleet, quickly slid down, and was soon standing beside his companion.

"That was well done," was the whisper in his ear. "For your life now not a word. Lie down in the bottom. I shall scull her softly out."

Eugene did as he was desired. Redmond, placing his oar against the side of the vessel that seemed to lift herself like a mountain above them, sent the little skiff spinning noiselessly through the water. Then with his hand he paddled her some distance so noiselessly that Eugene, lying in the bottom of the boat, could scarcely hear the sound.

They had in this manner got a considerable length from the vessel—so far, indeed, that Eugene, lifting his head to the rowlocks, could barely see her in the darkness, looming like a huge spectral figure on the breast of the waters.

Over the darkness suddenly a trumpet sound rang out!

"Jump to your oar, Eugene! Quick!" said Redmond, in hurried tones. "We have been discovered. There's the signal. For your life, man!—quick!"

The bugle rang a second time before Eugene was able to get his oar into position. He had some difficulty in getting it from under the seat; he had a further difficulty in getting it into the rowlock, the clanking iron of which made a considerable noise.

Meantime they could hear by the calls and cries and other noises on board the distant vessel that there was considerable running about; and lights flitting to and fro hurriedly appeared on her decks.

"Don't make so much noise, Eugene, but pull with all your strength. Pull for your very life! They are launching other boats. See!"

A red sheet of flame burst out from the side of the ship, and long before the report reached them a shower of grape struck the water near, throwing up a column of spray.

"That was a random shot attracted by the noise, Eugene; but how near it was to doing its work! Pull! the tide is with us, and they will hardly find us out in the darkness."

It needed no words of encouragement or command to make Eugene bend on his oar. Freedom and liberty were before him—imprisonment and bondage behind. He was from long habit a skilful oarsman; and whilst his eyes watched the many moving lights on the deck of the vessel, betokening the haste that was made to put after them, the little skiff flew along the water in obedience to their nervous and vigorous strokes.

"How far have we to row to land, Redmond?" he asked.

"Three or four miles; but there is no use running in close at once. They will sweep inwards along the shore looking for us. There is an island further up for which I think we should make—that, or pull Nor'ards keeping this distance out."

"The latter will be, I think, the best plan; we had better keep pulling whilst the tide is with us."

By degrees the lights on the ship grew dimmer as the distance from her increased.

Occasionally a cry of some seabird or a noise borne from afar came on their ears, startling them into the belief that the pursuing boats were on their track, and they leant on their oars in breathless suspense to ascertain if their fears were well grounded. Finding they were not, they pulled on again vigorously, until, after the lapse of a couple of hours, they had so far increased their distance from the vessel that her lights were invisible.

"We are approaching land," said Eugene, as the noise of surf came on his ears, and he turned his head around, to look over his shoulder.

"So we are," said his companion, looking around also; "this must be the island I told you of. The Thunderer passed it up and down repeatedly recently."

"What shall we do now?"

"We are safe here for a while. Their boats must have made for the shore in the belief that *we* would have rowed straight therefor also."

"Shall we remain here?"

"Yes, I think so; for some time at least. We are a long time from daylight yet. We can get out here and rest our legs. I am perfectly crippled with sitting so tight in this little boat."

"And I, too," said his companion. "But are we safe?"

"There are nooks along these cliffs that they would find it perfectly impossible in the dark to find their way into, or in which to discover our boat. Besides, they would never dream that we should make for this place with the shore so much nearer and safer."

"Very well; pull along, then. I shall be glad of room to stand up."

"Steady, now, Eugene—we are in the surf. A little this way! Now!—we are in the deep water again. We are right under the cliffs. There is a little bay here, apparently. Easy, Eugene—back water. Here we are; nothing could be better."

"Nothing," said Eugene, as the boat, swinging around a projecting cliff, ran into a little narrow but completely land-locked harbour, with high precipitous cliffs projecting thereover. "It was specially marked out for the safety of fugitive British seamen," added he, laughing.

"I am glad to see you in such spirits, Eugene," said Redmond, as he stepped out on the narrow fringe of strand, covered with heaps of seaweed, beaten in by the waves.

"He should be more dull of heart and gloomy of disposition than I am who would not rejoice at escaping from the Thunderer, and the long captivity that lay beyond her. This, indeed, is liberty—I never really felt what freedom was before," he said, as he stepped out, threw up his arms, and drew himself to his full height.

"And by the way," said Redmond, as he suddenly placed his hand on his breast, "here is—is it not wonderful I never thought of it during our long row?—something that will add to our sense of relief."

"What is it?"

"A flask of brandy——"

"No!"

"Nothing less."

"Well, God bless whoever invented that precious liquor. I think it never came to more parched lips before."

"But that is not all."

"I think it must be all," said Eugene facetiously—the airy character of his French nature developing itself at once. "I fancy at this moment the world possesses nothing more valuable."

"Except these—cigars."

"You don't really say so. You are an angel of deliverance, Redmond. You are indeed. It is not an able seaman before the mast but High Admiral of the English fleet they should have made you."

"I am not very ambitious of that either. But here, take something—a little to refresh and strengthen you. You must need it very much. We have a long row yet before we touch land, and Heaven knows how we may fare then."

"Leave that to Heaven. Sufficient for the day is the evil thereof, and sufficient for the present that we have escaped from the Thunderer. And now for a cigar. How shall we light?"

"I have provided that, too. Here are flint and fusee."

"Good again. How long it is since my lips were blessed with the fragrant weed! I feel like a giant refreshed. I could keep the oar going without ceasing until daylight."

"You will need all your strength and vigour," said

Redmond, as they stamped on the strand to circulate the blood in their stiffened limbs. "We have a long row before us."

"The longer the better if it will but put us further away from the sides of his Majesty's line-of-battle ship Thunderer. We shall find friends on shore, I warrant you. French officers are not unwelcome visitors on Irish soil at present."

"I believe you are right—I had not thought of that," said Redmond, pausing in his exertions. "And that being so," he continued, "I daresay the best plan is to get to land as speedily as possible."

"I think so," said Eugene cheerfully. "Who knows how soon fate and good fortune may bring us to Seamore?"

"It is almost too much good luck to hope for. And that puts me in mind, Eugene, of the conversation we had on the occasion of our first strange meeting on the Thunderer. I have often thought of your words since. And, what is more—I am almost inclined to agree with what you said of Mortimer."

"Say not almost, but quite, Redmond. I too have thought over the matter since, and I have come to the conclusion that he is at foot of all our misfortunes."

"What motive could he have?"

"It is hard to fathom any man's motives. It is difficult to get at the inner life of any man; but that he——"

"Hush!" said Redmond in a tremulous whisper, laying his hand hurriedly on the other's shoulder.

"What is it?" whispered Eugene, after a pause of dead silence in which neither scarcely breathed.

"I heard a voice whilst you were speaking."

They listened again for a considerable time.

"Your ears deceived you, Redmond," whispered his companion. "There is no boat on the waters near us. It was your imagination."

"Perhaps it was—but I certainly thought I heard a voice calling."

"It must have been the spirit of some drowned fisherman or sailor, then," said Eugene, unbelievingly, as, after cautiously walking to the projecting rock, and looking around it, he returned to where his friend stood, "for there is not a living thing to be seen around."

"I am quite certain I heard it. A weak voice calling or moaning."

"If you did it was no living voice."

"By Jove, Eugene, I feel quite an eerie feeling creeping down my back. I suppose my anxiety led me astray. Still!——By heavens! there it is again. Did you hear it?"

"Yes," said Eugene, quite as startled as his companion, "I heard it. Somewhere near us, too."

"Yet there is no one near us."

"No, there is nothing around but the cliffs."

"It is very singular."

"Very," said Eugene solemnly.

They listened for a short time.

Again the voice came. It was the weak voice of one in great agony.

"By heavens, Redmond," said Eugene, "it comes from the seaweed. From that heap yonder. It is some drowning person the tide has washed in."

"I believe you are right," said Redmond, moving quickly towards the spot.

"Good God! Eugene come here?" cried he, as he bent down. "It is a girl buried in the seaweed. Come here—come quick!"

Going there, Eugene saw indistinctly what his companion had seen before him—the form of a girl lying on the masses of seaweed. Her dress was black, and as she lay with her face apparently buried in the soft mass under her, she was undistinguishable, in the darkness, from the surroundings.

"Heavens! how could she have come here? She breathes!—she is living, but unconscious! What could have happened her?"

"I'll tell you how it is, Eugene," said Redmond, as he assisted to lift the senseless form of the girl, and turned her bruised and bleeding face upwards; "she has fallen from the cliffs. Her life was saved by falling on this mass of seaweed, else she should have been dashed to pieces. It was the providence of God that sent us here to save her. Merciful heavens!" he added, as he glanced at the precipice above him, steep as the wall of a house, "what a fall the unfortunate girl must have had!"

"Her face is cut and bleeding, too, poor thing. Heaven help her! what a frightful accident must have happened her! What shall we do? Have you anything left in the flask?"

"A little, but sufficient for the purpose. Hold her in your arms, Eugene, for a moment."

Redmond poured, as well as he could in the gloom and darkness that surrounded them, a few drops of the liquor into her parted lips. The light barely afforded him power to do so. An answering pulse of life through her form rewarded his efforts, and reassured him that it had not been wholly quenched.

"What shall we do, Redmond? This poor creature cannot be allowed to die here."

"No; certainly not," said his friend.

"What do you propose?"

"I'll tell you what we shall do—row directly to the shore. We shall find some means, once there, of bringing her into succour and help. Mayhap her friends are at this moment wondering where she is."

"I think you are right—even though we fall in with the search-boats of the Thunderer."

"Even though we should. Better have *us* retaken than that we should allow her life to be lost without an effort to save her."

"Such a thing is not to be thought of," said Eugene promptly. "It would be murder."

"Are you able to resume your oars?"

"I am able to row," said Eugene bravely, "until morning, if the need be."

"Good fellow!—Assist me to lift her into the boat. Gently. There!"

"Now," said Eugene, as he took off his coat and folded it around her, and under her head for a pillow, "let us get the boat apast these rocks, and she shall have a fair chance for her life. Poor girl!"

They got the little skiff out into the sea once more, and, turning her head to the shore, pulled with all the vigour of brave and gallant hearts. In a short time the little rocky islet disappeared from their view, and they were once more on the open sea, the night-clouds and darkness alone around them. Still they rowed on with unceasing exertion, spurred thereto by the low moan of agony that at intervals broke from the unconscious form lying at their feet.

"Who can tell," said Redmond, "what frightful sorrow and trouble her friends may be in, unknowing what has become of her."

Who, indeed? Not they, two, surely—rowing athrough the dark sea to the unknown coast, the beat of whose surf on the rocks grew more strongly each moment on their ears.

So strangely fate weaves her threads! So wonderfully involved are the golden web and woof of human lives!

CHAPTER XXIII.

THE CRY FROM THE CLIFFS.

A FEW weeks saw Helen Barrington and Kate Howard in the latter's comfortable home at Inch. Here, in the midst of new and agreeable surroundings, the former gradually began to forget her troubles, or, if not to forget them, to bear them better. The roses came back into her cheeks, and the old winsome smile into her eyes.

So also a short time saw the old deserted mansion at Grey Abbey being put in repair. It had been long disused and neglected, but now its broken windows were new glazed, and the place rapidly put in order. And no sooner was it habitable, than, to the surprise of Kate Howard, but not at all to that of Helen, Trevor Mortimer made his appearance therein.

Inch House lay in a sheltered nook some distance—half a mile or thereabouts—inland, protected from the sea-storms by an intervening hill. Its topmost windows alone gave view of the sea. Grey Abbey stood along the coast about a mile distant and near the strand. Between lay the ruins of an old monastery, whose walls, spray-swept and whitened with winter storms and bleached by summer heats, propably supplied to the builder of the lately ruined, but newly tenanted, mansion its picturesque name. At some time, so remote in the lapsing centuries that history had lost ken of it, the abbey must have been built a distance inland, but the action of the ceaseless sea had gradually swept away the cliffs, until now it stood so nigh that some of the walls had actually fallen over.

It was rather a matter of wonder with the people living in the neighbourhood, to see Grey Abbey refurnished, and most persons were disposed to look on its new inhabitant as a sort of government official guarding that part of the coast—a not extraordinary guess, considering the troubled condition of Wexford at the time.

"And who have you living with you, Sir Trevor?" asked Miss Howard, one day when he rode over, for the first time after his coming, to pay them a visit.

"Only an old housekeeper," said he gaily. "I mean only to use it as a shooting box, or rather, I should say, a fishing-box, while my friends remain here."

"How delightful it will be to visit and explore the old mansion! One can imagine ghosts and skeletons starting up out of old hiding places of years."

"I shall be glad to show you over the old fabric when it is ready, but at present it is scarcely fit for ladies' eyes to see—not to speak of the fact that my housekeeper is not at all disposed to do the honours of so uninviting a mansion."

"Well, let us know when you are prepared to receive us, and we shall be glad to pay you a visit."

"With the greatest pleasure."

The subject was dropped, and to Mortimer's great satisfaction was not resumed again for some time.

Meantime, however, his visits grew frequent to Inch House, and as, in consequence of the disturbed state of the country, many of the gentry had gone to reside in the metropolis, and society was therefore scarce, his attention was very acceptable, as tending to relieve the *ennui* of the place.

Helen began once more to be pleased in his society. Somehow the events that preceded and followed the disappearance of her brother and Eugene had tended to make his presence more or less distressing; but now she was beginning to look upon the past as irrevocable, and to regard the previous relations that existed between Mortimer and herself as undisturbed.

Wherefore it was that she was constantly in his company whenever he came, and if he were a day or two absent, almost felt lonely for his presence. Thrown, almost without further society, into his company, it was no wonder that his old power over her and her old liking for him began to be restored. And insensibly his statements constantly repeated began to impress her with the force of conviction, until whenever she thought of Eugene, it was with a shudder for his dreadful and unaccountable treachery and ingratitude.

Mortimer was delighted. He could not conceive that so welcome and fortunate a change could come for him from this visit to the country. Instinctively he began to find that her old regard for him, which seemed abating, had returned in greater strength. There was no need that she should tell him so; he knew it by mere intuition. And, so knowing, he resolved to profit by it—by pressing his suit as earnestly and vehemently as he could.

And so one evening, as they stood on the brow of the hill that intervened between Inch House and the sea, he urged her to be his wife without delay—and she consented. He pointed out to her her isolated condition, the long understanding that subsisted between them, the unreasonableness of further delay, the approbation with which her brother had looked upon their projected union, and after some objections on her part—put forward faintly and waveringly, but beaten down or waived aside by his passionate pleadings—she consented.

Immediately she gave her consent other preliminaries were arranged. She was to return to Seamore in a few days, and once there the marriage was to take place without any unnecessary delay. Indeed, now that her adhesion to his wishes in the principal matter had been concluded, there was no reason why there should.

Thence afterwards he was constantly at Inch and unceasingly by her side. A gayer or more agreeable suitor it would be difficult to find. Miss Howard was in delight that her friend was likely to be soon so happily placed.

and, whilst mourning over the disappointment her own heart had sustained by Redmond Barrington's disappearance or death, rejoiced unselfishly on account of Helen's happiness.

But if Trevor Mortimer was so joyous and light-hearted in his betrothed's presence, he was torn with very different feelings when away from her.

There were so many things to interrupt this chance of good luck that offered itself to him. There was one who might, at any moment and unexpectedly, turn up to mar his prospects. If he once were married to Helen Barrington he could afford to despise her threats. He could repudiate the French marriage with her It was not the law in this country, nor would there be many under the circumstances at present existing between France and England to think ill of such repudiation. As to what Helen thought, once he was her husband and master of Seamore and its rich estates, it would matter very little to him. She might think well or ill of it just as she pleased. He would take care that it should give him very little trouble or concern.

But until he really were married how many circumstances might turn up to ruin him! *She* had not come according to his arrangement with her. Who knew but she might, hearing how matters stood, present herself before Helen and warn her that she was already his wife. That would be utter and certain ruin. That would be a final and impassable barrier to his hopes. That would be a final ending to their engagement. His heart filled with malignant terror at the idea. The love—if it could be called love—that once he bore her had turned to implacable and burning hate. She came to his mind as the bearer of ruin to him; the demon would have seemed to his inflamed thoughts as less abhorrent.

There was a further source of trouble around him in the sense that some knowledge of his gambling propensities and his heavy debts might come to Helen's ears. There was also the pressing necessity for paying his debts of honour to his gambling associates in Dublin—else his name might be suddenly posted in the clubs as a blackleg, and his name ostracised in Dublin society.

But these latter became merged in the more dangerous trouble caused by the possible appearance before Helen of —of—*his wife*. It was with a curse of vengeance that this name occurred to him. If he could only be rid of her—if he could only——

It was in some such abrupt and malignant manner of thinking as this that one morning as he opened the hall-door of the dilapidated mansion of Grey Abbey there presented itself before him the form of—*his wife*.

If a thunderbolt had suddenly fallen from the skies at his feet he could not have been more surprised, although he had expected and arranged for it, and although he often feared she would not come. He had been on his way to Inch, and her appearance was furthest from his thoughts.

But he was equal to the occasion, and promptly recovered himself. The look of dark displeasure and surprise quickly vanished from his face, which became immediately wreathed with smiles.

" Come, at last, Alice dear ?" he said, embracing her. " How long and how anxiously I have expected you!"

"I could not come earlier, Trevor," she said, tears of rejoicing bursting to her eyes at the warmth of his reception. "I came as soon as I was able—for I have been very ill."

" I am sorry I have not a more suitable house to entertain you in and welcome you to, Alice, darling, but your stay will not be long. How did you come ?"

" By the night mail. You know you wished me to come privately."

" So I did, Alice. Such a good girl as you are—so true and loyal. Did anyone travel with you ?"

" No, no one. There was none but myself in the mail. It was so lonely a journey—oh! so lonely! But I was cheered by the thought of your welcome—of seeing you

"And you shall be still further cheered and rejoiced, Alice, darling. Come in.—Moya, Moya !" he called as they entered, " see who has come—see who has come, Moya !"

Alice was delighted with the warmth of her reception and the excitement her coming had caused; and as the old woman hobbled towards her she overcame her repugnance and threw her arms around her in a burst of gratitude and affection—as fervent for the moment as if it were around her dead mother's form she twined her arms.

Leaving her after some time, during which his delight was manifested in many ways that filled the weary wanderer with new feelings of joy, he took his departure for Inch. There he impressed upon Helen Barrington the necessity of her speedy return to Scamore. He had not much difficulty in inducing her to accede to his wishes, and the next day, or at furthest the next but one, was fixed therefor.

That arrangement made, he returned.

Alice and he walked, during the late afternoon, along the more unfrequented way towards the sea, and in the direction of the ruined abbey. In ecstacies at her new-found happiness, she hung upon his arm and listened with the old rapture to his honeyed words.

To one not burthened with his feelings at the moment she would have seemed a graceful and handsome girl, her pale olive face contrasting finely with her black hair; and her handsome black Provençal eyes flashing with the light of new-found love—one, indeed, who but lately must have looked striking and impassioned, although now a certain air of suffering pervaded her appearance.

The sea looked so glassy and beautiful—not a ripple ruffled its surface—that Alice could not help admiring it. The afternoon light fell on its waters, giving them a ruddy glow that turned them into molten gold.

"How beautiful!" she said, leaning on his arm. "It reminds me of the sea on the Southern shores of France. Shall I ever see it again, I wonder."

"You admire this, Alice," he said, pausing in his walk, as a sudden thought struck him. They had been walking towards the cliffs whereon the ruins of White Abbey stood—overhanging the sea.

"I do!" she exclaimed enthusiastically "It reminds me of the happy days before—before I loved you, Trevor."

"Would you like, Alice, a sail on the waters, this evening? There is an island yonder—you can faintly see it from here—whereon the sunsets are perfectly—surpassingly—beautiful. You will think you are looking at dear

San Grande again. It will be so delightful to be alone on the sea as we used to be there. Would you like it?"

"Of all things—with you," was her reply.

"It will be so pleasant, and remind us so of old times," he said, as they turned to walk back.

Returning to where his boat lay anchored under the mansion, they entered it, and, fixing the sails, were soon on their way over the dancing waters.

The sail was to her entrancing. It reminded her of many similar ones on a foreign sea. Hundreds of miles lay between the two scenes, but the happiness her heart experienced was the same.

Similarly entrancing was the walk over the high and grassy cliffs of the little island, when they reached it. How perfectly beautiful was the aspect of the sea as the golden sunset threw its flood of rays over it, reflecting in its breast the crimson sky overhead!

"Trevor! How glad my heart is!" she said, as they stood on the uttermost verge of a cliff looking far over where the waters of the Channel joined and became lost in the broad waters of the Atlantic. "How little I dreamt a few weeks ago that I——"

*   *   *   *

Watchers—if there were any around the little islet—might have been startled as a cry, such as in its concentrated terror and agony seldom issued from human lips, suddenly burst on the silence around! The cliffs, as if frightened at the fear, and horror, and surprise, and affright that were blent in its piercing power, gave it back in weird echoes!

The storm-birds, terrified from their sleeping crevices in the rocks, flew around and around in shrieking surprise. Such cry had never come before on their hearing —even from the lips of drowning sailors or fishermen!

But the shriek of agony died out unheard on the voiceless waters; the echoes ceased; the sea-birds abandoned their whirling flight and once more sought the repose of the beetling cliffs; silence—the unearthly silence of fear and death—and the growing dusk, wrapped the cliff and crag and harbourlett in weird tranquility.

What was that awful cry? What heart affrighted or in mortal agony gave utterance to it? Why was it quenched so suddenly.

Trevor Mortimer returned alone to Grey Abbey.

The old hag glanced at his pallid lips and white haggard face.

" Well ?—Is she ——"

" Moya," said he hurriedly, " I shall not sleep here to-night. I shall stop at Inch. I shall not return again. You will close up and come away as soon as you can."

CHAPTER XXIV.

A STRANGE DISCOVERY.

With quick and nervous strokes the two men swept the boat over the reach of sea that intervened between the islet and the shore.

They were not long in reaching the latter, but as they approached they were considerably startled to see lights moving over the water further inshore.

" Stay your oars, Eugene," said Redmond, as the light fell on his eye; "These are the man-of-war's boatmen pulling along the shore in search of us. Keep quiet as death for a while. Let the boat rock along with the tide."

" It is not a boat," said Eugene, after they had left theirs drift for some time; "it is a light moving along the strand. I hear no sound of voices, and that motion is not the tossing motion of a light on sea. It is someone walking on the strand with a lantern."

" I believe you are right," said his companion, after an earnest and attentive gaze at it, " and, see ! yonder, higher up, is another and steadier light. That is in some house. We are near succour. Thank Heaven, for the poor girl's sake."

" Shall we pull in."

" Yes, I think we may."

" Lay to, then."

They bent to their oars in order to carry the boat swiftly and strongly through the surf and ground her on the sand safely.

Just as Eugene thought, the light was not on sea but on shore ; their skiff headed for the latter—it advanced to meet them ; and when, after a rapid run through the white surf, the boat grounded firmly on the strand, the light and its bearer stood but very little away from them in the darkness. Save and except the light, however, very little of the bearer was to be seen, for the gleaming white phosphorescent foam made by contrast the darkness around blacker still.

Eugene stepping out on the strand, addressed the bearer of the light :

" We are strangers here. We are in great need of assistance—in urgent need. Can you——"

But to his infinite amazement the light was suddenly extinguished, and they were left in utter darkness.

Redmond called to him

" Steady the boat, Eugene, or it will turn on its side. Help me out with this poor girl first."

Eugene did so, and with difficulty they lifted the still unconscious form out of the boat.

" What shall we do now, Redmond ? Where was that light ? Was it not most strange that it was extinguished ?"

" Very. It was more worthy of wreckers in Cornwall than of our Irish people. They do not usually act so to people in distress."

" What step shall we take now ?"

" Why, the first thing would be to shove the boat out, and let waves and tide bear her whither they will. If we leave her here she will be a clue to where we are."

" Very true," said Eugene, as he caught hold of the prow, and with a vigorous push sent her spinning, stern foremost, into the boiling waves. " I had not thought of that. There she goes. She will have drifted miles away before daybreak."

" And the next thing is to bear this poor thing to the shelter of that light we saw higher up. I trust it will be of more service to us than that which has so singularly disappeared."

"Will you be able to bear her weight, for I must confess I am not able?"

"With the greatest ease; she is not the weight of a feather, poor girl."

Fortunately the ground sloped, a little nigher up, to the cliffs above; and after some searching and groping their way, Eugene going first and acting as leader, they reached the top, whence the light again became visible, steadily burning as before.

"You are right, Redmond; it *is* a house. That light is burning in a room—perhaps for someone ill. If so we shall have further assurance of sympathy and shelter."

"Let us push on; this poor thing breathes heavily. She may die in our arms before we get there."

They hurried on and reached the house, the door of which, fronting them as they approached, stood open. Without delay they bore her inside—into a large ruined hall empty of all but darkness.

Finding no one, Eugene stamped on the hall.

There was no response. There was no answering stir to indicate that anyone had heard them.

He stamped again with his heel.

But the echoes of the stone floor in the empty hall alone gave response.

A third time proved equally fruitless.

"Search for a door and knock at it. The house must surely be inhabited," said Redmond, who was beginning to find himself growing weak and faint from his exertions.

Eugene did as he was desired—found a door in the darkness and knocked strongly against it. But further than adding to and changing the form of the previous echoes, there was no result.

"Anyone here?" Redmond called aloud impatiently. "Is there anyone in the house? Strangers are here—needing assistance!"

His voice came back to him from distant corridors and rumbled up stone staircases; but it died out as they listened, and again all was silence.

"This is extremely strange;" said Redmond after a pause; "there seems to be no one living here. I declare I think we are bewitched."

"We are like people under some curious spell, certainly,' whispered Eugene. "What on earth is the meaning of it? Where can that light be? Here, Redmond, come here!" he added, as in groping around he opened a door. "There is a light yonder. And shelter. Come!"

Redmond bore his burthen to where his friend stood, and, glancing along a dark corridor, saw, where, at some distance, a light from a room leading off it was reflected on the wall.

Thither they advanced, calling aloud as they did so, but no person made appearance. Finally they reached the place, and pushing the door, which was ajar, open, entered.

There was no one there either. But the lamp burning on the chimney showed the room to be a bedroom, and very comfortably furnished. A fire blazed on the hearth.

"By Jove! this is extraordinary," said Redmond in dire amazement; "but it is very fortunate, all the same. It really seems as if we had arrived in fairy land, or that some special Providence is guiding us."

He deposited his senseless burthen on the bed, and took over the lamp to see how she looked.

Her long hair fell over her face, and neck, and shoulders to her waist. He put it back from her face, and tenderly wiped therefrom, also, the stains of blood and clay that crusted on it.

Eugene had discovered and opened a cupboard in which were a quantity of bottles of wine and other luxuries, and was about informing his companion of the fact, when an exclamation of surprise and horror from the latter drew him at once to his side.

"What is amiss, Redmond? She is not dead—is she?" he asked in affright.

"Alice—Alice Trainon!" said Redmond with difficulty, for his lips almost refused to perform their office.

"Who? Do you know her?"

"Alice—Alice Trainon," said Redmond incoherently.

"Who is Alice Trainon?" asked Eugene in much surprise.

"Alice Lefebre—your——" His lips refused to continue their office further.

"Your—your what? Speak, for Heaven's sake," said Eugene.

"Sister."

"My sister! Is that what you say?"

Redmond could scarcely nod an affirmation.

"Alice Lefebre—my sister! What can you mean?" asked Eugene, with a strange expression of surprise in his voice, placing his hand on the other's shoulder and turning him around.

"It is she, Eugene. Merciful providence of God! What could have brought her here?"

"You must be dreaming, Redmond. Alice is in France," said Eugene, with a cry of dismay and perplexity.

"It is she, Eugene, however she came to be here. I saw her lately. You have not seen her since childhood! It is she beyond all mistake."

Eugene stood in a stupor—a stupor in which astonishment and doubt, and boundless perplexity, nearly paralysed his every nerve.

"See Eugene! Stir yourself. She will die if we do not attend to her. Is there anything to drink in the room? Quick! get me some, if there is."

Eugene walked mechanically over to the cupboard, and brought over a decanter of brandy. Pouring out some into a wine glass, Redmond poured a few drops slowly between her lips. A stronger breathing showed that the stimulant had helped to revive her.

"Take off her boots, Eugene, and fill that bottle with hot water, and place it to her feet. There! Wrap them up warmly. I wonder is there any womankind in the house? Stay here for a few minutes whilst I see."

"Redmond, if you are right!—but you cannot be! It is impossible!——"

Indeed it was no wonder he concluded it impossible. The events of the night had been of themselves sufficiently strange, but this seemed so marvellous as to border on the region of coherency and dreams, so that Eugene appeared to himself to be half-dazed, and was in truth quite unable to realize the statement of his companion.

"I am correct enough," said Redmond, glancing again at the unconscious face. "Whatever extraordinary occurrence brought her here, it is surely she. Heaven save her!"

Tossing off a tumbler of brandy to strengthen him after his exceeding fatigue and the extraordinary shocks of surprise he had received, Redmond went on a visit of exploration, with a candle in his hand.

In a few minutes he returned.

"There is only another room in the house furnished, and that is untenanted, too," he said, when he returned. "The place seems a ruin, inhabited only lately for some passing occasion. I wonder where the inmates are. It is very strange," he added perplexedly.

"I had better close these shutters. This light may serve as a beacon in case our friends from the Thunderer may be searching for us," Redmond said again, suiting the action to the word.

"It seems to me as if I am only dreaming, and that I am on board the Thunderer still," said Eugene, when he had performed the offices for the patient desired by Redmond, and her more composed breathing indicating that she had profited by it, he took his seat by his friend at the fire, their tumblers full of the agreeable and highly acceptable drink, resting on the chimney-piece.

"Just the very thought that was passing through my head. Only that these"—pointing to the fire and the tumblers—"are not accessories found on board ship, I should certainly believe it."

"I have had a good many extraordinary adventures in my lifetime since I was carried away from school and placed as a midshipman on board *La Vengeur*, but they all pale before the events of this night. You cannot be mistaken here?" nodding towards the bed where the patient—whose heavy breathing was louder than their whisper—lay.

"No. I am quite certain."

"What could have brought the dear girl there? She could not have been coming across—on board a vessel that was wrecked."

"It would be useless guessing at present. Our first business when the day comes will be to get her proper assistance, and see if her life can be preserved. The next thing will be to place ourselves in a place of safety. For a diligent search will be made along the coast for us."

The daylight peeped through the closed shutter whilst they continued their subdued, but anxious and perplexed, conversation. It was impossible to throw light on this singular occurrence—and in a state in which Eugene could scarcely realize that he was not dreaming, or the subject of some singular hallucination, they awaited the dawn.

"It is time, I think, to extinguish this and admit the morning light," said Redmond, as he blew out the lamp, and walked over to and opened the shutter.

A flood of light burst into the room as he did so, showing that the dawn had long passed whilst they talked. It was, in fact, quite bright.

"We seem almost to be on a desert island," said Redmond, as he surveyed the scene before him; "there is nothing but rocks and ruin around."

"Hallo! Eugene, come here. Quick! come here. Look yonder!"

Eugene hurried to the window and glanced in the direction indicated.

His heart suddenly stopped beating. On the sea, about half a mile distant, the man-of-war's boat's crew was visible proceeding downward along the coast, and attached to the stern of their vessel by means of a rope was a small boat.

"We have had a narrow escape. What is that they have in tow? It cannot possibly be our boat?"

"It is nothing less," said Redmond, as he watched keenly the distant rowers; "it has drifted nor'ards with the tide, and they have found it. Furthermore, I fancy they are turning inwards. There—these confounded ruins shut out the view."

"If they do we shall be undoubtedly discovered." said Eugene.

"We shall, not a doubt of it, for we cannot abandon poor Alice, under any circumstances. I shall creep over to yonder ruins that now hide our view, and see what they mean. You remain here, Eugene, until I return."

Sheltering himself from observation by the rocks and

old walls which lay in his way, Redmond reached the ruined abbey. From behind a wall whose stone casemented window gave open view of the sea, he watched the enemy. At first they turned their helm towards the shore, and his heart throbbed within him. They seemed to be undecided what to do; divided counsels seemed to exist on board, as the boat lay motionless for a while. Finally, they turned her head once more to the sea, tacked around, and bore away.

With a genuine prayer of thanksgiving, Redmond watched the retreating boat as the wind filled her sails and swept her off.

He was about turning round to bear back the joyful news to his friend, when a rustling behind him caught on his ear.

A hand was laid on his shoulder, and a girl's voice said behind him:

"Luke."

CHAPTER XXV.

MORE MYSTERIES.

REDMOND turned around his face, for the voice seemed familiar to him.

As he did so, however, and before he could bring his eyes to bear on his accostress, a scream of surprise rose from her lips.

"It is Redmond!—merciful God!—It is the dead appearing!"

And without further stop or stay she fled.

"Who under heaven is this that knows me here?" said he, gazing with much astonishment at the retreating figure.

"This will certainly lead to discovery—certain discovery," he thought. "I must see who it is. We cannot always have these mysteries surrounding us—confound them! I shall see who it is at any rate."

The girl had disappeared through a broken doorway in

one of the ruined walls, with a flying speed that nothing but extreme terror could give rise to.

There was no time to be lost, if concealment were to be ensured, or if he were to elucidate this new mystery.

Whereupon with as much rapidity as he could, he ran over the fallen *debris*, the ruined tombs, and through the broken arches; and came up with her just as she was about emerging from the ruined abbey into the slope lying beyond it.

She had heard the step following her, and had in consequence redoubled her pace.

But when, having come up with her, he laid his hand on her shoulder, her screams were quite sufficient to have been heard by the boat in the distance. She fell on her knees, and covered her face and eyes with her hands, while her cries still poured forth unceasingly.

" Don't scream! I am not going to hurt you. Who are you that know me here? Speak! Because if you know me, I want your assistance very badly."

Seeing that she did not cease either in her affright or in screaming, and that this state of things, if of long continuance, might lead to further perplexities, he gently but firmly withdrew her hands from her face.

"Why, God bless my soul! it's Norah!" he cried in astonishment as soon as he got sight of her face, which he had much difficulty in doing. "Don't you know me, Norah? What on earth are you afraid of? I'm Redmond Barrington. Surely the world has not turned upside down that you should be afraid of *me?* Look up at me!"

The girl had, by the time he had done, ceased her screaming, tremblingly lifted up her eyes to his face, and took consolation therefrom. It was certainly no unearthly form that was speaking to her, but Redmond himself, and —though curiously dressed and much changed every way —still undoubtedly alive and in the flesh.

"That's right, Norah," said he, as he saw her satisfied glance. "Stand up, and tell me what brought you here, and why you screamed so. Why did you scream?"

"I—I—I thought it was your ghost," said Norah, shiveringly.

"My ghost!"

"Yes,"—with growing courage.

"Well, Norah, you see it isn't, but myself alive and well."

"Glory be to God for that!" said Norah, in trembling thanksgiving. "Where wor you, or where did you come from, Master Redmond?"

"That would be too long a story to tell you now, Norah. And besides," added he, as he bethought of Alice Lefebre, "I need your assistance badly. Will you come with me as far as yonder house, Norah? There is a young lady lying very ill there."

"There! Why, Master Redmond, that house—is——"

"No matter about the house, Norah. I want your help there—will you come?"

"All the world over," said Norah cheerfully, "I'd go for you. But sure I ought to go back an' tell——"

"You must go nowhere, Norah, but with me. You don't know how much your help is needed. I'm all impatience until you reach there."

Norah was so fluttered and frightened, and so out of breath with her race, and Redmond was so impatient to get back to Grey Abbey, and walked so hastily and swiftly for that purpose, that she had much difficulty in keeping up with him, and had no breath to spare for the question she was a-thirsting to ask him, or the information she desired to give him.

The confusion that existed in her mind was doubled and trebled when she reached the apartment where the injured girl lay, and where she met, to her great surprise and delight, Eugene.

Leaving the former to her ready and helpful hands for the present—and with no unnecessary conversation, circumstances being so pressing, Eugene and Redmond betook themselves to the upper rooms of the house, whence their eager eyes swept the sea and the distant horizon for some sign of the Thunderer; but there was none.

"She has probably left these waters," said Eugene after some time.

"I trust so. And now that that weight is off our minds for the present, I am anxious to know what brought Norah into this part of the world."

"She has probably got married during our absence. What I am anxious to know," said Eugene, "is, who are the good genii that left us this mansion thus fully fitted up for our needs?"

"Upon my word I had quite forgotten that," said Redmond; "in the multiplicity of strange events and surprises that have been occurring within the last dozen hours or so this had been quite forgotten by me. I wonder how it came to pass."

"Seeing that Norah lives in the neighbourhood, she may throw some light on it."

"She may, and no doubt will."

"Suppose we ask her?"

"No, not yet. She will call on us when she is ready. I told her where we were coming."

"But the great mystery of all remains incapable of explanation," said Eugene sorrowfully—"what brought Alice here? I have grave doubts still that you must be mistaken."

"There is no room for doubt, unfortunately," said Redmond. "I should know the dear girl's face among ten thousand."

"Hist! there is some one calling," said Eugene.

"It is Norah's voice. Let us see what she wants."

Norah's foot was heard on the ricketty stairs ascending, and she met them as they were about to descend.

"Masther Redmond," said she, "it would be well if you were to send to Wexford for a doctor. I am sure Miss Alice is in need of one. There is no sign of her recovering her senses."

"And how shall we send there, Norah? *We* dare not appear."

"Why, I'll go over to Inch," said Norah, sufficiently understanding, without being told, how matters were, and too anxious to have her advice carried out to need or ask for further information. "I'll get help enough there."

"Inch!" cried Redmond. "Are we near Inch?"

"Within a mile or so."

"And is it there you are stopping, Norah? Who is with you?"

"Miss Helen."

"Helen," cried both young men together.

"Unless she is gone out of it since I left. She was to go back to Seamore to-day."

"Good heavens, Norah! why did you not tell us all that before?"

"I was about tellin' you just after I met you," said Norah, "but you stopped me."

"And how long has she been there?"

"Some months."

"Well, thank God!" said Redmond gaily, "we are near friends at any rate. And, Norah, who is it that lives in this strange house, or did live in it?"

"Trevor Mortimer."

"Sir Trevor Mortimer!"

"He came down here," said Norah, in continuation, "when the young ladies came to Inch; but he was to go to Dublin this morning with Miss Helen and Miss Howard. They are all in great fuss about it; there's nothin' talked of but it."

"You must go at once, Norah, and tell Helen I am here—that *we* are here."

"Ill do that with a heart and a half," said Norah; "but I am afeard Sir Trevor was in such a hurry to reach Dublin that they'll be gone before I get back. It was to take place in a day or two."

"No matter, Norah; go at once. You will find some of the Inch people there, even if the young ladies are gone."

"Faix, an' its gone I'm nearly certain they are," said Norah; "for he was pressing Miss Helen to let it take place as soon as possible."

"What on earth are you talking about, Norah?" said Redmond impatiently. "*It! What is it?* You have mentioned that word half a dozen times."

"Why, don't you know?" said Norah, blushing rapidly.

"Is the girl gone crazy?" cried Redmond, in a fever of impatience. "Here is the day waxing; and so much to be done. What is this you are talking about?"

"The marriage."

"The marriage! What marriage?"

"The marriage of Miss Helen and Sir Trevor Mortimer. It's to take place as soon as they reach town."

Redmond blew a long, low whistle indicative of astonishment at this new feature that matters had presented, whilst Eugene staggered back against the wall, his whitening face and trembling lips showing how the unexpected information had affected him.

"Do you hear this, Eugene?" said Redmond, after a moment's pause of astonishment.

"Yes," was as much as the latter's lips would permit him to say.

"See here, Norah. Go as fast as you can to Inch. Tell Helen we are here, if she be not gone. And bind her to secrecy. If she be, tell some of my cousins to come over at once; and do not say who is here, but bid them come. Make all haste, for I must go to Dublin at once if Helen has gone."

"I'll do that sure enough," said Norah, "an' I'll engage the grass won't grow under my feet till I'm there and back again. So, stay wid the poor girl that's below until I return; an' here's a letter—keep it safe—that I got in the poor thing's breast. It's sealed, and was kept close, so see that it's safe for her by the time she recovers."

CHAPTER XXV.

IN THE CAVES.

Norah left Redmond and Eugene at the door, and hurried away with step as light and swift as a fairy, in the direction of Inch.

Her heart fluttered with the joyful news she was bringing to her mistress.

In the multitude of distracting things that had occurred to her within the last two hours she had been scarcely able to realise the wonderful character of the news she had learned; but now as she had more time to think, she began to recognise its importance, and her step flew so lightly over the sea-swept plain that, as she herself would say, "she'd hardly bend a lily with her step."

She was passing over a stile and had sprung lightly on

to the other side, and had resumed her speed again, when she ran right into the arms of a person approaching the other way.

"Where are you runnin' to, Norah ? or what's amiss wid you, or are you goin' distracted ?" said the new-comer, taking advantage of the accident which threw her into his arms, to give her a good hug. "Where have you been these hours ?"

"Let me go," cried Norah impatiently; "let me go, Luke Mahon. For the love of God, let me go," cried she, struggling to get free. "I have wonderful news for the young misthress."

"I'd rather you had some news for me," said Luke, determined not to let his prize go so easily.

"I tell you, Luke, let me go. You don't know the news I have or the hurry I'm in."

"I see the hurry you're in, an' the sorra fut you'll lave this or get out of my two arms until I hear the news too."

"Let me go, Luke—let me go! I can't tell you. I must see Miss Helen—at wance. Let me go !"

"Oh, the sorra fut," said Luke, "until I hear the news."

It was not to be wondered at that Luke hesitated to let her out from her imprisonment; for, what with her haste and what with her excitement, there was a glow of colour in her face and a brightness in her eye that made her the picture of rustic beauty and comeliness. He had, therefore, no disposition whatever to liberate her, and Norah instinctively felt that there was no chance for her without communicating some of the startling news to him.

"Will you tell me ?" said Luke facetiously, threatening her with an additional hug.

"Let me go, Luke, for the love of God. I have," putting her lips to his ear, "seen Redmond Barrington !"

"What?" cried Luke, releasing her at once as if he had received a shock from an electric battery, and falling a few paces back. "Redmond Barrington! Where?"

"I kem up this mornin' to the ruins, where I lost the ring last evening when you were tryin' to take it from me, to look for id. I thought it was you were standin' lookin' over the sea, and when I laid my hand on your shoulder and you looked around it was—Redmond !"

Luke's eyes were nearly ready to leap out of his head at this rather startling way of putting the information, and he crossed himself devoutly.

"Redmond! Was he alive?"

"To be sure he was alive, you *ownshuch*," said Norah breathlessly. "Let me off to tell Helen."

"Heavens and airth, Norah! You must be dhramin'!"

"Oh, the sorra dhrame," said Norah; "an' they're above at Grey Abbey this minit—himself and Eugene Lefebre."

"May the blessin' ov God be about us! that's the most wonderful news ever I heard in all my born days! But wait a minit, Norah," said Luke, as a thought struck him. "Where did they come from, do you know?"

"Sorra a wan of me knows," said she hurriedly, and preparing to resume her speed; "I never thought of askin', and if I did aself I hadn't time. But you'd hardly know Redmond in the dress ov a common sailor."

"Be the powers o' war!" said Luke excitedly, "that's it! I have it now!—They escaped from the man-ov-war, and they're the very two the sojers are lookin' for everywhere."

"The sojers!" said Norah, all her winsome blushes racing back from her cheeks into her heart, and leaving them pallid and white as snow. "The sojers!"

"The sojers, sure enough. They're searchin' everywhere for 'em, and if they're caught, the sorra fut they'll ever set on Ireland's ground again."

"Good God! What'll be done?"

"Run back, Norah, for the love of Heaven, an' tell 'em. I'll go back and bring the news to Inch."

"Do, an' God bless you! Don't tell any wan but Helen or Miss Howard, an' if they're not there, tell Mr. George Howard, an' no one else."

Without further delay, Norah raced back on her new journey, whilst Luke went with equal speed in the opposite direction. As Norah approached the house she was horrified to see at some distance to the northwards of Grey Abbey the red uniforms of soldiers on horseback. This sight, instead of paralysing her, however, only lent additional wings to her speed, until, quite out of breath and wholly unable to speak, she swept into the room where the injured girl lay and where Redmond and Eugene were conversing on very serious matters.

"You are back very soon, Norah," said Redmond, as the panting girl stood before them, one hand on the back of a chair, and making hurried gestures with the other—which gestures they failed entirely to comprehend.

"What's up, Norah? Why don't you speak?" said Redmond again, with impatience, as both looked at her frightened face and heaving breast, "Take your time, and tell us what has frightened you."

Norah made several attempts to speak, but her breath or her lips failed.

With an immense effort she at last spoke:

"Run! run! For the love ov the life that's in you, run! The sojers are comin'! They're yonder!"

There was no need to question; neither was there time. Every quivering motion of her form, every heave of her excited and panting breast, was eloquent of danger—of threatening and imminent danger.

"The ruins!" whispered Redmond hurriedly. "Come with me. We can shelter there."

At once they were on their feet; out through the hall-door, into the sheltering rocks that crept up on the cliff, and with many winding ways until they got within the ruined walls of the abbey. There they rested for a moment like hunted deer, and turned to look for the searchers.

The red uniforms of the soldiers shone in the distance, approaching the mansion they had a few moments before left!

CHAPTER XXVI.

THE SECRET LETTER.

WHEN Norah had left the cottage the two young gentlemen proceeded to inspect the carefully sealed letter which she had handed them.

"I wonder, Redmond," said Eugene, "if we should open this. It may throw some light on the circumstances attending the unfortunate position this poor girl is found in. Should we?"

"It seems like a desecration to open it," said Redmond.

"But it may be a clue to us as to what brought her from her quiet home in France, to be a waif cast away on the rocks here. When I think of it, it seems to be like a horrible nightmare which I am only dreaming and shall wake from shortly. I can scarcely realise it yet."

"It is real enough," said Redmond, "whatever may be the extraordinary circumstances that led up to it."

"There must be something unusually strange and singular about it," said Eugene—"something almost beyond what could happen in real life; and it seems to me that this letter might be a help and a guide to us in regard to it."

"No doubt, Eugene. But still it does seem, somehow, an unmanly and unwarrantable thing to do—particularly under the circumstances."

"But it is precisely under the circumstances I have the right and the need to open it," said Eugene, gazing at the letter, with its three red seals upon it. "Whatever it is," he continued, "the poor girl attached importance to it. The whole mystery lies enwrapped here. In the name of God—I shall open it!"

He walked over to the window, and broke the seals. He took therefrom a printed document with blank spaces filled up with writing.

He gazed at it like one in a dream for some time.

It would be impossible for the greatest master of word-painting to describe the look of blank amazement and horror that stood depicted on his face, as Redmond looked thereat for some indication of what the letter contained.

A pause of some minutes' duration ensued, in which Eugene's eyes were rivetted on the document he held in his hands, and Redmond's on *his* face.

"Redmond," said the former at last, in choking accents, "Alice—she was married!"

"Married!" cried Redmond, aghast. "When? To whom?"

"To—to—" said Eugene, with difficulty speaking, "to Sir Trevor Mortimer."

"To Sir Trevor Mortimer!" echoed Redmond, for the moment believing his companion had taken leave of his senses. "To Sir Trevor Mortimer!"

"Yes; here is proof of it. This explains everything. Can you read this?"

Redmond took the document mechanically, and gazed at it amazedly.

"Eugene," said he at last, "who would have believed this?"

"Married in Marseilles," said Eugene—"married in Marseilles!—my God! who could have dreamt of this? Who *could* have dreamt of this? Oh! merciful Heavens was there no pitying angel near to warn her? How could it have come about?"

"I unfortunately know now. He met her at Seamore during her visit. He must have followed her to France— he *was* there for his health during the Summer—and in some way induced her to marry him."

"Were they much acquainted at Seamore?"

"Not remarkably. He paid her attention—nothing more than one would pay to a graceful and handsome girl; and we used often joke with her about him, and laugh at how readily she blushed when he was mentioned. But it was the merest pleasantry."

"It was not all pleasantry for her!—oh, my poor sister! It is clear enough she fell into the power of the arch-devil when she listened to *his* words. Do you know what, Redmond? As surely as I stand here living, she was thrown off the rocks—flung off the precipice—and it was his hand that did it. He lured her here for the purpose."

Redmond nodded his head in assent. The same thought had flashed across his own mind.

"And do you know what further, Redmond," said Eugene, as he crumpled the letter, and, laying hold of the iron bar that had fastened the shutters, bent it with the strength of his hands—the strength of his feelings swelling every muscle in his arms until they stood out like whip cord. "He did the murderous deed to put her out of his way and enable him to marry Helen Barrington!"

"Stay, Eugene; don't say that!" a thrill of terror passing through every vein in his body. "You forget yourself when you say that."

Redmond was in the mood when anger, begotten of his own consciousness of danger to his sister, would have quickly supervened on his previous feelings.

"Don't be angry with me, Redmond, if I say precisely as I think," said Eugene, his own feeling warming pretty well into frenzy. "You know as well as I do that what I say is precisely what may at any time take place; and, moreover, it is to you that ——"

"To me—what?" asked Redmond, with fierce expression.

Just at the moment Norah burst back into the room with her breathless message, with what effect and result we have seen.

CHAPTER XXVII.

MIDNIGHT TERRORS.

When Sir Trevor left Grey Abbey in hurried fashion on that evening we have heretofore seen, he made his way with flying feet to Inch.

There he met Helen Barrington, and there he persuaded her to return to Dublin next day. Save and except from Miss Howard and her brother, all was for the present to remain secret.

Helen readily promised.

With continual entreaties from him—without cessation and without intermission—what was she to do? Her brother dead—how or by whose hand she knew not; Eugene, her presumed other friend, set down, with proof circumstantial enough, as his murderer—what was she to do? What other friend had she to look to?

Old Cauth's words came home to her—the words of wisdom from aged lips: "A girl's heart is aisily turned, an' it would be a sore day if you let it change from Trevor Mortimer, who loves the ground you walk upon."

No doubt at times, in spite of herself, forbidden thoughts of the handsome young Frenchman, so brave, kindly, chivalrous in his devotion to her, came before her; and in these moments her mind indignantly rejected the insinuations that had been made against him.

But she banished these thoughts on further consideration. They were purely temptations presented before her for the purpose of luring her from her good.

Wherefore Helen, not without some misgivings, gave her consent. She would start in her cousin's carriage early for Dublin.

Sir Trevor, to comply with the necessary formalities, would go by the early mail, and, in order the better to enable him to do so, he would sleep at Inch that night.

So far all went satisfactorily with him. His plans were working smoothly and without hitch. He had made a great venture, and, with the result attaching to all bold adventures, had succeeded. It was far advanced in the night before all these arrangements had been concluded.

Too excited, however, to retire to rest, he sauntered out nominally to enjoy a cigar, but really to cool his excited and heated feelings. He ascended the slight slope that sheltered the house from the sea-storms, and lit his cigar and smoked it mechanically.

The sea lay beyond him. The low murmur of the waves beating on the strand fell on his ear. Far over, in the cloud of darkness and night that lay on the waters, unseen and solitary, was the little island. A thrill like the searing of hot iron along his veins ran through him as he thought of it, turning presently into a chill to which the touch of ice would have been as heat and warmth.

That island! What form, mangled and torn, lay in the embraces of its dark precipices! That face so fair and winsome—those eyes so dark and flashing that looked up to his!—

A shudder of terror passed over him as he snatched the cigar from his lips and flung it on the ground. He would think no more of this. He would think of Helen Barrington—of the good luck that was in store for him in the future—of anything but the horrible thought that was in his brain, and the agonising cry that still rang in his ears.

He shuddered to find himself alone in the night and the darkness!

He would turn back and go into the house—into the light and heat and peace of the house.

He retraced his steps until the lights glimmering in its bedroom windows fell on his eyes. But they seemed no harbingers of Welcome now. Rather, they seemed like white eyes watching him intently.

He placed his hand on his brow. The bead-drops stood out thickly thereon!

He knew he looked excited—fearfully excited!—and feared to let any of the inmates see him in his present condition of terror and unrest. Why had he promised to sleep there? Why had he not said he would sleep in Grey Abbey for the night? What if he went there now? He could make excuses readily enough in the morning for his absence.

He turned away again from the lights.

Stumbling over the uneven ground as he hurried away, he hastened to place the slope between him and Inch.

Yet he did not turn to Grey Abbey. Reluctant as he was to sleep at Inch, he was still more reluctant to rest within the walls of the former. The very idea, when he was once more in darkness, was abhorrent to him—a nameless horror crept over his heart at the thought of it.

Mechanically his steps sought the direction of the ruins.

He would wander about until morning came, and with the welcome daylight—never so welcome to anyone in this wide world before—the mail car.

Oh! the horror of this darkness—and the sob of the sea! Oh! his terror of the storm-birds as they swooped by him, their shrill cries startling him in his feverish fancies as if it were the cry of ——

He feared to mention the name.

But that despairing, agonised cry! How it still rang in his ears!

Rang? As he walked along, stumbling over the rocks and *debris* that lay in his path, it seemed to him still to come from over the sea with appalling force—the rocks of the distant island, hemmed in by night and darkness, echoing it forth unceasingly.

Once, indeed, he thought it came so plainly—so really and unmistakably—that he paused shiveringly to listen!

He was fairly overcome with unmentionable horror and terror.

The clothes on him were wet with perspiration, and his

feet moved in his shoes with a splashy feel as if he had been wading through a quagmire.

Pausing to listen, however, his terror ceased—only to assume a new form. The dread of the supernatural vanished only to give place to a fear of pressing, immediate, and personal danger.

He stood beside the outer wall of the ruined abbey, and directly in front of an ancient doorway, broken and fallen.

He had scarcely stopped thereat to listen to satisfy himself whether the cry he thought he had heard was real, or whether the fears growing at his heart had not deceived him, when suddenly there rushed through it, in the darkness, a form; and before he was almost conscious of its presence it had flung itself against him!

CHAPTER XXVIII.

THE SEA GIVING UP ITS DEAD.

IT was a woman's form.

"In the name of the devil, who are you?" he asked. His thoughts ran instantaneously to the cliff on the island.

"Is that you, Sir Trevor," cried a palpitating voice.

"It is, Moya," answered he, much reassured, but still much frightened and surprised. "What brings you here? What brings you out at this hour of the night? Where are you going? And why did you leave Grey Abbey?"

"I was coming to see you," she said breathlessly, in answer to his many queries.

"To see me? What did you want to see me for? What have you to say to me? Is there anything wrong?"

"Yes, everything."

"Everything—what?"

"I have seen him."

"Seen who?"

"Redmond Barrington."

"Redmond Barrington! You are dreaming, Moya, or you're mad, or have grown frightened. No living eyes will ever see him again."

"I'm neither mad nor dreaming," said the fortune-teller; "and I have seen him; and Eugene—the Frenchman—too, and another."

"Another ? Stand a moment and think, Moya. Collect yourself. For heaven's sake think over what you are saying. I have enough cause for trouble without your unnecessary fears increasing it. Stay and tell me. Who did you see, or what; and where?"

"I seen thim, I tell you—seen 'em wid my two lookin' eyes this night—not ten minutes ago."

"Where?" asked Sir Trevor, incredulously.

Curiously enough, in presence of the alarm her presence and her news created, his former fears seemed to him most foolish and childish. He would have faced all the terrors of the supernatural now and scoffed at them if he were certain that Moya was only dreaming or merely frightened.

"Where? On the shore. There's where I saw 'em."

"What were they doing? What brought *you* there?"

"What brought me there?" reiterated the old woman, pausing to take breath. "I couldn't sleep—I couldn't rest. I did what I often did in Dublin when I couldn't rest aither—I walked about on the shore. An' to know my way back, I took the lantern with me. There now it's for you : but I saw 'em !"

An imprecation rose to Mortimer's lips, but it died there. He could not afford to quarrel with her, even though his terrified wrath rose to hear of her wandering about in the night, courting danger and exposure as it were.

"Well, Moya," said he, more quietly and soothingly, "what did you see—whom did you see?"

"Thim I tould you."

"Where were they?"

"Coming in—in a boat."

"In a boat! Surely not Redmond—not Redmond, Moya?"

"Ay, as sure as ever I saw him in life. An' the Frenchman wid him. And another—*her!*"

"Moya, I gave you credit for more sense than to perplex me thus with idle talk. There's no reason—there's no sense in that."

"Sense or no sense, there's the truth for you. I may not be sure about her, because I only saw the form lyin' in the boat—but somethin' tells me it is she. But I am sure about the others."

"You couldn't be mistaken. Moya? Eugene might by a miracle come ashore—he is on the warship guarding the coast here—but the others, never. No miracle could do that."

"I dunno whether a miracle could or not, but he is there, and, I make no doubt, she, too, sure enough. An' I was hurryin' as fast as my feet could carry me to warn you. Put as many miles as you can between yourself an' this place before the light comes, or ——"

"Assuming you are right, Moya," said Sir Trevor, a full consciousness breaking through his former unbelief that the old woman had some grounds for her statement, "I cannot leave before daybreak. I must await the mail. Helen Barrington comes to Dublin to-morrow to be my wife."

"Then if you don't hurry you'll never put a ring on her finger. The only ring will ever be put on is the ring of *skebeash* that goes around your own neck."

"Moya!" he said angrily, with a movement towards her as if he would strike her and so quench her malignant prophecy.

"Ay, that's what I say. If you're not out of this—she an' you—to-morrow, sorra ever you'll be master of Seamore, nor anything else except a grave in the prison-yard. You need not try to frighten me, Sir Trevor—you've enough on your hands to ——"

"See, Moya," said he, not having, in his own impetuous thoughts, heard one word of what she was saying; "you have possibly seen Eugene; that is likely enough, for he is on the guardship watching the coast here—perdition seize the souls of the Frenchmen that they did not sink her in the fight!—and he has maybe escaped; but, as for the other, you are mistaken—quite mistaken, Moya. Here is what you have got to do. Watch them, whoever they are. See where they have gone to—where they are hiding. I shall send word—or go with word— to Wexford before dawn, and send the soldiers on their track. You be their guide when they come here. Do you hear, Moya?"

"I hear."

"Very well, Moya. That done, come back again to Dublin. I shall be no more troubled with them if you do your work aright. Here is gold, if you should need it."

He passed his purse to her, merely deducting so much as was necessary to defray his expenses to Dublin, and turned on his heel to the high road that led to Wexford.

The dawn was breaking when he reached the barracks there and saw the officer on duty. In a short time after he had caught the Wexford mail for Dublin, which started at daybreak or a little after, and, with a host of emotions —of evil emotions—torturing his breast, was on his way to the metropolis.

CHAPTER XXIX.

THE RACE BEGUN.

The fugitives were fortunate in finding sheltering place. Underneath the ruins the encroaching sea had wormed itself into the cliffs. In times long gone, the former inhabitants of the abbey had dug for themselves underground recesses—catacombs, as it were—never dreaming that place so secure could ever be disturbed. But the never-ceasing wash of the sea had long ago found these out, and the storm beat and the waves lashed themselves with hollow moaning sound into the recesses thus laid bare.

Into one of these Redmond and Eugene, descending from the cliffs, made their way. Here they were perfectly secure. Not even one of the inhabitants around ever thought of making entry into these winding caverns, out of which the merciless sea at times washed ancient stone coffins and dead men's bones.

"Well, Eugene," said Redmond, as they rested themselves after their escape, and stopped to take breath, "we seem to be surrounded with dangers by sea and by land. How could these soldiers have come so quickly?"

"Unless the Thunderer sent word to Wexford," replied Eugene, thoughtfully.

"A very likely matter enough; but how should they come so accurately on the place where we were staying?"

"An impossible question to answer—for the present. It is only of a part with all the other incomprehensible things that are surrounding us. The question is what course now to pursue, assuming that we escape them."

They had sufficient food for conversation in the events already occurred to occupy the hours they spent in hiding. But the chief topic of discourse lay in the intimation conveyed by Norah of the approaching marriage of Helen and Sir Trevor Mortimer.

"See, Eugene," said Redmond finally, "the simple short and long of the matter is this: as soon as night sets in we must follow at once to Dublin—if Helen be gone there. My cousins at Inch, when they come to know of the circumstance, will take care of Alice; but we must at all hazards prevent the further machinations of this man taking effect."

"I agree with you. Time presses dreadfully on us, and it is simply maddening to be cooped up here, with such dreadful issues depending on a few hours. But listen—do you hear the noise?"

"It is the soldiers searching," said Redmond. "How clearly we can hear them above us! What a pity the power of defending ourselves even is not left to us. How thoughtless of me not to have brought a pair of cutlasses in the boat with me! It would have enabled us to sell our lives—should it come to that ——"

"There would not be much use in them, even if it did," said the Frenchman, carelessly. "It would be but a poor fight to fall in. I am not at any time much disposed to fly from danger; but I protest at this moment I would brook any stigma of cowardice and forfeit the brightest epaulettes in the French service to find myself unharmed and on the way to Dublin. It may or may not be bravery or gallantry, but I confess it is the feeling uppermost in me this moment."

"I wonder will Sir Trevor have any knowledge of our presence here?"

"He will have knowledge—clear and ample knowledge —of it the minute my eyes—if ever God gives me life and strength to do so—see the lamps of Dublin," said Eugene bitterly. "But—hush! Redmond! Is there not someone darkening the entrance?" inquired he, after a long pause in which both remained silent, occupied with their thoughts.

"Some shadow has passed over it certainly. Yes, I see a form—two. There are two of them—They are soldiers!" whispered Redmond hurriedly.

"It seems to me they know pretty well what they are about," whispered Eugene back, "for they are coming straight in this direction. If they are soldiers they seem to——"

"Why, I know them," said Redmond joyfully, as his eyes, straining through the gloom, recognised them. "That one to the right is Luke Mahon, and that other is George Howard."

In a few minutes they had come nearer and established their identity, to the great delight of the two fugitives.

When the first burst of welcome and rejoicing was over, Redmond asked:

"How did you manage to come unobserved by the soldiers around?"

"We first dispatched them on a false message towards Wexford, by informing them that a pair of suspicious characters," said his cousin, "such as you, had been seen taking their way in that direction. But you are quite safe now. You may come with us. My only regret is that Helen is not aware of the joyful news."

"Helen!" said Redmond, "is she not here?"

"No, she is gone."

"Gone—gone where?"

"Herself and Kate left in the carriage some hours ago for Seamore."

"Good heavens! Are they far on the road?"

"They must be more than quarter on their way by this time. They had two spirited, fresh horses under the carriage, that were pretty certain not to let the grass grow under their feet until they reached Arklow."

"Then. George, you must provide us with another pair

without delay. I must follow at once. It is a matter of more than life or death."

"Life or death?" laughed his cousin. "Why it's nothing more or less than a wedding. Are you aware that Sir Trevor Mortimer and Helen are about to be married, and are proceeding to Dublin for that purpose?"

"I know—I know—I heard that," said Redmond, with intense impatience. "It is to prevent them that I must hasten at once to Dublin."

"To prevent them, Redmond? Surely you would not signalise the joyfulness of your return by interrupting or marring their happiness?"

"Happiness! You do not understand what you are speaking about, George. He is married already, the scoundrel!"

"Married already! What are you thinking of? Sir Trevor Mortimer married?"

"It is not his fault that he is," said Redmond, "or that his wife is living. I am sure no one regrets it more than he. But explanation must come afterwards. At present the one thing necessary is to provide us with means of reaching Dublin without delay. More pressing need traveller never had."

"You do not propose to travel to-night. The dusk will be falling soon."

"To-night! This moment. If the road were as dark as Erebus we must go. An hour's delay would drive me mad."

"Very well, Redmond. This is most extraordinary news—incredible! But I suppose you have good grounds for what you say. Come and have dinner, and as soon as you have refreshed yourselves I shall have a carriage ready for the road."

They left the hiding place, and ascended the cliffs on their way to Seamore.

"Are you not coming, Eugene?" asked Redmond, as the latter paused for a moment when they had reached the heights.

"I shall come presently," said Eugene. "For the moment, I shall call to see how Alice is."

"How unthinking of me not to have anticipated you!"

Redmond said with momentary self-upbraiding. " So shall I. You must excuse me, Eugene, but my mind is quite astray with the number of things pressing on it."

"There are no excuses needed," replied his companion; and without further comment or remark they all deflected in the direction of Grey Abbey.

Alice was still in the same condition—living, but quite unconscious. Evidently some injury to the head—sustained how they were unable to tell—was the cause of her non-recovery.

A hurried consultation took place between them, ending in this—that Redmond, of himself and by himself, should proceed straight to Dublin; that Eugene—as he wished and willed it—should remain with his sister; and that George Howard should direct his way to Wexford and seek the best surgical advice he could get.

It was rather a sad and disconsolate council, save and except when Eugene's feelings burst into torrents of hate and vengeance against the man who had done him and his so much evil. In the which, Redmond, when he thought of Helen, was not much behind.

CHAPTER XXX.

AGAIN A PRISONER.

When Redmond Barrington left on his hurried journey to the metropolis, Eugene, who had been seeing him off, returned to Grey Abbey.

Troubled with many thoughts, he turned his footsteps to the old ruins to give himself time for reflection; and, the better to consider over the incidents that had been crowded into his life during the past few days, lit a cigar from the case which Redmond had given him, and, with slow and thoughtful steps, passed through the scrubby tangle that lay between him and the ruins.

Once there, he seated himself on the mossy rock, sheltered by higher walls from observation on the land side, but with full view of the spreading reach of waters that lay before him.

He had many things to think of—of the singular and most marvellous incidents connected with the discovery and rescue of his sister, which, now that he had time to reflect on it, seemed to him scarcely realizable, and more like a dream, or incident occurring to the heated imagination of a story-writer. There was also the projected marriage between her intending murderer and the dear, sweet girl at Seamore—the very idea of which sent a thrill of horror through his breast. He had, however, sufficient faith in Redmond's energy and untiring vigour to know that whatever man could do to save her from peril, and worse than danger, her brother's hand was surest to effect.

Then, there were also considerations as to other matters attending his visit.

"These papers!" he thought, "I wonder if they are there still. How important for me to know—and, oh! how fortunate I did not seek to bring them with me to France last time. Else, they were unavoidably gone— gone for ever. And how providential—what I thought so unfortunate at the time—my capture! Otherwise Alice, poor girl, were lying in lonely death this moment—untended and forgotten. How wonderfully the hand of God brought it all about! Well, a few days will bring us together to Seamore, where the past—the sorrowful past— shall be forgotten. I shall see if the papers, of which I have heard so much from the old lawyer in Versailles, and which are of so much importance, are still there. Pray Heaven, they be!"

The falling of some stones or the displacement of some triturated mortar from one of the ruined walls behind him attracted his attention. He turned his head around and was displeased and annoyed to see the form of a bent old woman hobbling away through a broken archway behind him.

"Some old creature gathering faggots," he thought.

But the presence of any human being disturbed his reveries; broke on the high tension of his thoughts, and made him uncomfortable; and he rose to leave.

The broad sea lay sleeping before him. Not a ripple broke on its surface, and scarcely a distant sail interfered with the bright monotony of its calm. Save and except where, on the white sands below, the slow-rolling wavelets broke in surf, lazily scattering itself on the level strand and as lazily withdrawing itself, everything was motionless. A gnarled rock projecting itself into the sea to his right prevented him from seeing the coast in the direction of Wexford.

"I shall go down the sands, climb up that rock, and see what the further stretch of coast yonder may be like," thought he.

Lighting another cigar, he took his way carefully along the dangerous and winding path that led down the steep declivity—in some places so very steep and requiring such caution that he had to hold on by tufts of grass or clefts of rocks to steady his footing.

At length, and with much difficulty, he gained the white strand and turned to look upward at the height from which he had descended. The action of the sea had so worn the face of the cliff away that not only was it in places steep as the wall of a house, but in others rocks on high projected over the denuded face of the bank beneath, and threatened at some not distant day to topple over.

As Eugene's eye rested on the most prominent of these latter it seemed to him as if a flag or coloured garment of some kind appeared for a second over it and instantly disappeared. This, in a careless way, caught his attention, for he had seen nothing of the kind whilst he sat above. He looked again, but there was nothing visible on the protruding rock.

Dismissing the matter from his attention, he walked slowly on.

"How curiously those caves are formed, and what an excellent place for hiding in! I fancy it would be difficult," thought he, as he gazed at the long caverns which the ceaseless action of the waves had made in the soft stratification, or, perhaps, which the ancient monks had made for burial purposes, "to follow an escaping prisoner through them. This rock prevents the view of the southern coast. How shall I climb it?—it is so steep? Stay, here is a crevice through which I can pass more readily—— What! How dare you? Hands off, fellow!"

He had been seized suddenly from behind, and his arms fast pinioned.

With a vigorous wrench he tore himself free from his assailant and thrust his hand into his pocket for the pistol Redmond had given him. Alas! it had been left behind in the ruined mansion. His captor, noticing and understanding his action, stepped back and quickly unstrung the carbine that was strapped on his back. Another moment would have been fatal Eugene threw himself on his foe, ere yet the barrel was levelled, and sought to wrest it from him.

Even while he did so the shrieking tones of a woman's voice came from the high rocks above.

"Seize him! That's the escaped prisoner. Seize him and bind him. That is the Frenchman that came to Seamore—and if you let him go, may your arms be paralyzed!—Moya watched him. Moya tracked him. Yonder he is! Yonder he is! Seize him—bind him fast and secure him or he will escape!"

Notwithstanding the struggle in which he was instantly engaged—nay, perhaps, because of it, for his senses were so strung to high tension that they were electrically alive to outer objects— every word of the old woman's shrieking voice fell distinctly on his ears.

Even whilst they swayed and struggled for possession of the gun—his weakened frame strengthened by the consciousness that it was a struggle for life or death, or at least for liberty or imprisonment—the meaning of the scene became apparent to him,

"Moya! That was the old fortune-teller at Seamore! What brought her? Why is she here? Why has she tracked me?"

In some such disjointed manner flashes of thought like these shot through his brain the while he struggled with his more burly antagonist.

Eugene was full of activity—the lithesome activity of a sailor—and but for his recent illness the soldier would have had no chance in his hands. As it was, whilst still wrestling for the gun, he placed his foot behind the heel of his opponent, and with a sudden and vigorous effort, flung him from him, and wrested the gun from his possession. In the effort, by some curious accident the firearm, which was held upright, struck against the ground. A burst of smoke and a flash of light blinded him for a moment, and the latter singed his eyes, as the gun exploded. An inch nearer and the bullet would have blown his temple off.

"That was a dreadfully narrow escape!" was his first sensation when the shock had passed; but, in the instant succeeding, a shriek of wild agony and despair came ringing from the cliffs above, and at the same time a rush was made from behind, and half a-dozen hands had grasped him at once.

Eugene had had scarcely time to realise that he was now assuredly a prisoner, when an exclamation from his captors and an upstretched hand from one of them caused him involuntarily to glance upward through the wreathing smoke which was dissolving itself into transparency.

A glance showed him the cause of the outcry.

Falling, tumbling downwards from rock to projecting ledge and then to grassy slope, and finally on to a steep and terrific descent which there was not rock nor bank to break, until it fell at his feet on the shingle—was the form of an old woman! A glance from her dying eyes, wild with affright and green with the deadly venom of unquenchable hate, met him as he looked in wonderment for a second at her.

"Moya is avenged! Helen Barrington of Seamore——"

Whatever more the old fortune-teller had to say or what threats to utter, remained unspoken; the last word was said with a shrieking effort; a convulsive movement passed through her mangled form, her lips parted, her eyes suddenly became glazed—and her life of mystery and misery and revenge was over.

Eugene had only time to notice a small blue mark in her wrinkled forehead—it showed where the musket so accidently discharged had sent its leaden messenger—when he turned away with a shudder of horror and disgust. The wrinkled lineaments of the hag, yellowing and hardening in death, seemed to gather unto themselves a greater and more implacable malignity.

"D—n her! she had no business here!" was the commentary of the sergeant of the party that had arrested him, as he turned from the repulsive object and gave his attention to his prisoner, who was now securely handcuffed. " Did you know her ?"

" I saw her once or twice," said Eugene, who, seeing that further resistance was hopeless, suffered himself quietly to be made prisoner.

" Well, she deserved what she got, the old ——, though only for her we should not have found you. It was she who gave us the information where you could be found."

" She !" said Eugene.

" Ay. She watched you for us, and was most anxious you should be taken. She had a nice liking for you—she had. But we had better be getting along. Whistle for the boat to come around."

" What shall we do with this ?" said the man addressed, motioning towards the dead form before them.

" Let her lie there and be ——," was the response.

A whistle from one of the men was responded to by the noise of oars from the other side of the rock, and in a few minutes the prow of a man-of-war's boat appeared rounding it.

" You have led us a nice dance these past twenty-four hours," said the sergeant, as, all parties having seated themselves, the rowers bent on their oars and the boat swept southwards. " You and your friend made a bold run of it, and were near succeeding. I never saw so clever a thing done before. It is almost a pity you did not get off."

" Where are you taking me to ?"

" The Thunderer. She is anchored off Carnsore Point. She should have sailed for Plymouth by this if the old hag had not brought in the news of your being here."

Eugene was silent—silent because of the rush of conflicting thoughts that crossed his brain. ' Alice—Redmond—Helen Barrington—imprisonment—the hulks—Moya. Ay, Moya! What had he done to incur the old woman's enmity—enmity that had proved to him so unfortunate ?"

In some such fashion as this the crowding thoughts surged on him.

" Don't be downhearted mate, said the sergeant, wrongfully interpreting his silence. " You'll not be lonesome. Your companion will be with you before long. The dragoons are upon his track already."

"The dragoons! What is that you said?" inquired Eugene hurriedly, the words banishing his abstraction. "What dragoons? Where?"

He had but half heard the soldier's words, and caught but indistinctly their meaning.

"To Dublin. Your companion has gone to Dublin—hasn't he?"

"Has he?"

"You know he has. The old hag told us so, and if her information is as true as in your case he will soon be beside you."

"When did she give you this information?"

"Same time as she told us about you."

"And ——"

"And," said the soldier, interrupting his unasked question, "the dragoons were despatched after him. He had some hours' start, but they will, unless he goes very fast, be likely to catch up with him."

A feeling almost of despair grew over the prisoner's heart. His own capture paled into nothing before this new danger. Redmond captured! Redmond, the only one that was left for the protection of Helen!

What if he were captured before he was able to see her!—before he was able to prevent the nefarious designs of Sir Trevor—before he was able to prevent the projected marriage—that marriage which would be the consummation of the ruin of his own earthly hopes and happiness! His head grew dizzy and his brain swam as the terrible thought presented itself to him. Oh! if Redmond could only know—could only be made aware—of the danger that followed so swiftly on his track!

With a fervent prayer for his safety and his unhindered arrival in Dublin—there was nothing else in his power to do—Eugene turned his thoughts to what lay before him.

"What will become of Alice?" he thought. "What *will* become of her. Ah, Norah!—Norah will see that she is attended. What a month of misfortunes."

But regrets were unavailing, and he banished them.

"How far are we from the vessel?"

"Yonder she is," said the sergeant.

Looking forward Eugene saw her. Her sails were in course of lowering.

"She will sail presently," said the sergeant, noticing his glance.

"Where to?"

"To Plymouth—for repairs."

"Is she going out of commission?"

"Only for a while—during repairs. Times are too pressing now to let her remain long idle."

"Have you many Irishmen on board?"

"Plenty," said the soldier with a grin. "But you will not get that chance again. I don't think you will again get that opportunity."

"I had no thought of it."

"Better not try it, even if you got the chance. It is not once in every hundred times that an escape is planned and carried out so safely as yours."

"Any French prisoners on board."

"Not now. We had one lately—a young fellow. Oh! I remember now. He was taken with you."

"Yes. What became of him?" asked Eugene eagerly.

"He was put on board the tender and sent to Plymouth."

"When?"

"A week or less after being made prisoner. But here we are. This is your old friend the Thunderer. They will be all glad to see you back again."

The boat came to the ship's side, and he once again stood a prisoner on board the vessel from which he had so recently escaped.

CHAPTER XXXI.

THE SWIM FOR LIFE.

It is needless to dwell on Eugene's second reception on board the man-of-war.

As the sergeant had stated, the prisoner was no sooner on board than the anchor was weighed, the sails unfurled, and the ship started on her way to Plymouth.

Once there Eugene was sent on board the hulks.

These were large, dismasted, worn-out men-of-war in which the French prisoners were confined, and anchored some distance out in the harbour, or in the man-of-war roads. Gunboats at either end of the tier of vessels thus used as hulks were placed with shotted guns at all hours, day and night, ready to put down with showers of grape any attempt at mutiny or sign of insubordination, much less of escape. To prevent any chance of individual escape, guard boats rowed sentinel-like around the prison fleet with unvarying regularity throughout the twenty-four hours.

When on board the hulks, however, he found that he was not to be placed with the other prisoners, nor to be treated like them. Some subtle influence was working for or against him, he could not tell which.

Abandoned to the control of a crowd of petty officials, much of whose perquisites were obtained from the plunder and sale of the provisions intended for the prisoners, the unfortunate Frenchmen, cooped up in the hulks, were slowly starved to death. Instances were not infrequent when the hungry men had been left for two or three days together without any food at all. They had not, as in the case of famine in a beleaguered city, excitement to sustain nature; and so, bereft of air, of liberty, of food, they pined and drooped spiritless, until the vital spark rather wasted into nothing than fled.

It was not an infrequent thing for a prisoner waking at morning to find his comrade dead of exhaustion beside him, and the dead body was suffered to remain there, before means were taken for its removal, until it became unbearable, and added still further to the terrible atmosphere of the 'tween decks. What made matters still worse was that the prisoners had nothing to do; there was no work to their hands; and after roll-call in the morning they were abandoned to themselves. Save the parties of guards that with loaded fire-arms stood at the ends of the decks, there was no further notice taken of them. With nothing to read and with nothing to do, time hung heavily on their hands at first; grew heavier as the imprisonment lengthened; until finally each hour seemed a day, and each day a year; and when to this was added the pangs of hunger, the sufferings of these imprisoned ones grew to be absolute hell.

The dull sloth and rusting idleness were so inimical to their active French nature—the fogs, that, rising from the harbour and settling around them in gloom and darkness, were in such contrast to the bright and joyous sun of France, that it was difficult to say which it was—the mind or the body—that suffered most. Repeatedly the reason of prisoners gave way—the delicate organisation of the mind failed under this never-ceasing torture—and day after day some unfortunate broke the bounds of prison discipline in his delirium. In these cases the result was summary. Any violation of discipline was visited with death. Any unusual case of insubordination was met by a levelled musket on the instant, which effectually quelled irrestraint for ever; in other cases by the court-martial, which sat daily on ooard, the usual finding of which was death. The offender was placed on the upper deck stern, and a platoon of marines did the rest. There was no day the report of musketry was not heard, or on which the smoke of guns was not visible

There was no classification of crimes; there was no such thing as inquiring into causes; oftener than otherwise the offender whose riddled body lay on the deck was unconscious of the crime he had committed. The mind in the mental blankness of his prison—in the eternal weariness of gloom and idleness—in the vain pining for home and freedom and sunlight and France—had gradually given way. That was all.

At other times a frantic desire to escape forced itself

simultaneously on many of the prisoners. Although perfectly assured that escape was as hopeless as climbing to the moon, an unreasoning longing seized on a body of them at the same time. Acting under the pressure of irrestrainable wish and intense yearning for freedom, they formed designs for seizing the vessel or the guard, or some other equally futile project—the outcome of their diseased hopes. The first revealment of this intention was answered by a fusilade from the muskets of the guard, and the smoke cleared off only to exhibit a number of the conspirators strewing the deck with their bodies. If necessary a second fusilade followed the first, until the half insane rioters were quieted. The living were forced to sew up the fallen in canvas sacks, to carry them on deck, and hurl them over into a barge beside, whence they were carried to land to be thrown into a pit in the prisoners' graveyard, or, as sometimes happened, carried out to sea, tied together and sunk. That done, the survivors were compelled to swab the decks wet with the blood of their brothers until they were completely free from stain, and after that they might again linger and mope in maddening idleness between the decks, the light wherein forming a dim compromise between daylight and dark.

It was into such companionship as this Eugene was thrown, and, although kept apart from the general body of prisoners, his weariness and dreadful sense of imprisonment were not lessened thereby. Indeed it was rather increased, for in the isolation of his position he had more time for reflection, and the misery of his fellow-countrymen added not a little to the agony caused by suspense and want of knowledge of matters that concerned him both in Ireland and in France, until death itself would have been deemed a welcome release.

So weary weeks passed over, which finally rolled into months, until his position became unbearable. There seemed to be no limit to the duration of his imprisonment. The sun rose and set, marking the progress of each day—but that was all. No news came to him of the outer world—no news from France and Seamore. Even the new French prisoners that were introduced were kept so far apart from him that he had no means of ascertaining how the armies of France fared in the desperate struggle for superiority that was rending the Continent.

At times fresh vessels were commissioned and despatched from the harbour laden with troops; at others battered and dismasted vessels—line-of-battle ships home and foreign—were towed into the bay, the victims of terrible sea-fights afar off. And Eugene's heart was pained to see more than once the towering men-of-war of his own nation—mere floating wrecks, with broken masts, battered hulls, and sails torn into ribbons—towed into port!

He felt that his heart and strength were going; that his mind often trembled unsteadily in the balance; and that if left much longer in this floating hell he would only return, if ever the day for his liberation arrived, a wreck in mind and body.

He therefore determined, come what would, to escape.

The prison arrangements had been much relaxed lately as far as he was concerned, probably because he had shown himself during his imprisonment so quiet and unobtrusive.

A small boat lying out towards the mouth of the harbour had for many days past attracted his curious attention. It was occasionally used during the day-time by parties outside the harbour for some business or other— who, he noticed, always when they returned, moored it at the same place. At times, however, it remained there for days untouched. But it always attracted his attention the first thing in the morning and the last at night. And of late it remained in his thoughts *all* night. It was to him as a little star beckoning him to the far-off land of France. The small flag that fluttered from its tiny mast appeared to wave him a welcome to freedom The pair of oars lazily swaying and balancing in the rowlocks seemed to invite escape.

With this little skiff before his eyes day after day the yearning on him to escape grew stronger and stronger, until it was finally irrestrainable. He could stand it no longer, and determined to essay the effort.

Death could be the only alternative, and death was preferable to his present unendurable position.

He had always been a skilful swimmer, and, unless his

imprisonment had taken the strength out of his arms, would readily be able to make his way to the boat.

Accordingly one evening when over a year had been spent in his floating prison, he waited on the deck until the dusk of a June night had settled on the waters. He had accustomed himself to do so of late, and there was no notice taken of him.

When it was quite dark he slipped off his shoes and stood in his bare feet as was the habit of the watch. Further, he contrived to doff his coat and supply its place with a jacket of the kind the seamen wore. Then he lay stretched as if in a slumber beside a coil of rope, as was often the manner of the guards on board also.

The sentry, musket on shoulder, marched leisurely along the deck, ready at the first movement to fire, and so bring a troop of soldiers to his side.

Eugene waited with breathless anxiety turn after turn of the vigilant guard, as he passed and repassed from one end to the other.

Often he essayed to make a rush to the ship's side where a rope hung swaying, but as often some imaginary noise stopped his attempt.

The sentry had passed him with measured step, and his form had almost disappeared in the gloom of the night at the other end, when lifting himself to his hands and feet Eugene made an attempt to move. But a pistol placed on the coil of rope, unperceived by him, was thrown down by his action, making a noise on the deck that seemed, in his ears, as loud as the report of a sixty-pounder!

He at once lay still on his face, expecting to hear the quick report of the guard's musket and the rush on deck of an armed force. But the noise, loud as it seemed in his anxious ears, was unheard or unattended to by the sentry, for no response came; the heavy measured tread in the distance still sounded in his ears, then returned with unchanged slowness, passed him and repassed.

Softly placing the cause of the alarm in his breast pocket he essayed the effort a second time—this time with more success. With cat-like movements he gained the bulwarks, crept noiselessly over them, caught hold of the rope, and swung himself down.

THE SWIM FOR LIFE.

Once under the side of the ship, he allowed himself to depend in complete motionlessness and silence—the step of the sentinel over head, and the soft surge and plash of the waters against the vessel's side, alone falling on his ear.

For a moment his heart ceased to beat as the steady tread overhead faltered when just above him, and the sentinel strode to the bulwarks and looked over. Evidently something had attracted his attention, for he paused a moment and stood still.

Every second—and seconds to Eugene seemed hours in duration—he expected to hear the warning gun fired. For an instant he doubted whether or not it would not be better at once drop into the sea and make a swim—unavailing or not—for life!

This dangerous resolution was as suddenly checked, for apparently satisfied that all was right, the guard again resumed his walk.

"Thank God!" was the fugitive's fervent prayer, as he heard the step repass overhead, and grow faint in the distance.

He slid quietly down the rope, until all but his shoulders was in the water; then placing his feet against the side of the vessel, gave himself, as he let go, a gentle move forward so as to bring himself out of reach of the suction of the ship; and with noiseless movements of his hands, drew himself into the darkness, where he lay as a log until the guard had again repassed.

Then, with bolder, more vigorous, but still noiseless, strokes he drew himself into the open water!

He was swimming, with fresh courage growing into his heart, albeit the unaccustomed cold water was chilling him, when suddenly an unexpected noise struck on his ear, making his senses grow dizzy. He let himself sink in the water until only his mouth was above it.

The noise grew swiftly louder on his hearing.

It was the guard-boat rowing around the hulks.

Louder and louder the plash of the oars grew, louder the whispers of the rowers—for they were not permitted to speak openly—and then the form of a boat swept into view out of the gloom and darkness!

He could almost distinguish the faces of the men, so near they were; and the oars, as they uplifted, dashed the water into his face!

But the boat swept by without its occupants noticing him, and once more disappeared into the gloom.

Beyond him in the night, far beyond, shone a watch-light. Of this Eugene had taken careful notice, for the tiny skiff lay in a line with it. Guided by this directing beacon, he swam stoutly in its direction. But his arms were unaccustomed to exertion, long and enforced idleness had enervated his system, and swimming in one's clothes is at all times difficult and fatiguing. More than once his strength failed him and he thought he was drowning.

But he cheered himself with the thought that France and freedom and Helen Barrington were in the future, and stoutly braced himself for further effort

His brave heart finally won the victory over his failing muscles, and a tide of fresh warmth and blood swept through his veins, as, out of the night and gloom and the dark water, rose the tiny skiff. Too tired to lift himself, he hung with one hand on its side, suspended in the water, to rest himself and take breath after the sustained exertion of his long swim. Then placing the end of an oar under a seat and using the other as a lever, he with much difficulty, wet and chilled, raised himself into the skiff.

Seated at last in safety, he took a long rest and looked around him.

The hulks lay moored afar off, only visible through the gloom by the lights that here and there flickered from the cabin windows. Further over on the shore, and up where the town ascended to the headlands, lights innumerable twinkled. To his left the friendly beacon that had guided him through the water shone with undiminished and encouraging brightness.

A prayer of thanksgiving swelled from his heart to his lips as the fresh air of the sea blew through the harbour entrance on his face. Heaven had guided him so far safely, and a bounding hope arose in his breast. The hand of God was more powerful than his enemies, and he felt certain that as he had been successful so far, so he should be in the future.

Much refreshed by his rest, Eugene rose to unfurl the sail. There was no sign of his escape having yet been detected, but how soon might there not be? Haste was urgent, and minutes now were of incalculable value. The breeze was beginning to rise, and with it rose his chances of success.

Once out of the harbour, a few hours under its freshening influence would place him far from the coast of England and nearing that of France.

Whilst yet engaged in unfurling the sail, the noise of muffled oars fell on his ears.

Could it be anyone in pursuit of him?

A sudden pang of dread shot through him. He suspended his work and listened.

The boat was undoubtedly approaching; still it might not be coming his way, so many boats passed—so many had occasion to pass—through the harbour at night.

In breathless suspense he ceased his work, and, to prevent his being seen, lay down quietly at the bottom of the skiff and waited—waited, oh! with what breathless suspense!

The boat came towards him almost noiselessly—but not noiselessly to *his* ears, for each drop and lift of the muffled oar-blades fell with clear distinctness on his hearing.

All doubt of their object and their mission was at an end when, with a shock that was to him as a volley from a platoon discharged at his breast, the prow of the advancing boat struck against the little skiff in which he lay!

CHAPTER XXXIII.

THE PURSUIT.

A SHORT time found Redmond, with Luke for driver, speeding swiftly on his way to the metropolis.

On the journey he learned much from his companion of what had happened both at Seamore and Inch during his absence, and the news did not serve to appease the haste and impatience that possessed him. He now saw in a clearer light than ever the evil intention that possessed the baronet in his regard. It seemed as if a cloud had previously overshadowed his understanding, as if a web of mist had been drawn over his eyes through which he could see nothing.

But it had departed now, and he looked back on the past with a clearness and a light which revealed all to him thoroughly. But the more he understood the more his anxiety to get forward increased.

Dusk found them at Arklow. Here there was no change of horses to be had. Previous comers, together with the necessary change for the mail, had bereft them of the available stud.

" Previous comers—who were they ?"

" Two ladies and a gentleman, proceeding with all speed to Dublin."

" Two ladies and a gentleman," said Redmond turning in dismay to Luke, who nodded his head in intelligent sympathy, " The gentleman, now—what was he like ?"

" Gentleman," innkeeper thinks, " was about five-and-thirty years of age or thereabouts, tall, well-dressed, fashionable, and spoke with an English accent."

" Mortimer !" ejaculated Redmond, glancing again at Luke, who again intimated his assent by a nod.

" The ladies—what sort were they ?"

Innkeeper could not say—they were so closely muffled up. " It was after dusk, too," innkeeper explains, "and there was but little light to see them with. They did not even leave the carriage, they were in such haste."

" Heavens ! how often people rush unconsciously to their own undoing !" said Redmond, giving utterance to the thought that struck him.

" They were not rushing or going to Dublin," innkeeper says, mistaking his words ; " they spoke of Seamore."

" Just as I said, Luke," said Redmond, aghast. " Mortimer and the girls. No persons else."

" He was not with them leaving," said Luke ; " they were coming by themselves. Was the gentleman with the ladies when they arrived ?" This of the innkeeper.

Innkeeper thinks so ; nay, more, is sure of it. Saw

them come up, in fact, in a handsome carriage with two horses; but the latter dead beat and worn after a furious drive.

"He was to go by the mail," Luke says. "He must have waited for the young ladies and got into their carriage on the way."

"Good heavens, Luke, they may be—nay, are—in Dublin by this time, whilst we are waiting here. What shall we do?"

Innkeeper thinks they must wait until a change of horses can be provided; which they most reluctantly do —most reluctantly, for Redmond is possessed by the belief that the soldiers may be on his track. They had come at such furious pace that pursuers, if such they were, would be left far behind. But delay here might give them time to come up.

Gold can at all times work wonders. Redmond's purse was in speedy requisition, and with such *largesse* as innkeeper had never seen before given for posting fare, he was induced to make greater efforts to provide the necessary steeds. And with success.

Even so, however, some time must elapse before the horses can be provided—which period seems to Redmond an age. His mind is tortured with impatience— with thoughts of what may be taking place in the city whilst he is constrained to remain in this remote village. But there was no help for it, and the slow-consuming minutes pass on, whilst he, restless and unable even to converse, awaits their ending in a state of feverish unrest.

At last they are on the road.

"Pray Heaven it be not too late," thinks Redmond. "Now, Luke, for the love of Heaven! let the horses go as horses never went before. If we can reach Seamore by nightfall I shall be content."

The blue peaks of the Wicklow hills sentinelling the Irish coast pass them in quick succession as their smoking steeds pace along the highway.

Changes of horses take place; wayside stations, little villages, creep up on their horizon and are left behind them as they pursue their rapid way.

The dusk falls upon them as they pass Dunleary, and night throws her dark pall as they pass into the gates of Seamore, and sweep up to the hall-door.

Wearied and tired, and from long sitting scarcely able to stand, Redmond dismounts from his seat and rushes into the hall. The first his eye falls upon is the old housekeeper.

"Cauth! Grannie!"

Her back is to him, but his familiar voice rings in her ears. She turns around.

A cry bursts from her lips.

"Redmond, Redmond! is it you come back again? Is it yourself that's in it, or ——?"

"It is I myself, Grannie," said Redmond, hurriedly, gently disengaging himself from the embraces of the delighted henchwoman, who had thrown her arms around him; "but where is Helen?"

"Helen!" said the old woman. "Redmond, asthore, you don't know the way the world has gone here since you left—an' sure it's the light that comes into my old eyes to see you come back again to ——"

"I know, I know, Grannie," said Redmond, kindly, but with excessive haste and impatience; "but forgive me—I want to know where is Helen? Tell me at once."

"Helen is in Inch, Redmond, darling; she went there ——"

"I know she did," he said, almost thrusting her from him with his impatience; "but she came back last night or this morning. Where is she?"

"Came back! What's amiss with you, Redmond, honey?" cried the old woman, judging from his fierce gestures, uncouth appearance, and rambling words that he was demented. "Sure she is not to come back until May."

"Oh, my God!" said Redmond, clasping his forehead in his hands in the bitterness of his agony, "my worst fears are realised! They are married!"

"Redmond, dear," said the old woman, in pitying sympathy for—as she thought—his mental derangement, "come in and rest yourself. Don't you know you're in Seamore—your old home, an' where we're all glad to see you. God knows, my poor boy, how often I prayed for you to come back safe an' sound—from the time the stars came out in the sky until the dawn came over the tree-tops—but sure I never thought you'd come back like this. Oh! Redmond——'

"Grannie," said Redmond, understanding even in his terrified impatience, the thoughts that were running through her mind, "there's nothing wrong with me, but don't worry or interrupt me, for I cannot bear it at present. Helen has come back—come back some time last night or this morning. If she has not come here, she must be married. And if she has, Grannie, it would be better that she were drowned in the Deadman's Bay a thousand times over!"

"Married!" cried Cauth, "married, did you say, Redmond?" as a sudden thought struck her. "Oh! not to Eugene, Redmond—not Eugene—I always knew sorra and trouble would come of him. I always knew that——"

But Redmond had turned away from her unheedingly, and had passed once more out through the hall-door to where Luke was standing with his trap and horses.

"Luke," said he in a hoarse whisper—so full of despair and excitement was his heart—"Luke! she is not here. They must have been married, since they have not come. Heaven protect me! What shall I do? Do you know the Eagle in Eustace-street?"

"I do."

"Will your horses take us there without a change?"

"At once?"

"Yes, without a second's delay."

"Hardly. They'd be all the better for a change, Masther Redmond. They've had a long journey an'——"

"Yes, yes, of course; but can they do it?"

"To be sure they will. If they must, they must."

"Then drive me there at once," said Redmond, springing into the trap. "It is the only place where I can find tidings of him. Even if the horses fell dead when you reach, let me down at the door in the shortest time their strength can make it."

Whipping his steeds into a trot, which their previous long drive made them but scantily able to accomplish, they passed once more out through the gates of Seamore, out through the carriage sweep of winding oaks on to the high road, and, as the horses grew warmer, with increasing speed until they got within the circle of the city lamps. Thence by the shortest and quickest ways until the carriage swept down the uneven and ricketty pavement of Eustace-street, and stopped opposite the gleaming coloured lamps of the Eagle—the latter in all respects unchanged since last he saw it.

The excitement now pervading his frame had rendered him insensible to fatigue, and had much the same effect on his limbs as active exercise would have had. Wherefore he lightly leaped from his seat and entered the hotel.

"Hallo, Barrington," said a gentleman, as he entered, "you're quite a stranger here lately. Have you heard the news this afternoon?"

"What news?" asked Redmond, at once understanding that the question in some way affected him personally. "What news?"

"What news! Why where have you been that you have not heard it?"

CHAPTER XXXIII.

ESCAPING.

"Safe at last," whispered a voice, as a hand was laid on the side of the skiff.

"Yes, thank God! at last."

"Step in quickly—there is no time to be lost!"

"What shall we do with this boat?"

"Let her go adrift."

"Shall we take the oars with us?"

"No. Don't you see there are oars here?"

"All right. Step in then, in the name of God."

A form from the other boat stepped on the rower's seat of the skiff.

"Here, take this valise. Be quick—there is not a moment to be lost!"

"All right. I have it. Come in. Send the other boat adrift; she may be in our way presently."

As the first of these whispered sentences fell on Eugene's listening ears, something in the voice of the night-farer struck him as familiar. When the conversation continued this familiarity grew stronger, until with the force of an electric shock the recognition flashed upon him!

With a cry of joy he raised himself from his prone position!

But his sudden appearance had an unexpected effect upon the strangers.

An exclamation of affright and apprehension burst from them simultaneously, and the bright flash of a naked cutlass swiftly drawn, fell upon Eugene's eyes in a twinkling.

"It is I, François! It is I!" Eugene cried, as he threw himself upon the uplifted right arm of the other.

"Who is this. Who knows me?" was the surprised exclamation that followed. "Who are you? Hold a moment, MacNevin!—do not fire! Who are you?"

"I am Eugene, François. Don't you know me."

"*Mon Dieu!* it cannot be—yes, it is—Eugene! Eugene Lefebre! In the name of all that's wonderful," whispered François in utter and bewildered astonishment, "what do you here?"

"Escaping," whispered Eugene in return, withdrawing his hold of the arm that held the cutlass.

"Philip—Philip! Here—come here quickly! Was there ever such a meeting as this?" called in a low, but emphatic voice, François to the third party, who, having pushed out in his boat a little from the skiff, was looking with intense dismay at this most unexpected *rencontre*.

The party addressed, somewhat reassured, pulled in until the two boats lay alongside.

"Do you know who this is, Philip?"

"No. Who?"

"Eugene—Eugene Lefebre."

"What! our fellow-traveller on the Albatross."

"The same!" cried Eugene, in frantic delight.

"Where did you come from, M. Lefebre?" asked the captain hurriedly. "Have you dropped from the skies, or risen out of the water, or come from the grave?"

"I am escaping. I have swum from the hulks," said Eugene.

"So are we," whispered François, "though we have not come from the hulks. And there is not a moment to be lost. Discovery may come at any moment."

"Yes, at any moment," urged Philip. "Liberty or life may hang on an instant of time."

"Eugene," said François, "what shall be done? This skiff will hold only three—two to work and one to steer. I have it! I shall return in the boat, and you three sail at once—make your escape while there is yet time."

"You will do nothing of the kind," said Philip emphatically. "I shall return in the boat, and you three leave—and leave at once."

"Philip," persisted François, "it is I that shall return. You will be more needed and more useful on the way."

"Certainly not. There is not time for discussing the matter. *You* must go and *I* shall return," said Philip emphatically, pushing away his boat. "Good-bye all! Good-bye, Mr. Lefebre! We shall meet in happier times. Don't lose a moment in putting yourself beyond the pierhead. For God's sake make haste! Good-bye!"

The speaker, taking the oar in his hand, soon disappeared noiselessly in the distance, and the night shut him out from view.

"He speaks aright," said François. "Help me, Eugene, to spread the sail. There! Take the tiller. You are handier at this than we. Now! There—we are under weigh. Turn her head to the harbour-mouth. The breeze will aid us. Heaven sent it. Now! she is gliding easily. Not a word—but dead silence!"

The skiff, as he said, glided easily along. The three took their seats; and silently as a phantom bark the little boat sped through the gloom. Not a word was spoken, scarcely a breath was breathed, as with vigilant eyes they passed out—the pier-head rising frowningly above them in the darkness.

Out into the open sea, where the breeze grew stronger —out, shooting like an arrow, into the Channel, where the fog lifted and the long reach of swelling waves became visible

On—and on—and on: every moment leaving the shore behind them, and the wide waste of visible water growing continuously larger. On and on, until an exclamation from François—the first that broke the silence—drew attention, and he pointed to where in the east a rift in the night-clouds on the verge of the horizon showed the first faint approach of dawn.

"Glory to God! who has led me thus far!" was the heartfelt prayer that burst from Eugene's swelling heart, as the dim light, beginning to spread about like a faint whiteness, showed no sail near.

"Eugene!" said François, from where he sat holding the cord of the sail in his hand.

"Yes, François."

"It has been a long watch we have had."

"It has. Heaven be thanked! it has been successful."

"I think we may speak now. I may fasten this sail. There is no need to alter our course. Keep the helm as it is, and anywhere we strike the coast of France will serve our purpose."

"Yes, anywhere. Any place will suit us."

"Eugene, it is a long time since we saw one another. Let me see how you look. Merciful Providence! how ill you seem!—or is it this cold grey light that makes you look so?"

"I suspect I look so—because I am so," said Eugene, gravely. "Twelve months in the hulks is not calculated to improve one's appearance."

"Did they send you to the hulks after your capture?"

"Not then. I stood on Irish ground since."

"On Irish ground?"

"Yes, but was retaken. It is a long story—too long to tell now."

"The hulks have left their story written on your face. You have grown years older—and look very ill."

"A swim from the prison to the skiff, François, was not calculated to improve one whose only exercise for twelve months was confined to a few feet of the deck of a ship. Nor is sitting for hours without stirring, in wet clothes, the best restorer after that exertion."

"Good heavens! Eugene, I had completely forgotten

that your clothes were wet. How forgetful of me! But my whole thoughts were upon the sail, my ears for sounds of danger, my eyes for an approaching enemy."

"Speak no more of it, François; I had forgotten it myself. Like you, every sense was absorbed in listening and looking for symptoms of danger. We have had a marvellous run of good luck."

"Marvellous; there is not," said François, "a sail within sight. We have earned whatever there is in this,"

He produced the valise referred to some hours before, and drew therefrom a flask, which he opened.

"This is brandy, Eugene, and of the best. The Commissariat-General who last owned this never expected it would be used by escaping prisoners. Try it. Why, man, you look as if you were swooning. Try this—quickly!"

Eugene indeed felt as if but little more were needed to stop the action of his heart for ever, so thoroughly weak and exhausted was he. The revivifying liquor, untasted by him for twelve long months, sent a sensation of warmth through every vein and fibre of his body.

"There, Eugene; that's better. That brings the colour a little back into your face. Change seats, and I shall take the rudder awhile. But first let me introduce you to my companion: Monsieur MacNevin—an Irishman, escaping from imprisonment like ourselves. And now for some of the grateful brandy."

The conversation warmed as the skiff sped along in the opening twilight.

"Now tell me what became of you after our capture, François?" asked Eugene. "I often wondered what had happened you."

"So did I of you. The captain, I, and the two men were transferred to the tender, and brought to Plymouth. There I, being a good French writer, and I suppose being too innocent a youth to possess much guile—was employed in translating French despatches. Captain Philip and his two friends were put on board a man-of-war."

"How did he turn up to-night?"

"His vessel came in last week to refit, in company with, I grieve to say, some of our liners they had captured in a deperate fight off Ushant."

"We are never destined to be successful at sea," said Eugene.

"I fear not. Some fatality seems to hang over our fleet. Although carrying everything before us on land——"

"Ah! what of affairs in France? How goes the tricolor? What are our armies doing?"

"Doing! What a question to ask, Eugene!"

"My dear François, remember I have not heard a word from France, nor from the outer world, for a year and a-half.

"A year and a-half, Eugene! Why the map of Europe has been entirely changed during that time."

"What has happened? Tell me, François! I'm thirsting for news from France. What has happened? Where are our armies?"

"Armies! Everywhere; tramping to victory over every high-road in Europe. Bonaparte——"

"Ay! Bonaparte. What of him?"

"Bonaparte has conquered everywhere. The light of victory has never left his banner. The tricolour with him marches from triumph to triumph. He beat the best Austrian general in Italy, until the great nation bent to her knees to him at Campo Formio. Castiglione, Bassano, Arcola, and Rivoli, are new names inscribed on our banners since you saw them. He has brought the banners of France within sight of the Pyramids."

"Egypt! He has not gone there surely!"

"But he has. Syrian and Egyptian land is ground hallowed to France since the days of Saint Louis."

"This is marvellous news. What has he done there?"

"Won battle after battle over Saracen and Englishman, conquered Malta, and made his name famous to all time."

"And the fleet, François?"

"Your arm of the service has sustained many disasters. The old nobility that officered it, when they fled as *emigrés*, I greatly fear, bore the naval skill and renown of France, with them. At least the newer race of officers do not bear out its old repute. But the armies have more than made up for this, for their bayonets have carried everything before them, everywhere; and even now Europe echoes to the tramp of our battalions, as they pass over the frontier to further victories!"

"This is glorious news, François. What of Ireland? What became of the expedition, or did it ever sail?"

"The expedition sailed, but met with immense disaster."

"To Bantry Bay?"

"Yes—to Bantry Bay. The seizure of our little craft prevented the destination of the fleet being altered."

"And so they sailed?"

"Yes, and failed to effect a landing. The weather, so calm for weeks before, broke into a hurricane almost before the ships had cleared the passage of the Yroise, and scattered them completely on the voyage. Not half the expedition turned up at Bantry Bay; and the ships bearing the ammunition—the powder and firearms and cannon—not at all."

"That was very unfortunate."

"Unfortunate!" cried François. "That is hardly the word to apply to it. It is shocking, miserable, disastrous. The furies seemed to be in wait for the fleet to sail to set heaven and earth and sea in motion. It had not fairly got into the open sea when the Seduisant ——"

"The Seduisant—yes! I was midshipman once on board of her. What of her?"

"Capsized. And the *deuxieme* regiment of infantry—one of the finest in the service—was lost in her. Not a man was saved; not a musket, not a cannon, not an ounce of powder."

"Good heavens!"

"You may well exclaim! The Fates seemed to fight for England—the winds and storms against France."

"And what of Ireland all this time?"

"I can speak but little of Ireland," said François. "It is French matters that have passed exclusively through my hands. But our friend here can give you some information."

"My information," said MacNevin, who had been listening with much interest to this conversation, "is not very recent. It is many months since I set foot in Ireland—since I was arrested. I and the other prisoners were imprisoned in Fort Augustus, Scotland, whence I escaped some weeks since, and made my way through England to this port."

"An adventurous journey!" said François gaily.

"How did you manage to pass through an enemy's country and not get re-arrested?" asked Eugene.

"I had little difficulty," said MacNevin. "If it were not for the way I travelled I should probably have been detected and arrested; but with my violin under my arm I played the entire way. There was but little necessity for explanation with that."

"Not every one has such a fortunate way for travelling as you MacNevin," said François.

"Yes, I paid my way like a nobleman, without a farthing in my pocket. In return for their largesses I entertained the English boors with such strains as never before entered into their half animal souls—the olden Irish love airs or battle marches—soft with melting passion or thrilling with martial ardour; and so I passed from the Scottish border right through the length of England until I came here."

"How did you become acquainted with François?"

"Why, I was perambulating the streets one day, strongly dissatisfied that not the faintest opportunity of escape presented itself, when my eyes happened to rest on his face. In a moment I recognised him, although I had never seen him but once, in the council chamber over Nell Dowling's shop."

"Why, now I understand," said Eugene warmly. "I could not remember where I saw you before. It was there."

"I don't remember having seen you ———"

"Why, MacNevin—don't you remember? The 'ambassador' of whom we have talked so much?"

"What!" cried MacNevin. "The ambassador. It cannot be."

"It is, nevertheless," said Eugene, smiling. If 'ambassador' you call me."

"Well, I thought I had a good memory for faces, but I should never have known you, you are so much changed and altered! It is a good omen of the future that we should have met together again."

p

"That is what I am curious to hear," said Eugene—"how you two met."

"As I told you, I remembered François' face, and took opportunity of making myself known to him. He knew Captain Philip, and as we were all anxious to escape, we fixed upon that little skiff of the harbour-superintendent's that lay so cosily and invitingly rocking at the harbour mouth. So we stole out last night—never thinking that we should find anyone in the boat before us—least of all you."

"You did certainly astonish us," said François. "I fairly thought my heart would leap through my mouth when you rose like a dark spirit from the bottom."

"I had need to be pretty quick. There was not much time for explanation, with your cutlass flashing through the dark."

"Ay, Eugene," said François gravely, "you came pretty near it that time. A second later and our friend the ambassador's dreams of escape were over. If my cutlass failed to do its work, MacNevin's pistol ——"

"Well, that would have been a last resource," said the latter. "We should have a thousand pursuers before the echoes of the shot had died away."

"At any rate," said Eugene with a smile, "between you both I ran a pretty narrow risk for my life. The only one whose hand did not happen to be raised against me was the captain's."

"Ah, by the way," said François regretfully. "I wonder what will become of him."

"He is in a very dangerous position this moment," said MacNevin. "If the slightest suspicion attaches to him—and I don't see how it can fail to—he will be summarily shot on deck or swung from the yardarm."

"You see, Eugene," broke in François, "we never expected to be forestalled in our possession of the boat, which only carries three."

"So he sacrificed himself for us."

"It is only on a par with his whole conduct. I never knew one so unselfish or so self-sacrificing. But see! What is this bearing down on us?"

François pointed with outstretched hand to where a

small two-master came sweeping down upon them at some half a-mile distance. Half cutter, half yacht, she came towards them at tremendous speed, the brass carronade on the poop reflecting the morning rays from its burnished surface. Her enormous sails spread to their full extent and filled with the breeze that had sprung up, were so large and extended in comparison with the diminutive size of the craft, that they made her look like an immense sea-gull. As she came pacing along half on her side, the white cleaving lines of foam swept back from her prow in two lines of glinting light.

A graceful bird of the sea, her swift motion and magnificent spread of sail caused an exclamation of admiration from Eugene.

"This one is coming to capture us!" broke out MacNevin.

"She appears to be coming on business certainly," said François, eyeing the approaching craft distrustfully yet intently.

"She seems to wonder what brings a craft of our size in mid-channel, and is going to satisfy her curiosity," said Eugene.

"And see!" interrupted François, "look yonder on the horizon! I shall be much surprised if these are not men-of-war."

"You are right, François. They *are* men-of-war— English line-of-battle ships, too," said Eugene, after a keen survey.

"And this confounded pinnace," said MacNevin in much alarm, "is coming from them. What a pity that——"

"You are wrong there; this cutter is French. The English never hang their halyards so; it is a trick of our sailors, and a bad one—but they will not give it up. Yes —she is French! But see! there she comes to speak for herself."

The cutter glided towards them with the ease and grace of an eagle swooping through the air, to which bird, with its extended wings, her large sails bore no small resemblance.

"*Ohe! Abauer les voiles!*" snouted a strange voice from the prow of the pinnace, as she swept past.

"*Bien,*" cried Eugene, in ecstacy at the language in which he was addressed.

"*Qui etes vous,*" hailed the officer again, as he lifted his cap in salute.

"*Français,*" cried Eugene in response.

"*Do'ù ?*"

"*Une prison Anglaise.*"

"*Echappement ?*"

"*Oui l'chappement.*"

At these words the crowd of curious faces that lined the bulwarks doffed their caps, and an enthusiastic cheer went up from many mouths.

"*Bummuez de voiles et benez à bord,*" shouted the officer again, with singular sympathy in his tones.

"That we shall with the greatest possible pleasure," said Eugene, with delighted energy, to his companions, as he heard the request.

If an archangel had called to François, the invitation could have fallen on no more eager ears. The cutter slackened her sail, and the skiff, altering her helm, ran up under her lee.

In a few minutes all three had clambered on board, the skiff was set adrift, and the cutter once more proceeded on her way.

"Your name?" asked the officer, who wore the gold epaulettes of the French naval service, but looked quite a youth.

"François Delavigne, sous-lieutenant; once of General Clarke's staff, and lately a prisoner in England."

"And yours?"

"Edmond MacNevin, Irishman, prisoner of war also in England."

"Desirous of reaching France?"

"Yes."

"We have a good many of your nation there. You will find many comrades to welcome you. And yours?"

"My name is Eugene Lefebre—once of the Republican line-of-battle ship, *La Vengeur.*"

"What!" cried the young officer, as he started back, dropping in his astonishment the log book in which he was entering the incident and names. "Not Eugene

Lefebre who was to command the Seduisant under Hoche in the ——"

"Yes, Carlo; and who was midshipman with you many years ago in her."

"Eugene! Eugene!" cried the officer, as he threw himself with French affection and rapturous delight, into the other's arms. "How delighted I am to see you! How glad to meet you! We all thought you had been drowned at sea. But how changed you are! I should never have known you."

"I am all the better for meeting you, Carlo, in a double sense," Eugene said, when the first burst of delight and greeting was over, "as an old friend and present rescuer. But, Carlo," as he saw his friend about to break forth with a fresh burst of exclamations, "remember that we have been all night at sea in that little skiff, that I have had to swim for my life, and have consequently been sitting in wet clothes all the time."

"A thousand pardons! I was so pleased to see you I had not noticed the circumstance. Yes, your dress is wet. Come down to my cabin. But first—do you see these sail yonder? Can you carry your eye so far?"

"Yes, we have seen them already."

"Can you tell me if they are English?"

"They certainly are," said Eugene.

"Not Spanish?"

"No, undoubtedly not."

"I don't know the rig out of these vessels," said Carlo, "and portion of my business out this morning was to see to what nationality they belonged. We have been expecting our allies, the Spanish fleet, from Cadiz. I half believed these were they. If I had not seen your little boat on the water, and become curious to know what it was, I should probably have run up to them."

"It would have been a serious business for you if you had, Carlo *mon ami;* but as they were the means of bringing you out this morning I shall have a greater regard for his Britannic majesty's ships than I ever had before."

"Here you are, gentlemen," said the vivacious young officer, as they descended into his apartment, "welcome once more to French ground. Oh; by the way, how you do shiver, Eugene; you are thoroughly chilled. Take a glass of this—it is champagne—that will put fresh vigour into your veins; it must be long since you tasted any. Fill your tumblers, gentlemen, and then into bed. You all seem worn out, and a rest will do you no harm. Nay, not a word," added he, as he saw Eugene about to speak. "I shall tell you no news—no, not a word—until you waken in the harbour of Brest. It would be as much as your life is worth to remain as you are. Come! Take your tumblers! the sparkling champagne will make you sleep the more soundly, should you need anything for that purpose—which I doubt. A French captain is monarch on board his vessel, and must be obeyed."

There was no ignoring the friendly orders of the kind-hearted young officer—thus overflowing with delight at seeing an old friend under such circumstances, and full of frank hospitality—and so having quaffed the reviving wine he poured for them, they turned into their hammocks.

Eugene was not sorry to get rid of his saturated clothes that clung as tenaciously as if they were glued to him; and, as sleep closed his eyelids, he felt for the first time for twelve long months the sense of freedom breathing on his forehead, and the heavy, dull sense of imprisonment lifted from his heart.

In the grateful warmth they were all three soon fast asleep; and the sun was in the mid-sky, and the pinnace anchored at rest by the Artillery-pier in Brest Harbour, before their slumbers were broken.

"Are you awake, Eugene? Are we dreaming, or is it a reality? Is that the glorious language of France I hear spoken on deck? Oh! glory to high Heaven that I hear its music once more instead of the barbarous Saxon jargon! That language, Eugene, was only meant for speech of savages. Do you hear?"

"I hear," said Eugene, drowsily waking. "Is it really actuality or am I dreaming?"

"It is actual and real enough, Eugene," said François, jumping up. "There goes a military band playing 'The Marseillaise.' Magnificent strain! Where could it be conceived but in our glorious France?"

CHAPTER XXXIV.

IN FRANCE.

EUGENE's awakened faculties soon became aware that the pinnace was the centre of much attraction.

The buzz of conversation on deck was distinctly audible through the open windows where their hammocks swung; and boats were constantly passing with officers whose uniforms showed them to be of high rank. On the whole, it struck him that the arrival of the cutter, for some reason or other, had occasioned considerable *furore*.

Which, indeed, was the case. The singular news that the boat had been found in the wide waste of waters—a little waif extruded from the night and sea—with her adventurous passengers, fugitives from the horrors of an English prison; that two of these fugitives were French officers; and that one of them was Lefebre, the chosen right-hand man of Hoche in the expedition to Ireland, created such a sensation in Brest, then full of military and naval officers, as could not well be described.

The news flew like lightning through the town. Eugene was well-known to the officers of the fleet as one of the most promising therein at the time of his sudden disappearance. Why he had disappeared, or how, were matters of which none of them had cognisance; and, as is usual in times of great excitement and enterprise, he had soon dropped out of men's minds. The world was moving swiftly, great events were in course of accomplishment, and one man's life was of no more account than a grain of sand on the Bretagne coast.

But the news that he had escaped from an English prison in which he had been confined; that he had swum for his life from the hulks; that he had tempted the dangers of the furious sea that runs in the Channel, until by good providence the tricolor of the Normandie cutter had sheltered him, elevated him at once into the position of a hero of romance.

"You have had a fine sleep, gentlemen," said their

friend entering, just as the strains of the Marseillaise fell on their ears.

"You have come to anchor, Carlo?"

"Anchor!—yes, hours ago."

"For heaven's sake," said François, "open that window and let me look once more on French land. Let me see the surf breaking on the French shore. Let my eyes behold the tricolor floating once more on the hills of France. Quick! I tell you, or I shall die. You do not know what it is to be nearly two years absent."

"Well, François," said the officer, laughing, "I think breakfast should be far preferable at present."

"Nay," said François, leaping from his hammock, rushing to the window, and throwing it open, "you don't —you can't—know the delight of seeing France again after two years of imprisonment and home-sickness. Two years! Think of it! Yes! there is France again—thank God I have lived to see it! How gloriously the water sparkles!—it never shone like that, Eugene, in that dreary, foggy Plymouth. How exquisitively fresh and clear and picturesque everything looks! Don't you think so, Eugene?"

"Beautiful—exquisite—superb!" were the exclamations of Eugene, as the two gazed long and exultantly on the bright and busy scene around them. "Is there anything unusual afoot to-day, Carlo? for I notice an immense number of officers in full uniform passing and repassing —and the line-of-battle ships are lined with streamers. Has anything unusual occurred?"

"Something very unusual has occurred," said Carlo, with quiet gravity

"Unusual—what? Has there been a victory somewhere? What news? Tell us!" asked both officers, turning around from the window.

"No; no battle has been fought—that would not occasion the slightest excitement. Triumphs come now as a matter of course. A ball given by our officers in a captured capital to a beaten sovereign and his generals does not occupy an inch of the *Moniteur*. It is something more than that."

"What?"

"The wonderful news that three escaping prisoners have been rescued from perfidious Albion—one of them the former captain that was to be of the Seduisant and the future Lord High Admiral of the French fleet."

"Cease joking, Carlo, and tell us what it means."

"I assure you I am not joking. It is true what I say. All Brest knows it by this time, and the conquest of Prussia would not create half as much enthusiasm. The deck is crowded with old companions in arms, and with all the high and mighty naval chiefs in harbour—waiting to pay their respects."

"Come. Be serious. Cease joking, and let us learn the good news there is."

"I am as serious as the president of a court-martial, Eugene. They are all eager to see you. But if Bonaparte himself were on deck, he must wait until you have breakfasted. Come. There is no particular need for careful toilet. Your clothes are dry, and your breakfast waits."

The snowy linen and the appetising viands of the breakfast-table were acceptable to the hungry travellers—who, after their rest, were ravenous as wolves.

The meal once over they went on deck.

Three battered and scarecrow looking persons they seemed amid the glitter and pomp of the gorgeous uniforms that crowded the pinnace from stem to stern. It was a splendid sight, the crowd of officers—many of them bearing the great historic names of France, whose deeds were household words through Europe—their myriad-coloured uniforms making the deck one shifting kaleidoscope—surrounding the three ragged and tattered sea-farers, and doing homage and giving welcome to them as if they were monarchs in all their regal pomp just arrived.

Nothing could equal the warmth and welcome poured upon them. They were the heroes of the hour. Exhumed after long months out of the prisons and fogs of that barbarous land at the other side of the Channel, they were looked upon by the French officers pretty much as the Spaniards looked upon Columbus when his sea-tossed galleys came back from the mysterious bounds of the unknown ocean into the ports of Spain.

When the reception was over, and the officers had

demonstrated their delight and welcome, Eugene and his two friends were invited to a ball to be improvised in their honour that night in the Hotel de l'Europe. It was necessary, therefore, at once to provide uniforms, for the dress of an escaping convict, whilst interesting at first sight, was hardly fitted for the gaiety and grandeur of an officers' ball, or for mixing with the beauty and fashion that were certain to be present thereat.

They had hardly dismissed their costumier when a skiff passed under the window where they stood. Its occupant, whose face they did not see, ran swiftly up the ladder and on deck.

In a moment after a marine tapped at the cabin door and handed in a card.

It bore the name, "Theobald Wolf Tone, Army of the Sambre and Meuse."

"Wolfe Tone!" said Eugene eagerly. "Where is he? Send him in at once."

An officer in uniform entered. A little above middle size, slight and agile in form, thin and sallow in face, but with an eye that, at once bright and resolute, bespoke vigour and resolution, and impressed him with an undeniable character of resolve and determination—the newcomer advanced with outstretched hands. A smile of exceeding warmth lit up his features, and there was no mistaking the thorough welcome he had for the fugitives.

"Well, gentlemen, I am delighted to see you! Welcome—a thousand times welcome to France again!"

"How kind of you to come, Tone," said Eugene, as he and François grasped a hand each. "How well you are looking! When did you hear of our arrival?"

"About half an hour ago. I just arrived from Havre to find the town ringing with the news. And how are you François? How you have grown! Why, it is colonel of cuirassiers you should be, from your inches."

"Thank you, Tone. I am all the better for hearing your cheerful words again. But not colonel, please; I mean to have the marshal's baton yet."

"Well, the other must come first, François. And how are you, Eugene? Not looking so well as when I last saw you. Good reason for it, I make no doubt."

"Prison life does not help appearances."

"No more it does, Eugene. But it might readily have been worse. I had long given you up as lost. What became of you after leaving Dublin?"

"You heard of our sailing?"

"I did—long afterwards. Woe worth the day that your errand failed! It was a grievous loss to Ireland. But more of that anon. What happened?"

"We were not well out of sight of the southern coast of Ireland when we were captured by the British vessel Thunderer."

"And the Albatross!"

"Sunk with a cannon shot."

"Ah me! We believed it had foundered. And the captain?"

"If not shot or hung since we parted him last night, is in bounding health and spirits."

"Where?"

"On board the Thunderer—refitting at Plymouth."

"An invaluable sailor lost to Ireland," said Tone gravely. "And so, Eugene, all the time we thought you had gone to the bottom in the Albatross you were in an English prison. It seems to me as if you had suddenly risen from the depths of the sea, so long I have been accustomed to think you there."

"And so the expedition sailed, Tone?"

"Unfortunately it did."

"And with disastrous ending?"

"Most disastrous. Ah, Eugene! If you had been spared to bear your message to the Directory, what a change there would have been in the destinies of Ireland. Little the millions of Irishmen knew what fortunes for them your vessel bore as she sailed down the Channel."

"The forces did not even effect a landing?"

"No—not even that. But the story is too sad and too long to tell at present. Why! whom have we here? What? you, MacNevin! Is it possible, you here too? Why, it is a perfect gathering of old friends!"

"You were so busy conversing with my friends that I forebore to introduce myself," said MacNevin, grasping the proffered hand.

"What a shame for you not to have introduced yourself!" said Tone, laughing. "I thought you were in Scotland—in prison, too."

"There has been a sort of general jail-delivery latterly," said MacNevin drily. "We took French leave, and very properly, as you will say, seeing that we were coming to France."

"Broke the bounds also, MacNevin."

"I fear so. I believe that's the way they would phrase it in England."

"Probably. And what news from Ireland?"

"News! I have not heard a word these six months. You may well believe I did not make many inquiries during my pilgrimage through England."

"You haven't heard then?" said Tone, eagerly.

"Heard what?" asked all three at once, impressed by Tone's manner that something startling had happened.

"The insurrection has broken out in Ireland."

"What!" cried all three together. "Impossible!"

"The country is up. Lord Edward Fitzgerald has been arrested, and is now, I fear, dying in jail of his wounds. The Wexford men have taken to arms, and ——"

"And what of France?" cried Eugene eagerly. "What is she doing? What aid is she sending?"

"France has not yet sent a man or a gun," said Tone sadly. "The people are fighting unaided—however long or short they may be able to continue the struggle."

"What are the Directory about? Why have you not urged them to send aid?"

"Urged!" cried Tone. "Urged! I am weary of urging."

"And what are they doing?"

"Nothing."

"Nothing?"

"That—and that alone."

"What do they say? What reason do they give?"

"That they cannot send a large and they will not send a small force."

"Where are our armies?"

"Across the frontiers, or with Bonaparte in Egypt."

"And our fleets—where are they?"

"With Bonaparte also."

"Damn Bonaparte," said Eugene, impatiently.

"With all my heart," said Tone; "but that will not help us much."

"Who is admiral here?"

"Bruix."

"Our old friend. Will he do nothing?"

"He can do nothing without orders from the Directory."

"Who is war minister?"

"Kilmaine."

"What of him?"

"The same."

"Merciful heavens!" said Eugene, in dismay. "This is awful! Is there no succour whatever?"

"I fear not. I am perfectly heart-broken trying to push on matters. With your assistance the business may go faster."

"Well, Tone, I shall meet Bruix to-night in all probability at the ball. He is under obligations to me for services long ago. I shall see what I can do with him."

"And I," broke in François, "am off for the Minister of War in the morning. I shall see if they will suffer an insurrection that they themselves encouraged and half induced, to be crushed without a trigger being pulled to aid it. It is monstrous."

"How long would it take to fit an expedition?" asked Eugene, after a pause in which he was engaged in deep reflection.

"So much depends upon the number of men and the amount of arms and ammunition forwarded, so much upon the heart and energy thrown into the business, that it would be very difficult to say."

"How long are the Irish people likely to be able to resist the forces of England."

"Equally difficult to say. A great deal depends on whether the insurrection is general or only partial. Remember, they have to contend with the whole might of England."

"Unfortunately, yes. You do not know to what extent the insurrection has spread?"

"No. You must remember," said Tone, "that the coast is so blockaded now that not a single letter or item of news can reach us from England or Ireland. This much has reached us vaguely and indirectly *via* Hamburg."

"I was not aware the blockade was so close."

"That is so. The English fleet sweeps the coast. Not later than yesterday two of their frigates bore down within cannon-shot of the fortifications at Havre."

"Communications come readily enough from here to England," said Eugene bitterly. "I know that."

"They must be traitorous communications, then," said Tone.

"A very great many of them were. English gold seems very powerful."

"Well, gentlemen," said Carlo, entering, "you have had a long time for discussion. You have some time yet before it will be necessary to go ashore. I vote for a cigar and a glass of Burgundy before dinner. You will dine with us, Tone?"

"I have no objection. I came here by request of Admiral Bruix to see him; but the interview can wait. I had little idea that I should see our lost friends here. By the way, Eugene, are you aware that you were appointed to the command of a frigate in the Irish expedition?"

"Yes, Morand de Galles intimated as much in the message François brought."

"Did he tell you the name."

"No—which was it?"

"The Seduisant."

"I remember her well. Where is she now?"

"At the bottom of the Yroise. She capsized before the fleet was ten hours under weigh."

"Capsized! Good heavens! how was that?"

"Ran on a sunken rock, going at full speed with all sails set; capsized, and every man on board—she carried the *deuxième* regiment of infantry—went down with her. So that you see your captivity was not altogether an unmixed evil."

"Well, I am not sure that I should have embraced the alternative I am sorry for the Seduisant—I served as midshipman on board her," said Eugene, as he lit a cigar and took a seat.

The conversation became general. Carlo—and indeed Tone—had much to say about the deeds of the great armies of France; the campaign of Italy and Holland; the sudden departure of Bonaparte for Egypt, whither the eyes of all France were at present turned with eager interest; to all of which the three late prisoners listened with intense eagerness. They had been so long shut out from all news that they heard with rapt attention the recitals of the astonishing victories of the French arms. It seemed to them like news from the other world.

By the time dinner was over and that it was time for them to put on their uniforms for the ball prepared in their honour, they were pretty fully acquainted with French military history for the past two years.

"How well the marshal's baton would hang at your side, François!" said Tone chaffingly, as the tall, slender form of the youth looked to fine advantage in his new uniform.

"And it shall hang there yet—remember that!" said François seriously. "I always told Hoche so, when I was a drummer boy."

"By the way—Hoche!" said Eugene, "I had quite forgotten to ask for him. How is he?"

"Dead!" said Tone sorrowfully.

"Dead!" cried the former with a start.

"And not on the field with the colours of France around him as he would have wished to die, but of consumption."

"Then there died a gallant general, and the first of French soldiers," said François.

"And the best friend of Ireland that stood on French ground," said Tone.

The feeling of sadness that this news evoked gave way to the necessity of preparing to go on shore; and in a short time the two officers had descended the side of the cutter and put off to the pier. The magnificent hotel standing on the terrace overlooking the harbour was alight with lamps and coloured arches, the reflection of which in the waters of the bay gave an appearance of unique beauty and chequered magnificence thereto

Tone and MacNevin elected to remain on board the cutter and discuss home matters.

They had much to speak of, much to think over in regard to things in Ireland; and Tone felt that it would be almost a desecration of the cause he had at heart to attend festivities in France while his brothers in Ireland were engaged in a life-and-death struggle with English forces—whilst they were pouring out their blood freely in one more gallant stand for liberty.

CHAPTER XXXV.

CITIZEN CARNOT.

THE ball passed off with great magnificence.

The enormous banquet hall of the Hotel de l'Europe was arranged for dancing purposes; it was lit with innumerable coloured lights, and the banners of many nations drooped from its walls. It did not take long to improvise the festivities—Frenchmen are particularly quick at such work; and, perhaps, from being got up with such excessive speed, more heart than usual was thrown into it to complete its success.

All the superior officers of both arms of the service were there in full uniform, as also their wives and daughters, looking only as French ladies can, in their wealth of exquisite fashion, good looks, and renowned names. For miles around the local gentry poured into the place, until the carriages blocked the streets of the town.

But regal as was the scene got up in Eugene's honour, brilliant the uniforms, and bright the glitter of golden epaulet and polished scabbard, bewitching the smiles and welcomes bestowed upon him by lady friends and acquaintances, the gorgeousness and gaiety of the scene soon passed from his mind, and he—as soon as he, with due courtesy to his friends, could—tore himself from the joyousness of the occasion to direct himself to other interests.

For this purpose he sought out the admiral, whom he found smoking in the conservatory overlooking the bay, and apart from the ball-room.

"I thought you would come to see me, when you grew weary of dancing," said the admiral gaily, as he embraced his friend.

"Why did you think so, admiral?" asked Eugene.

"Because I fancied you looked a little distraught in the ball-room. I warrant you I can tell you what was in your mind."

"What?"

"Ireland."

"You are perfectly right," said Eugene laughing.

"And now, admiral, as you can guess so well, perhaps you can also tell what brought me—independently of the wish to see an old and kind friend—to search you out?"

"I can. It is to help on Tone with his wild and Quixotic mission."

"Wild and Quixotic! These words from you, admiral!" said Eugene in tones of dismay and disappointment—"from you who sailed with the former expedition."

"Times have altered since then, Eugene. Then we had a powerful fleet. Bonaparte has taken all that with him to Egypt. We have no ships here to spare."

"We should not want many vessels. Quick-sailing transports to disembark men and muskets and artillery. That is all we need."

"You forget England is a great naval power. When France prepares to strike her she must not do so with a solitary brigade and a few guns, but with a powerful division of her army and battery upon battery of artillery. And ships innumerable will be necessary to carry these."

"But we cannot hope to get these. France cannot spare them. It would be worse than idle to delay for or expect them."

"Wait until Bonaparte returns from his absurd expedition to Egypt. It is to him we must look. The Directory is effete, moribund—it will do nothing."

"Until Bonaparte returns!" exclaimed Eugene in dismay. "That may not be for months, and think how urgent times are! Ireland is in the throes of battle Now is the time to send her aid. Even ten thousand men, with fifty thousand stand of arms, sent now from France, will kindle the flame of insurrection from one end of Ireland to the other."

"It cannot be done, Eugene. I tell you the Directory will not do it."

"They must," said Eugene vehemently. "The honour of France is concerned. France has through her officers urged the Irish to this effort. It would be an act of national dishonour to abandon them. It is even in the interests of France, military and commercial, to aid them. They are a gallant and martial race of six million people— and would be, if aided to freedom, a powerful ally to France. I tell you now emphatically that Bonaparte has wasted the blood and treasure of France; has shamed folly by his foolishness—and he will live to say so yet— by striking at England in Egypt instead of in Ireland. England is powerful, as Rome was, in her extremities— her great fleets make her so—but strike her at home at the heart, and she collapses. There is no strength, no vitality there. It is the case of a strong man whose arms can give death-dealing blows, can mock at swords and lances and battle-axes, but a tiny needle driven through his heart paralyses his strength and renders his arms feeble and useless."

"Well, Eugene, granting all that you say—and you put it vigorously and well—what can we generals and admirals do? We are but the machines that carry out the orders of the Directory."

"You can advise them—urge it on them. Admiral, plead the cause of the hapless land struggling for freedom with the dagger of the tyrant at her heart. If you carry out the orders of the Directory, you can also inspire them to give these orders."

"Well, I cannot say that you have not influenced me, Eugene; but as I know the difficulty in making the Directory take up a fresh idea, come with me to Paris in the morning. I am going there. I shall give you an introduction to some of the leading members of that body, and if you with your local knowledge can influence them you may reckon on me for ready support. And now tell me something of your adventures in England."

The conversation was continued, and only broke up when the bustle and stir in the courtyard beneath announced that the ball was terminating, and that the brilliant carriages rolling away, whose flashing lights brightened the streets, were conveying to their homes the fair dames that graced it with their presence.

Tone and MacNevin slept on board the yacht, and were wakened early in the morning by Eugene.

"Tone, my dear fellow," said the latter cheerfully, "I am off to Paris with the admiral. I shall see the Minister of the navy. François has started already to see Kilmaine. All may come right in a few days. You and MacNevin had better follow as soon as possible. We may want your information in the shape of statistics, and so on. Good-bye. Call for me at the Ministry of Marine. I shall be glad to see Paris again after such a long absence. Good-bye."

He was gone.

"Things are beginning to look brighter," said Tone cheerfully, as they sat at breakfast. "I came to Brest yesterday from Havre with scarcely heart enough, from continued disappointments, to walk the streets. Now I seem to see in the near future the accomplishment of our hopes."

"If energy, good faith, and enthusiastic bravery can gain success, our cause is in good hands," said MacNevin, "Meantime, as there seems nothing to be done here, I scarcely see what good purpose can be subserved by remaining. I am anxious to see Paris."

"Very well. We shall start to-day if you wish."

"I have no objection."

"What time do you say?"

"Any time that suits you will suit me."

The evening saw them on top of the diligence on their way to Paris.

Things did not move more swiftly, however. The Directory, as Bruix had said, were slow to move. The power of Bonaparte was overshadowing them, and they hesitated in his absence to make any new motion. Eugene plied the Minister of Marine with unceasing supplications. François urged General Kilmaine, the War Minister; and Tone was in constant negotiations with both. Inquiry and inquiry was made of him as to the positions, resources, and prospects of success of the Irish insurgents, to which he gave most elaborate returns; but nothing came of it all.

Meantime, however, the war was raging in Ireland, and no aid was reaching the insurgents.

While these negotiations were going on, the heart was being crushed out of Irishmen—cannon and muskets were only opposed by pikes, and the result could scarcely be doubted.

Tone was in utter dismay. But to all his energies the inertness of those in authority opposed a victorious resistance.

"Well, Tone, the French nation, or rather its rulers, are strangely altered since I left France, short as the time has been," said Eugene one evening, as Tone and MacNevin visited him at his quarters in the Ministry of Marine. "I cannot put any life into them."

"Nor I," said Tone despondingly; they require report after report, return after return, but when these are furnished nothing comes of them."

"There is no energy in the Directory. There is less evidence of interest in Irish affairs this day than was manifested yet. I would Bonaparte were back. If his vigorous mind caught the idea, what a stir on all sides there would be!"

"In the present condition of things, and in this do-nothing state of existence," said MacNevin, "I am not quite sure that imprisonment in Scotland were not quite as enjoyable."

"Well, things are hardly quite as bad as that," said Eugene gaily. "Existence in Paris must have grown very unenjoyable when imprisonment in that land of mists is preferable to it. But we cannot mend matters by talking here—can we? I am going to Montemartre.'

"If talking could have mended them they would have been set right long ago," was Tone's response.

"That being so, I vote we have a cigarette and a

stroll through the streets. Anything to break the cruel monotony of disappointment. We shall be together some distance."

Agreeing to his proposal. the three friends emerged on the streets.

The footways were crowded with citizens enjoying the balmy air of an August evening, and Tone wondered, as he looked at the gaiety of all around, and the laughing conversation that rippled along, to think that this was the metropolis of a land that might be said at the moment to be at war with all Europe.

The windows overhead were thrown open, and clusters of fair faces were chatting thereat and gazing indolently on the moving crowd below. The *cafés* were bright with the glare of lamps and crowded with customers. Occasionally, to give piquancy to the scene, a troop of lancers, with the bannerets of the tricolor at the points of their lances, cantered gaily by, or a squadron of hussars, their jackets of braided gold setting off their smart forms finely, flashed the light of the lamps from their lifted sword-blades.

"Certainly this does not seem like war," he thought. "I wonder if the streets of Dublin are gay like these, or its people as light-hearted?"

In the midst of these reflections he found that he had lost his friends. However, as he knew the direction in which they intended going, he was not much concerned. feeling certain of meeting them later on. So he strolled carelessly on, taking note of the many strange things that presented themselves to his view, until he found himself in one of the narrow and crooked streets that led from the Boulevards to the Seine.

"There is a short cut, if I remember aright, in this direction to Montemartre. Eugene and MacNevin will have gone there. I shall try and overtake them. This route will probably bring me in advance of them."

Tone merely knew the general direction, and, as often happens in great cities, when he got into the network of narrow, unlit, and tortuous streets, he soon lost even that. The bustle and life and light of the great thoroughfares were unknown here. An oil lamp, swung from the

corners of the streets, alone showed a glimmer of light in
the long, dark alleys, for the dense darkness of a summer's
night had fallen on all around. The denizens of these
streets seemed to have all long since retired, for there
was not a traveller visible. Occasionally, indeed, from
narrow courtways and in some street corners there were
lights visible, and brawling voices were heard—betokening
where some wine-shops, still open, were the scenes of
noisy roystering. But Tone instinctively avoided these;
the Revolution and the subsequent wars had produced in
the more disreputable haunts of the city a class of
characters undesirable to meet. Two years previously
Hoche himself narrowly escaped being assassinated in one
of the streets at night. Wherefore he kept a safe distance
between himself and the dangerous beacons hung ont
from these places.

Walking swiftly, he turned from one street to another,
from one courtway to another, without seeming to make
progress.

At last the conviction forced itself on him that he had
lost his way and was rambling around in a circle. It was
long past midnight, and he began to grow considerably
uneasy. The hour at which the wine-shops closed was
near at hand, and their occupants would soon be turned
into the streets—very undesirable parties to make acquaintance with in the worst quarter of the city, and on a
lightless night.

He felt himself tired with this purposeless walking, and
when he got into one of the wider streets stopped irre-
solutely to consider what to do.

His attention was suddenly arrested by a strange series
of cries in the distance, at the further end of the street.

Not at all at his ease, and believing it to be some midnight brawl, from which the further he withdrew the
better, he turned on his heel in the opposite direction.

The cries increased so quickly and were of such curious
import that he could not forbear turning again to look.

To his surprise two lamps seemed to be hurrying in
the distance swiftly towards him. At the same moment
the beats of horses hooves came on his ears, sparks of fire
seemed to fly from the pavement underneath the lamps

—and then, almost instantaneously, he knew what it was!

There was but little time for thought. The two thoroughbred horses, in some manner broken loose from their driver, came pacing along the street with the fiery speed that maddened and affrighted animals alone can.

It was an open carriage, and a lady's form in white was perfectly visible in the dim light, sitting therein in mute terror. A crowd of people, as is usual in such cases, were hurrying as fast as they could in pursuit, their calls and exclamations but making the runaways go at still more terrific pace.

It would be over in a second.

The street at its nearer end sloped rapidly and turned a sharp curve. Once there the frail carriage would be smashed instantaneously into matchwood, and the occupant hurried into eternity.

The sparks flew under the horses' feet as they approached, in continuous coruscations!

The panting of the flying steeds came distinctly on his ears. They were near enough for him to see the foam that covered their mouths. But no word or cry came from the lips of the occupant in her imminent and deadly peril. She had evidently swooned.

Tone was no coward. He would not have been engaged on the mission he was, if he had been. Danger always called up with him the excitement of fiery daring; so stepping into the road along the centre of which the carriage was flying with the velocity of an arrow, he waited a breathless second until it came up—and, as the smoking breath of the nearest steed was on his face, sprang forward and grasped the reins!

It was the veriest risk for life or death ever man took: but his clutch proved successful. He caught the reins near the bit just as the fore legs were in the air, and the sudden check, with his additional weight, brought the nearest horse propelled furiously forward on his head.

Tone felt himself jerked violently forward; but in the space of a heart's beat he was the centre of a confused mass of struggling horses and an overturned carriage—

and then a sudden blow coming on his temple, he grew unconscious!

For a little while only, however.

He felt something cold on his face, and a voice fell on his ears:

"That will do, Antoine. You need not bathe his face more. He is recovering. His pulse is coming back."

"I am delighted to hear that. I would not wish for half the wealth of Paris anything should have happened him," said another.

"Not one man in every thousand would have essayed that feat," said the first speaker, who held his wrist.

"And not one in a million would have succeeded," said the other.

"If he failed he would have known what the secrets of the next world are by this time, and ——"

"Is he much injured do you think?" asked a girl's voice in soft musical accents.

"He can answer for himself by this time," said the first speaker, as he saw Tone open his eyes. "How do you feel?"

"I have been a little stunned, I think."

"So you have. It is well it was no worse. Take some of this."

He held a glass of brandy to Tone's lips, and the latter feeling very much revived thereafter was helped to his feet. A crowd stood around at a respectful distance.

"I have to thank you," said the second of the two speakers, "for your brave and successful effort to save this young lady's life. But for you ——"

"I hope the lady is safe," said Tone earnestly.

"She is. But for your gallant heart no power on earth could save her life. But she will record you her thanks by-and-by. Is he able to travel, doctor, do you think?"

"Oh, yes. I think so. He has received no serious injury."

"Then I shall be obliged by your coming with me in this carriage. My own is, as you see, scarcely fit to journey further? Look there!" Looking there, Tone saw some men holding the trembling horses, now shivering with fear at their own mad career, and, near where they were standing, the broken carriage. Looking also, as another carriage came up, he noticed intuitively the exceeding deference and respect paid by the assembled crowd to the gentleman who spoke and to the young lady that, pale with her recent fright, hung on his arm.

"You will do me the favour of coming with me—with us?"

"I will be most obliged," said Tone, who felt himself still dull, unsteady, and confused.

"Thanks. There Marie. Let me help you in. Now Monsieur let me give you my arm, too—for you seem not over strong yet."

With a word to the coachman the crowd fell back, and the carriage moved on.

After a profusion of thanks from the gentleman—and a few words from the young lady—in tones so sweet and silvery and cultured that Tone knew at once they were people of distinguished position—the former said—

"You are not a Frenchman, I think?"

"No—not by birth at least."

"An Englishman?"

"Well—not quite. An Irishman."

"Yet you wear the uniform of the French service?"

"I do. I am an officer in that service."

"Indeed?"

"General Bonaparte gave me my commission."

"Bonaparte—heh?" said the gentleman, with interest. "Would you pardon me for asking your name? This young lady," said he laughing, "has a right to know her preserver's name, and I—I have an interest in hearing it."

"Tone—Theobald Wolfe Tone!"

"Oh! I remember now. I am quite familiar with your name. I am doubly glad to meet you. I have read your reports to the Directory with great interest."

"Read my reports, Monsieur," said Tone with quick uneasiness. "I did not know they were published. They were forwarded by me as secret information."

"Published! No, of course not. Why would you think that?"

"Pardon me for a moment," said Tone as a thought struck him, "may I have the pleasure of knowing whom I am addressing."

"I thought everyone in Paris," said the gentleman gaily, "knew me—at least every officer. But I see I am not as distinguished as I thought. My name is Carnot—Citizen Carnot."

Tone sat spell-bound for a moment or two as the famous name fell on his ears. Could this be Citizen Carnot—Carnot the great organizer of victory, whose bright brain and fearless heart had guided the French revolutionary armies to triumph before even they themselves knew their marvellous and matchless strength? Whose name was second not even to Bonaparte's own in the French Military Councils. To whom he had so long and so often unavailingly sought for an introduction. The one man of all others in France the most potential for the cause he had at heart! Could it be really he?

"I am extremely glad, Citizen Carnot," said Tone, wakening up from his reverie, with the sense pressing on him of the desirability of making himself more intimate with his distinguished acquaintance, "to have the honour of making myself known to you—even under these undesirable circumstances. I have been long anxious for a personal interview."

"So?"

"Yes. I wished most anxiously to speak with you on public matters—on Irish matters."

"I could hardly refuse any request to one who has done me such signal service," said Carnot, as he turned a look of intense affection on his daughter. "This is my house," as the carriage stopped—"If you will do me the favour to accept my hospitality we can talk over matters."

Tone did not need further invitation—did not need the kind entreaties which the young girl joined to her father's —to accept the proffered hospitality; and, accordingly with bright spirits and high hopes, which completely banished all sense of pain or dulness, descended from the carriage with them and entered the palace.

Seated together at table, the impetuous Irishman lost no time in placing before his illustrious host a vivid statement of Irish affairs.

He told him in eloquent words of the downtrodden condition of the Irish people; how ready they were for revolt; how already a partial insurrection had developed itself; how all that was needed to make it successful was ample and timely aid from France; and pointed out to him that the heaviest blow that could be struck at England would be in Ireland.

To all of which Carnot listened with rapt attention.

"I am sorry, M. Tone," he said, at the conclusion, "that I did not possess this intelligence long ago. I never heard the case so clearly put before. I thoroughly concur in what you say. But we labour under this difficulty: The real ruler of France at present is in Egypt. This is in confidence. The Directory, nominally the governing body, possess no power—none. They cannot —dare not—take any step, least of all one so important as a large expedition to Ireland, in his absence. When he comes back —— Will this insurrection last until winter is over?"

"It will be crushed out if foreign aid does not arrive, long before winter commences," said Tone, decisively.

At this moment a gentleman in the uniform of a general officer entered.

"Welcome, Humbert. I am glad to see you," said Carnot. "You are an early visitor."

"What is this accident I have heard that has happened you?" asked the visitor.

"Oh, it is a mere nothing! I was coming from Augeran's quarters, and just as I was about to step into the carriage, and before the driver was well in his seat, the midnight gun, fired near the horses, startled them and they were off."

"Who was in the carriage?"

"The Citizeness Marie."

"The dear girl is safe, I trust?"

"Yes, thanks to the bravery and fearlessness of this officer. Citizen Tone—General Humbert."

"We could hardly permit any trouble to befall the organiser of victory yet awhile," said Humbert pleasantly. "I think I have had the pleasure of meeting Citizen Tone before," said he with cordial greeting.

"Then you are the very officer I want to see this moment. Citizen Tone will tell you his mission himself."

Which Tone did, dwelling upon every point which he thought would interest and attract one whom he knew to be one of the most rising and energetic of the French generals.

" What say you to that, general ? There is a new field for an enterprising commander. What if the *baton d'Irelande* lay in the future ?" asked Carnot.

" I would I had ten thousand men to lead, and," said the general, who had caught up Tone's enthusiasm, " I should soon see the tricolor outhung on Irish ground."

"Precisely what I expected," said Carnot, laughing. "Well, let the matter rest in my hands for a few days, Citizen Tone, and we shall see what can be done. Meantime, let this be in confidence."

Leaving the two to discuss other matters, and with a promise to call again, Tone took his leave in high heart that he had succeeded in enlisting the famous senator in the behalf of Ireland. Reaching his apartments, he retired to bed and was soon fast asleep, dreaming of Ireland and of the French banners unfurled theron.

Late in the afternoon he was awoke by François, who came in high good humour.

"Why, Tone," said he, "there has been quite a revolution in our favour to-day. There has been nothing talked of in the War Office but Ireland. Your reports have been asked for again and again."

" How does that arise ?"

" Heaven knows. I don't. Possibly some recent news has come to the Directory from Ireland with which I am unacquainted."

"And what has been done, François? Is there any result?"

"That I cannot say, but I am under orders to accompany General Humbert to Rochelle. And so are some Irishmen in Paris."

" This is a sudden movement, François."

" So it is. Everybody is wondering what it means Have *you* heard anything from Ireland to-day ?"

" Not a word."

" Then I wonder what it can be?" said François, gravely. "But at any rate there is no time for wondering or surmising now. We start to-night."

"To-night?" said Tone, in undisguised amazement.
"To-night. That's the oddest thing about it—it is so sudden. Take my word for it, Tone, there is something on foot, however it has arisen."
"I have no doubt there is. What forces are at Rochelle?"
"That I cannot answer you. And now there is not a moment to spare. Good-bye!"

The light step of the young officer, as he descended the stairs, whistling a bar of the "Marseillaise," was in Tone's ears as he rose and dressed.

"This is marvellously quick work on the part of Citizen Carnot," thought he. "It is worthy of the alertness of the man who guided the half-trained armies of the revolution to victory. Heaven grant he may not be too hasty this time. But he cannot be. Everything now depends upon speed."

CHAPTER XXXVII.

"VENGEANCE IS MINE."

THE gentleman—Lord Kingston—at the Eagle, in Eustace street, to whom Redmond Barrington so impatiently put his question, "What news?" leisurely replied:

"You have not been much about town this afternoon or you would have heard that—but I remember now you have been a complete stranger here lately. And that puts me in mind, was there not some fuss about your singular disappearance, some ——"

"My lord, I am very much pressed for time now, and have not much leisure for conversation," said Redmond, rather curtly. "You spoke as if there was some news that concerned me?"

"Egad, your absence has not improved your courtesy, Barrington," said Lord Kingston with undisturbed good humour, "but the news does concern you, or I expect it ought. I am surprised you have not heard it."

"I am awaiting that favour at your lordship's convenience," said Redmond, who knew of old that the reckless but high-spirited nobleman delighted in retailing a story which had a spice of the personal in it, and therefore was prepared to put a stay on his own impatience in order to humour him.

"Egad, Barrington, the world is changing so much latterly that news of the forenoon is old by evening. Who would have thought of Mortimer ——"

"Yes, yes, what of him?" rapidly inquired Redmond.

He was about retreating from the gossiping nobleman, as believing that his long-deferred anecdote had no connection with or interest for him, and was hastening to other quarters where he might glean some of the intelligence he thirsted for.

But the concluding words of the speaker drew him back to his place as if a pillar of loadstone stood before him.

"What of Mortimer, my lord?" he asked again, scarcely giving time to his lordship to continue his narrative.

"Why, Barrington, you take one's breath away with your hurried manner of questioning. Mortimer, this afternoon ——"

"Who speaks of Mortimer?" said a gentleman passing by, whose ear caught the words of his lordship.

"I, my lord," said Lord Kingston, extending his hand to the new-comer. "I was about telling Barrington of ——"

"Barrington!" said the other interruptingly and glancing at Redmond in amazement. "Why, so it is! Where have you been all the time whilst this work has been going on about you? Why, we all thought you had been drowned, or murdered, or made away with in some shape or form. Where on earth have you been? But that," said his lordship, "is not exactly the question at present. You can tell me all about that another time. I want your presence immediately."

"Excuse me a moment, Lord Edward; I wish to hear from Lord Kingston the news of ——"

"Nay, nay, not now," said his lordship; "not now. Come with me." And, placing his arm within that of the other, he drew him by force away.

"I have something of importance to tell you, Redmond. Your sister, Helen Barrington ——"

"Yes, yes, what of her? Where is she?" broke in Redmond impetuously, as he stayed his friend in his course, and stood stock-still before him, awaiting an answer.

"Helen was married this morning," said his lordship.

"Married!" cried Redmond aghast, as he staggered back a step or two. "Married! To whom? But I need not ask. Merciful Providence! that I should have come so late!"

"Yes, if you had been here earlier, his life might have been saved, and matters might have been made all right. I am extremely sorry, but I certainly thought he held a keener finger on the trigger. And he had his choice of ground too."

"Would it be any offence to ask you, my lord," said Redmond, in angry impatience and perplexity, "to speak a little more plainly. What are you referring to?—for I know nothing of what you are speaking about;—and where is Helen? If she were married this morning, and that you are aware of it, perhaps you can tell me where she is. I tell you the news is to me and to her a matter of the highest moment. Where *is* Helen?"

"Helen Barrington, or Helen Mortimer—as we must call her—is with Lady Pamela at Leinster House, Kildare-street."

"At Leinster House! What should have brought her there? Why did she go there, my lord?" cried Redmond fiercely, as it seemed to him that the meshes of perplexity were being woven more tangledly around him. "Let me go there at once!"

"Your question demands an answer, Mr. Barrington," said Lord Edward haughtily, completely misconstruing Redmond's impatience through ignorance of the motives thereof, "and it shall have it. She came to us as the daughter of an old friend, and as one without relative or protector. To whom else should she go on her wedding morning? There is an old kinship, though you seem to forget it, between our families, and it was most right and befitting that she, a simple, unbefriended girl, should come to us in the supreme moment of her life."

Redmond heard but little of this statement. In the intensity of his anguish he paid no attention to the warm and eloquent words of his lordship, but pressed his hands over his throbbing and beating temples.

"Mortimer—poor fellow!"—continued his lordship.

"Ay, what of him?" asked Redmond fiercely—the name wakening him up from his tempest of passion. "Is he, too, at Leinster House?"

"Mortimer," said his lordship quietly, overlooking the sneer evident in the latter portion of the question, "Mortimer is not at Leinster House, as I thought you knew already. His eyes shall never see that nor——"

"What has become of him? Where is he?" asked Redmond, now grown almost furious by the repeated delays in getting the desired information. "Half a dozen times already I have asked this question, and failed to get an answer. Once more, where is Mortimer? I have an account to settle with him that must not be delayed for a moment. Where is he?"

"You will settle no account with Mortimer, Redmond, in this world at least?"

"Why? Will you be good enough to say why, my lord?"

"Because, Redmond," said his lordship, sinking his voice, and with much kindliness and gentleness of manner, "because—but I am quite unable to explain now. You must come with me, I am quite overpowered."

"My lord, I shall not stir one pace from this until you answer my question. Where *is* Mortimer? Where is the scoundrel? Is there no friend who will answer my question? Are all leagued against me?"

"Redmond," said Lord Edward in a tone of great emotion, "this is not a moment for——"

"One thing, my lord," said Redmond with savage harshness, "it is not a moment for—it is not a time for trifling with *me*. Are you prepared to answer, or shall I have to seek the information from others?"

"If you will but have patience—and hear me—you —"

"Patience! my lord!" exclaimed Redmond, drawing abruptly back a step or two. "Is this a time to preach patience? My lord, I should have expected that you and yours would have stretched out the right hand of friendship and protection to my sister; you have failed in that. But I am here now; and by my father's soul! I shall see that she is protected though all the world were leagued with Mortimer. Once more: Where is he?" He was quivering with impatience and passion. The muscles stood out like whip-cord on his forehead.

Lord Edward Fitzgerald stepped up to him and whispered a single word in his ear.

"What!" exclaimed Barrington his whole manner changing of a sudden, and falling back a pace or two.

"True enough, Redmond," said the other with visible marks of astonishment on his face, and in his voice.

CHAPTER XXXVIII.

THE FRENCH FLEET SAILS.

AWAITING further commands from Carnot, Tone spent the next few days in great unrest. Bound by his word to the Director, he was unable to communicate the secret of the recent stir in Irish affairs to Eugene, who was in high delight, but in much bewilderment, over the swift turn which matters had taken. For, whereas before the name of Ireland was not even mentioned, now the name was constantly on the lips of the high officials of the War Office. A hundred surmises were broached as to the cause of the sudden change, but all equally futile, and dismissed after a moment's consideration. For Tone kept carefully locked, even from him, the knowledge he alone carried in his breast.

They were seated in Tone's apartment discussing affairs one evening shortly after, when the landlady came up with a letter for the latter, which a messenger had brought. It was marked " In haste, and confidential."

"I wonder who is this from," he said as he glanced at the superscription. "It is unofficial and I am unacquainted with the handwriting. Here goes, however," he added carelessly, breaking the seal.

He had read only a few lines, however, when he started up and paced the room.

R

"Why this is wonderful, gentlemen! This is astounding!" he cried excitedly.

"What is it—what is the news?" asked, simultaneously, MacNevin and Eugene.

"Here is the letter—read it," handing the note to the latter.

"Why, it is from François," said Eugene, glancing at the signature.

"Read it aloud. Let us hear what it says," said MacNevin impatiently.

"Here it is:—

["'Private.]
"'Rochelle, Friday.

"'CITIZEN TONE—This is to inform you that we sail from Rochelle to-morrow for the Irish coast—1,600 men, with artillery and ammunition. Humbert commands.

"'FRANÇOIS.'"

MacNevin gave a long whistle, whilst all three looked at one another in much bewilderment and astonishment.

"What *is* the meaning of this, gentlemen? Are the fates playing us a freak of fortune, or is the letter a bogus one?"

"The letter is genuine enough. It is François's writing, and he does not usually play pranks—at least not in matters of moment."

"What do you make of this, Tone?" asked MacNevin again, after a pause. "Is it the work of a good or an evil genius?"

"It is difficult to say," said Tone perplexedly.

"Sixteen hundred men! They might as well send a corporal's guard. Of what earthly use are sixteen hundred men?" insisted MacNevin.

"It depends upon circumstances. It is a small force no doubt, but if landed on the coast of Wexford or Dublin"——

"I venture to say that is precisely what they will *not* do," broke in MacNevin impatiently. "And if not they might as well send them to Iceland."

"Surprising that François does not say where they are destined for—what part of the coast," said Eugene.

"Very likely he does not know," said MacNevin irritably.

"More likely he did not like to run the risk of stating in a message coming by hand."

"It is most tantalising—this skeleton intelligence on such a weighty matter," said Eugene, with a vexation almost equal to that of MacNevin.

"I would venture a wager," said Tone, "I can guess the cause of your annoyance, Eugene."

"Easily guessed. It is the utter want of information," said Eugene.

"I doubt it."

"Well, what is it?"

"That you are not sailing with the expedition yourself."

"I confess," said Eugene, laughing, "there is something of that at foot of it. But they might, at least have offered me command of one of the frigates."

"There is a higher command awaiting you mayhap."

"It is not the rank of the appointment I care about. I should rather go as seaman before the mast than be left behind."

"Do you know what I think?" said Tone, after a few minutes' pause.

"No. What?"

"This expedition is but the forerunner of a larger one —a mere decoy-duck to distract attention."

"Perhaps so. I hope in heaven it may be so."

"You will find it is. It is out of the question to think that the Directory would have dispatched such a force on such a mission."

"But they might at least let us know what they were doing. Who should they consult but us?"

"What character does Humbert bear?"

"Excellent. A skilful, intrepid general. If circumstances are favourable, he will give a good account of treble his number."

"If it be not too late ——"

"Hallo!" interrupted MacNevin, who had risen, and was standing at the window looking down on the street. "Here comes a hussar with a dispatch for one or other of you, gentlemen."

"So there is," said Eugene, walking to the window also, and looking down. "An orderly from the War Office. His message may throw some light on the business."

"A letter for Citizen Tone," said the landlady, entering with a large official letter in her hands.

"Well, Tone—what is it? Who is it from?" asked MacNevin, as that gentleman broke the seal and read it.

"It is from Carnot—Citizen Carnot."

"From Carnot!" exclaimed both.

"That's the writer's name"

"For heaven's sake what does he say? The Directory must be pretty much in earnest," said Eugene, "when *he* writes."

"He wishes to see me immediately," said Tone, handing him the letter.

"It is laconic enough. It is in his handwriting, however. Citizen Carnot does not waste words, no more than powder and shot."

"He used these latter to some advantage," commented Tone, as he proceeded to arrange his toilet.

"Yes, he managed to make the most of his bullets in the early days of the revolution. He had not much ammunition—nor men either—to throw away."

"What can he have to say?" queried MacNevin. "I hope it may be that ten thousand men are being mobilised at Havre for embarkation."

"Heaven knows."

"Well, the mystery will be soon out," said Eugene. "Meantime do not keep us too long in suspense, Tone. Come back as soon as the interview is over."

"Nothing worries me like suspense," said MacNevin. "I vote we have a cigar and a glass of Burgundy to while away the time."

"Here are both—at your service," said Tone. "And now for Citizen Carnot. Pray heaven he may maintain his old character as organiser of victory this one time."

Arrived at the war office, in the Hotel Louvre, Tone presented his card. He was quickly admitted, and ushered along corridor after corridor until he was shown into an ante-chamber, magnificently furnished, and filled with generals in full uniform and other high officers awaiting an interview.

Tone, under other circumstances, would have been more or less embarrassed at the distinguished company in which he found himself—generals, ministers of state, foreign ambassadors, naval officers of high rank, all in glittering uniforms and with their insignia of rank. Here was an eastern ambassador with quaint fez and burnouse, and diamond star sparkling on his breast. There a distinguished general who had clutched honour, position, and renown from the ranks by desperate valour, as his empty sleeve well attested. Standing at the fire-place, in deep conversation with the Russian Ambassador, was one whose name and fame were European, but whose ending was to be so ignoble and terrible—the general who carried his army safely in their famous retreat through the Black Forest—Moreau. And many others then undistinguished, but who were afterwards to fill Europe with their fame and their deeds of prowess.

But a passing glance at some of the more prominent and renowned was all that Tone vouchsafed. Personal matters were pressing at his heart and absorbed his whole thoughts. What project was on foot ? Was there really a determination to send sufficient aid to Ireland ? and, if so, when, from where, and how !

Whilst these questions were revolving themselves in his head the door leading from the ante-chamber was flung open and a herald cried :

" Citizen Tone !"

The animated conversation at once ceased, and for a moment Tone, so filled was he with his own thoughts, doubted the name that was called.

" Citizen Tone !" the herald called again.

Tone presented himself as the others fell back.

The herald beckoned him forward.

Passing the door, which closed after him, Tone entered the inner ante-chamber, and thence into a richly furnished room, where, under the soft light of a chandelier, sat at a round table, covered with maps and papers, two gentlemen —one in uniform, the other not.

The latter was Carnot, who with warm courtesy stood up to welcome his visitor.

"You see I have not forgotten you, Citizen Tone," he said, pointing to a map of Ireland that lay on the table. "We have been discussing Irish matters, and we want your assistance and opinion."

He paused. Tone bowed.

"This is General Hardy."

Tone saluted the general. He had never seen him before, but was well acquainted with his name.

"It is right to tell you, Citizen Tone, that there sails this day for the Irish coast, an expedition under General Humbert, whom you met with me last time. He is an able and energetic officer. The expedition is a small one, and the general sails for the western coast."

"The western coast!" repeated Tone disappointedly.

"Yes; I should indeed have asked for your advice previously, but that the business here is so multifarious, and I was unfortunately unacquainted until this evening with your address. The reason it was dispatched there is this —I find from recent reports that have reached us from Ireland *via* Hamburg, that it is along the eastern coast" —laying his finger on the maritime counties of Leinster— "that the war of insurrection rages. Further, I find that the insurgents are being severely pressed. To make a diversion in their favour by causing the withdrawal of the royal troops, and to excite revolt in a district which seems quiescent at present, I have directed them to land here" —pointing to Killala Bay—" where there seems to be a capacious harbour and good anchorage. What do you think of the project?"

"I think it is ably designed," said Tone, much struck with the reasoning.

"I am glad to have your approbation."

"But," said Tone, hesitating, "but it is a very small force—small to send on such an important mission."

"I anticipated that observation. General Humbert brings with him but an advance guard. More could not be done in the extreme haste. General Hardy is under orders to sail as soon as ever he can from Brest with three thousand men, and effect a further lodgment on the northern shores—somewhere here," pointing to Lough Swilly. And General Kilmaine is to mobilise a further corps, as soon as may be, of some ten thousand men to effect a landing on the eastern coast as near the metropolis as possible. What think you now?"

"I think you have assured the independence of Ireland," said Tone, whilst his heart beat rapidly and exultantly at this magnificent intelligence.

"If there be staying power in your nation they shall get sufficient help."

"If there be," thought Tone, with a choking feel in his throat as the dread possibility occurred to him of the revolt being crushed out before even the first of these detachments could arrive.

"By the way, there is a young naval officer recently escaped from England. Do you know him?"

"Citizen Eugene Lefebre."

"Yes; he is a good officer I am told, and knows much about Ireland. Do you know where he is to be found?"

"I have only just parted from him."

"Very good. Tell him to report at once to Admiral Bompart, who will command the fleet. It will sail from Brest or from Camaret. Meantime—I suppose *you* would wish to go, too?"

"Go!" said Tone earnestly. "For two years I have been longing, yearning for the day to come."

"I see!" said Carnot, smiling. "You Irishmen, are all so enthusiastic! You will, in that case, place yourself under General Hardy's orders. You will have your present rank. The expedition will sail as soon as ready. Report to General Hardy in the morning. Good-bye! I am sorry I cannot discuss the matter further with you, but there is a large number of people waiting for audience. Once more—good-bye, and success to the Irish cause!"

"Well, Citizen Tone—for I suppose Carnot has imbued you with thoroughly republican notions by this time, if you did not possess them before," said Eugene, on his return. "What news? What says the brain-carrier of the French nation?"

"The news is capital," said Tone, paring the end of a cigar, as he prepared himself for a long smoke and chat in the highest of good humour.

"I am glad to hear it. We have had such a recurrence

of calamitous information that a rift in the clouds is most opportune. The expedition has sailed?"

" It has."

" Where for ?"

" The Irish coast."

" And with what intention? What does he think it will do?"

" Keep the insurrection alive until a large force sails."

" Right. Citizen Carnot—though my family is under but scant obligation to him—is a right vigorous worker for all that."

" Do you know him, then ?"

" I might say he knows me anonymously."

" A rather indistinct knowledge, is it not ?"

" I don't know that I could express the acquaintance more aptly. But that is of no consequence at present, for ——"

" On the contrary, it is of consequence."

" Ah, how ?"

" He made inquiries about you."

" He did—eh ?" exclaimed Eugene, suddenly.

" Yes."

" What did he say ?"

" That you were a capable officer, knew Ireland well, and requested you to report at once to Bompart—who is to be admiral of the next fleet."

" Oh, that's all—is it ?"

" That's all. The information seemed to alarm you."

" Why, so it did, Tone. It is only the recurrence of an old sensation."

" It is the first time I **knew** you were subject to alarms."

" Why, my good friend, when one has lived for months —indeed I might say for years—with the dread of the guillotine on him, he is apt to be readily startled. I remember a time when a call, ' Midshipman Lefebre is wanted on deck,' seemed to be forerunner of a journey to the Place de la Greve, and an introduction to Dr Guillotine."

" You were not an *aristocrat*—were you?" asked Tone chaffingly, as he threw himself into an arm-chair and lit his cigar.

"I dare say they would readily impeach me as one then—rightly or wrongly. And so I am to report to Bompart?"

"Yes. Do you know him?"

"Perfectly. I sailed with him to the Indies, where he knocked to pieces the English fleet, with two line-of-battle ships and two frigates. I remember the battle as if it were a thing of yesterday. So I ought. We ran out a broken mast from our vessel, *La Vengeur*, to the British 74, and our fellows raced like wild cats along it in their bare feet, and boarded and captured the Englishman. I wish you saw the scene on that deck when in the middle of the smoke that canopied the ships, our men leaped in. I fancy tougher work was never set to Frenchmen. It was cut and thrust of cutlass at close quarters, and I wager you more men died in that quarter of au-hour's fight than ever died in the same size of space before or since. Yes, Bompart is not likely to pull down his colours without just and sufficient cause."

"Were you one of the boarders, Eugene?" asked MacNevin, whose interest had been aroused by the speaker's words.

"I was second on the mast, and first to leap on board. De Fournieux, a brother middy, was first to race along the mast—they guillotined his father, a naval captain, in Paris, a few days before, but the poor lad never heard of it—and, a bullet striking him, he fell, before I could grasp him, between the two vessels. This mark will serve as rememberance of it (he pointed to the cicatrice on his temple), for an Englishman's cutlass left it there on that occasion."

"What experience of the world and of life you sailors must have!" was the admiring comment of MacNevin.

"It was no pleasant experience, I assure you. With the very atmosphere of France saturated with suspicion of treachery, with every French mind electrical with dread of betrayal, it was no joke to lose a battle or a ship. Courtmartials made short work of defeated admirals, and every man, gentle or simple, on board was bound to do whatever lay in him to win victory. I tell you men valued their lives at little moment in these days. But we have been rambling away from the subject. When am I to report?"

"In the morning."

"But Bompart is in the Bay of Camaret."

"You will have to travel thither without delay."

"Well, thank heaven I am on active duty once more. Continued idleness here were nearly as bad as being on board the British hulks. And now, having heard this joyful news, I think I shall retire. I shall sleep more soundly to-night than I have done for a long time; the murmurs of the sea on the Irish coast will be in my ears."

"I wish it were really and actually in mine," said Tone. "It is odd that whilst everything was uncertain and changeful, I was strong in hope, but now that everything looks promising I begin to feel chokeful of unrest and uncertainty."

"The result of too much anxiety, dear Tone. It is a feeling you should banish. When men have done their best they should leave the rest to Providence. It is not in man to control the future."

"Shall we see you again?" asked MacNevin, as Eugene prepared to depart.

"I fancy not. I have some calls to make and some little business to transact in the morning, and the diligence starts early."

"We shall see you at Camaret, then."

"And the sooner the better. I wager you Bompart loses no time if Hardy does not. What a beautiful moonlight night—how bright and silver-like the moonbeams fall on the carpet! Good-bye."

CHAPTER XXXIX.

THE STORM.

WITHOUT delay Tone reported himself to Hardy.

Thenceforward his time was fully taken up in aiding his chief in the details of the expedition, acting constantly as the general's secretary. It was only then he began to see some of the difficulties in connection with the fitting out of an armed force of the kind

So many things had to be arranged, so many matters to be provided for. There was the selection of the regiments best fitted for irregular warfare, such as that in Ireland might chance to be ; the gathering together of these from the different divisions with which they were brigaded through France ; the selection of suitable artillery ; the packing up of cannon-balls and powder and fire-arms and bullets ; the storing away of thousands of muskets, and carbines, and spears, and swords ; the selection of horses and accoutrements and the proper storing of them—in a word, the embarkation of three thousand men. The number might look small on paper, but before they were ready the impatient Irishman had full time to see what responsibilities attached to the proper carriage and provisioning of even that number closely packed for some weeks on board a limited number of ships, and in the face of an enemy vigilant and all powerful at sea.

With superhuman energy he worked both night and day to hurry the expedition. His heart lay with the gallant men in Wexford and elsewhere making an unavailing struggle against overwhelming forces. No matter likely to affect the expedition's welfare or success was left untouched or unattended to ; and it was with a heart delighted and joyous, but with a body weary and worn, that on the evening of the 19th September, 1798, he dined for the last time with his wife and children and MacNevin, previous to his departure the next day for Camaret, where the fleet was gathered.

The evening, nathless the sorrow of separation in the morning, was full of pleasure, and all were bright with hope and promise.

" You will wait for Kilmaine, MacNevin," he said, as they separated at a late hour. " He holds nine thousand men in reserve to start with as soon as possible after news of our successful landing reaches him."

" I should much rather go now."

" I am sure you would, but Hardy wishes it. And I, too. The Directory will need some one to consult, and there is no one here so reliable as you."

"In that case," said MacNevin, disappointedly, "I suppose I must; but I do so with great reluctance. I am thirsting to see Ireland again. I am longing to see the green flag at last unfurled on her hills."

"You will see it in good time, and all the surer that it will lie in your power to hasten Kilmaine's force. You will be the good genius at his elbow to hurry him on. Carnot has given you a commission in his brigade, and attached you as aide-de-camp to his staff."

"I am obliged to him, but, as far as that is concerned, where Ireland's cause is at stake, I should as freely fight in the ranks. It is not my own honour I look to, but my country's freedom. It has been the solitary star that shone on my life—the one bright hope that beckoned me on."

"Unless the fates are more than usually unpropitious the hour has struck when her freedom cometh," said Tone enthusiastically, as he parted from his friend. "The sound of French cannon on Irish hills will ring the knell of tyranny, and the flash of the guns will kindle the light of freedom never to be quenched again in her valleys."

"Heaven send it," said MacNevin; and they parted.

September 18, 1798, Bompart sailed from the Bay of Camaret. The fleet consisted of one first-class line-of-battle ship, The Hoche—so named at Tone's special desire in honour of the dead hero who had so strongly testified his admiration for Ireland and his unaccomplished desire to aid in recovering her freedom—and eight frigates. A reconnaissance by Carlo in his swift sailing pinnace had shown that for some reason—probably because they had gone to the coast of Spain to watch the Spanish fleet—the English vessels were nowhere to be seen.

The day was beautifully fine as the nine men-of-war spread their sails above the water, attended by an immense crowd of transports. Not a cloud broke the clear arch of summer sky, and, save where the favourable breeze disturbed the surface of the water, the azure above was reflected in the brightening sea beneath.

Taking a long sweep to the westward, the admiral sought to avoid coming in contact with the British fleet. In this he was successful, but he met a fiercer foe.

For some days the fleet sailed on in splendid order, a magnificent sight to behold.

"If this weather lasts, Eugene," said Tone to his friend, who had been appointed captain of the commander's vessel, "we shall see the headlands of Ulster shortly."

"Look yonder, Tone. Do you see that sunset?"

He pointed to the west, where, on the far edge of the distant horizon, there rose above the rim of the Atlantic a black mass of clouds, the edges of which were turned into fiery redness by the beams of the sinking sun, and so made the centre to look of pitch blackness.

It was a weird sight to see, and so Tone thought.

"Have you ever seen the like of that before, Tone?"

"I don't think I have. It is very remarkable."

"It is something more than remarkable. It is dangerous."

"Indications of a storm?"

"I never saw such a sunset as that," said Eugene gravely, "but one, and that was in the East Indies. I shall long remember it."

"Preceding a storm?"

"Preceding such a storm as rarely sweeps the surface of the sea. When it was over, the Orient, a 74 man-of-war, had foundered with all hands, and the Fundroyant was high and dry ashore—a complete wreck."

"I hope there is no occasion to dread anything of the kind now," said Tone anxiously.

"I hope so, but I doubt it. What think you, admiral?" —to Bompart, who had joined them.

"That is an ill-looking sky, Eugene," said the admiral quietly. "It means mischief."

"Just what I have been thinking."

"It is spreading even now."

Tone glanced westward. The cloud did indeed seem to be spreading, like a funeral pall, its intense blackness over a larger portion of the sky.

"Eugene, I think it were wiser to signal the fleet to sail in more extended order. Abundance of sea room will be wanting to-night."

"I quite agree with you, admiral. There is a storm, and a dangerous one, imminent."

Orders were immediately given from the flag-ship for the fleet to sail more widely. The order was immediately obeyed. Most of the captains had already noticed the sinister and threatening cloud, and had already anticipated the direction.

It was surprising—surprising to Eugene even, who had long experience of the sea and storm—to see how rapidly the night fell, how swiftly the dark sky flung its forbidding hue over the water.

"Look, Tone! look yonder! There goes the beginning of heaven's artillery."

A rift seemed to have formed in the centre of the blackness, from which came, like the glow from a wizard's cauldron, a streak of reddish grey weirdly illuming the water.

"That is the hurricane, Tone; the lightning will come presently."

Springing from his side, Eugene issued the necessary instructions to furl the sails and let the ship run under bare poles.

Whilst they were executing the order Tone watched the wierd light travelling over the surface of the water, which latter seemed to grow grievously disturbed under its influence.

Suddenly the clouds gathered together, and at once out from their centre a red flash of lightning shot, streaking with sudden fire the black background of sky. At the same time a burst of thunder smote their ears, seeming in its extraordinary violence to peal beside them and to rumble along the atmosphere until it died away in the distant sky.

"We are in for it now," said Eugene, as the coming grey light rapidly approached. It was the hurricane sweeping along the water, and as it struck them its force would have blown the men off their feet had they not held on to the rigging.

The vessel keeled over on her side under its influence, and the few topsails that remained unfurled were torn to pieces as if they were made of cotton.

Thence afterwards it was one continuous storm.

It was difficult to say whether the ceaseless roar of the

wind and waves, the rolling discharges of thunder, or the red flashes of lightning sweeping in grand relief against the background of pitch-black sky, were the most astounding. The great man-of-war rolled and tumbled on the mountain waves as if it were the veriest cockleboat. Except for the flashes of lightning that for a heart's-beat of time lit up deck and mast and top-gallant yards with a fierce glare, they were plunging through sea and atmosphere black as Erebus.

So passed the night—a night of unspeakable horror within the huge unmanageable vessel. The only thing that inspired admiral and captain and seamen with confidence was that they had plenty of sea-room. There was but little danger from rocks or a lee coast, and unless she sprung a leak, or a huge gun broke from its fastenings and falling through the hold tore a hole in her bottom, she was sure, owing to the precautions, to weather the storm.

Day succeeded the terrible night, but the storm abated but little. And when it did it made up in duration for its slight cessation of violence.

For days heavy head winds continued on a violent sea, and it was so far in advance as the 9th of October when the storm entirely ceased, as it had arisen, at nightfall.

The admiral and Eugene took the bearings, and declared the vessel some eighty miles off the northern shores of Ireland.

CHAPTER XL.

DEFEAT OF THE EXPEDITION.

NEXT morning as the rays of the sun tipped the summits of the masts and the sea broke forth into brightness, a whistle came from the masthead.

"Ahoy! What is it?" shouted in response Admiral Bompart, who was standing with Tone and others at the poop.

In the surge of waters and the noise on deck the words

came, scarcely heard, or with vague indistinctness on their ears.

"What does he say?" inquired Tone eagerly.

"The fleet, I believe," said Bompart, with a quick glance around.

"No, I think not," said Tone. "Whatever it was, it was not that."

"We shall soon know," said the admiral impatiently. Then through his speaking trumpet he shouted aloud:

"We cannot hear you. Call louder."

"Land!" came in clear response from the top.

"Land?" echoed all around in tones of high delight. Short as their time had been at sea, the soldiers were delighted to find themselves once more near land.

"Ireland! Beloved land!" cried Tone, as his eyes strained through the circling horizon in front to get a glimpse of the land for which he had worked so earnestly, and towards which his thoughts had oft so yearningly turned.

But the sharpest eye could as yet detect no sign of land. The grey white mists of morning, curving over the brightening surface of waters, hid for the present further view from their eyes.

Meantime the stately ships, with all sails spread to catch the fresh breeze setting in from the north, ploughed their way through the yielding sea. The foam swept up as they careened over, in the swiftness of their going, to the bulwarks; and as the early fresh rays of dawn fell upon it they seemed to turn it into green and gold. It was a setting of snow-white pearls in rubies and sea-green amethysts, with here and there a placement of sun-red cornelian. High up, in the great rim of heaven, the white cirrhi were purpling with the fresh rosy beams, and were rapidly vanishing into the deep blue. It was at once a sight enlivening and glorious—one of nature's wondrous masterpieces—and enough to make the human heart leap responsive. A thrill of rejoicing seemed to stir in the hearts of the group of officers gathered on the poop.

"It is a pleasant augury of our expedition to Ireland," said Bompart, who had often enough seen dawnings at sea, but never anything to equal this

"It is magnificent," said General Hardy, as his eye, taking in with one sweep the glowing expanse of sea, fell on the wide space of sails now gorgeously coloured as with the pencil of an old master.

"It is only a foretaste, gentlemen, of what this land you are coming to is like," said Tone, exultantly.

"So very fair as that?" asked Bompart, laughingly.

"Fairer you never saw. Fair in the springtime when the grass grows green, fair in the summer when the hills bask in the sunshine; but when, in the autumn, the trees grow to brown and golden, sweeter land to look upon there never was."

"Pity its people did not fight for its freedom, then!" said an old officer, with a half sneer.

"So it is," said Tone. "They often did, but unfortunately they were always cursed with incapable leaders. But now," added he, "their destinies seem to be altered, and the flag of France lifted on their shores or on their hills will give them a new light to victory."

"If there be any worth in them it assuredly will," said Hardy eagerly. "And talking of shores, is that a cloud I see yonder, rising blue over the grey mists, or is it augur of further storm? Heavens knows we have had enough of storms."

"It is not sign of storm," said the admiral. "There is no sign now but that of fine weather. It is—land."

"Land!" cried a dozen delighted voices in unison, as all eyes turned to that mysterious island—to many of them a *terra incognita*—which had been so much in their thoughts for the past three weeks.

"Ireland—Innishowen!" cried Tone, as he looked at the chart to find out their position, and knew from a glance at the map that the peaks now rising bluely from the bosom of the mists were the hills of the peninsula just named.

Eugene had been standing apart during the conversation, looking at the mists receding before the advancing vessel and steadily disappearing before the morning sun.

The words fell on his ears with startling effect, arousing him as if with an electric shock, from his reverie.

"Land—Ireland!" he repeated after them—"where?"

s

"Yonder, my dear captain—yonder," said Tone, catching his arm in delight. "Do you not see the cloud-like peaks rising from the sea right to the south?"

"I do not see them," said Eugene, his eyes failing him partly because of their eagerness to catch the long looked for objects.

"Do you see that small boat to the south?"

Eugene nodded.

"Lift your eyes a little above it and see where the sun-rays are just now brightening the hills."

"I see them! I see them!" cried Eugene delightedly. "Hurrah for Ireland and Seamore! At last my eyes are blessed with a glance at its green hills."

"You seem to be as glad as I am myself," said Tone, laughing at the enthusiasm of his friend.

"Glad! I could not be more entranced if it were a vision of Paradise that fell on my eyes."

"Yet it is not your native land—nor are you as long from seeing it as I am."

"Nevertheless," said the captain, "I doubt if anyone could rejoice more at seeing it. It is simply delightful to think that to-day we shall tread on Irish soil, and sleep to-night on Irish ground."

"There is an old maxim in Ireland," said Tone, whose first enthusiasm had given way to a fit of depression, "that there is many a slip between the milking of a cow and the tasting of the butter; and without at all seeking to throw cold water on your high-heartedness, I must confess I am not at all sanguine that we shall."

"What is there to prevent us?"

"Why, for the matter of that, anything—everything. Under any circumstances I am glad to see the shores of Ireland again. But look how we come! After a disastrous voyage of three weeks rounding the northern seas, we come within sight of Ireland with one line-of-battle ship and three frigates. Think what an invading force that constitutes! It is the old story of the Bantry Bay expedition over again."

"I should not have expected these words from you," said Eugene disappointedly.

"Nor should I, perhaps, have spoken them. But I

cannot conceal the disappointment I feel—and I never realised it so thoroughly as now, when after a long absence my eyes fall on Irish hills again—at the nonsuccess of my efforts on Ireland's behalf. It sinks like a leaden weight at my heart."

"A smaller force has often worked wonders in other countries."

"So it has; but the day has passed for that in Ireland. Four months ago and it would have been different."

"You are unnecessarily downhearted."

"Perhaps I am. But I shall not be so any longer," said Tone, with a quiet, sad smile, as his eyes rested on the headlands of Innishowen, now coming gradually nearer and looking beyond measure lovely as the slanting rays of the morning sun fell on their sides, mantling them with rosy light. "It is not for one who for years has not looked upon his native shore to feel long disheartened when such a sight as yonder meets his gaze."

"Is it not beautiful—superb?" cried Eugene enthusiastically. "And so the admiral thinks, too; see how intently he is gazing at it. Let us join him."

"Is it not magnificent, *mon admiral?*" said he, when they had joined the party.

The commander and several of the officers were gazing through their glasses in the direction of the shore, and Eugene, tapping the former on the shoulder, emphasized his remark.

"Magnificent, Eugene?" said the admiral, turning around with a questioning look on his face.

"The scenery—that noble range of hills rejoicing in the morning sunlight. I fancy there is nothing in the world to surpass it."

"Oh! the scenery. It is fine, very fine, now that you draw my attention to it," said Bompart with a smile; "but I confess I was not thinking of that, nor looking at it."

"There must be something else strange in view?" said Eugene, becoming querist in turn.

"There is—something that has greater attraction and interest for us just now than your Irish scenery. Take that glass in your hands, look over the western shoulder of that hill that fronts you, and tell me if any object strikes your view."

Eugene took the telescope, and, having adjusted it, glanced in the direction indicated. For some time he gazed in silence, then suddenly lowered the glass and turning round, said :

"The semaphore."

"Precisely. It has been working rapidly for the past quarter of an-hour. They are signalling some information."

"Can no one read it ?" asked Eugene.

"Unfortunately no. The book containing the English code of signals was mislaid in the hurry of our despatch."

"They are signalling our advance ?"

"They are ; but whether giving warning to forts or to a fleet, we are, owing to the absence of the book, unable to tell."

There was a pause of some duration, during which the vessel, steering to the west, left the signalling semaphore far behind.

Standing close in by Malin Head and leaving the little island of Innistrahul to the right, the fair expanse of Lough Swilly began to open out before them.

Suddenly an exclamation burst from one of the officers as he pointed with outstretched hands in the direction of the Lough. All eyes followed his motion, and as they did a thrill passed through the assembled group.

For standing down the bay, with close set sails, and with decks apparently cleared for action, was the British fleet.

Striking and imposing they looked—six sail of the line, one razee ship of sixty guns, and two frigates.

"That explains the working of the semaphore, gentlemen," said the admiral quietly, as he looked with long and eager glance at the stately liners moving towards the opening of the bay.

"And ends the expedition," said Tone.

"I should think so," said Bompart, turning his head around to look at the three frigates, the remnant of his fleet, that sailed some distance behind him. "We are too few to win, and too near to escape."

"Small chance of winning with that splendid force of vessels to contend with," said Eugene, glancing with admiration at the fleet as it sailed forward in far-extended order.

"None whatever," burst from many officers at the same moment. The fact was palpable to all.

"Well, gentlemen, this is somewhat untoward, though not unexpected. Our frigates behind may escape; we cannot. Surrender is out of the question. What shall be done?"

"Fight her while she lasts," said Eugene, and as he spoke a cheer arose from the band of officers assembled, announcing their hearty concurrence in the proposal.

"I thought that would be about your decision, gentlemen," said the admiral, "and, that being so, I think we had better prepare for business and signal the frigates to make their escape. Their mission here is ended."

"I fancy their mission anywhere is ended. There is but little chance of their escaping," said Eugene.

"They must take their chance for that. It would simply be a sacrifice of the soldiers they carry to bring them into action here. Signal the Roise to come near; we shall transfer to her the line regiment from our own vessel. They would only cumber us during the action, and be needlessly slaughtered."

The frigate was accordingly signalled to draw near, which she did, and in a very short time the troops on board the Hoche were re-embarked on board the Roise, whilst the officers, sailors, and marines of the former worked with untiring energy to get the vessel into fighting trim.

When the Roise was about to put off, the admiral walked over to where Tone was standing watching with lonely indifference the transfer of the troops.

"Another day of evil to Ireland," Tone said, as the former took his arm.

"It cannot be helped," said the admiral, with deep sympathy for the disappointed patriot.

"Not now, I daresay," said Tone bitterly.

"The fates will have it so," said Bompart. "I grieve for your many disappointments—I assure you I do—but there is little use in grieving against what is decreed. And there is but little time for talking over the matter just now—or sorrowing over it. Why I come to you is this: To prevent the inevitable sacrifice of these regiments, we are sending them—if we can—back to France. The Roise is a good sailer and will outrun their fastest vessel. She is pretty certain by making a wide sweep to reach France or a friendly Continental port in safety. You must sail in her."

"I?" queried Tone, turning sharply round and facing the admiral, his anger at the suggestion showing itself in his pale face and whitening lips. "I?"

"Yes, my dear Tone. Do not be angry. *We* are Frenchmen and shall find a soldier's death on the open deck or in the sea; but you are not called on to do so—for this fight—battle it cannot be called—can avail naught for Ireland. It can only preserve the honour of France and her fleet."

"And you therefore suggest that I should fly from Ireland, now that I have, after many years' absence, come almost within swimming distance of her shores?" Tone asked disdainfully.

"Do not be angry with me, my dear Tone," said the admiral deprecatingly, but with gentle and chivalrous courtesy, as he saw the hot blood rush into the pale face of the speaker. "There stands on the deck of the Hoche to-day none readier to sacrifice his life in a good or brave cause than you. But consider. We fight now for our honour—not for Ireland. Our guns are shotted for the stainless honour of our flag. The expedition is at an end. We Frenchmen shall die on the deck, which is still French land, or we shall go down with our vessel. You have no cause in all this—no share in the national honour. *You* may still hope to work for your country."

"I have no choice to make," said Tone resolutely, but with a voice that trembled not from sorrow but the anguish of disappointment. "I have come within sight of the shores of Ireland and I shall not fly from them."

"There is another consideration," said Bompart gravely. "If the Hoche should be captured without being sunk, and that those of her crew living are taken prisoners, they would be treated as prisoners of war. How would *you* fare under such circumstances? I think it right to put this view before you. You shall be tried, possibly— I know these English well—as an Englishman in arms against his country."

"It matters not. I shall not go from the shores of Ireland now that I am come within view of them, let what will betide. I said I should come in the next expedition if but a corporal's guard sailed for Ireland, and I have come, I shall not leave the Hoche—you willing— whilst a plank of her deck holds together or a gun is able to send a bullet to the foe. Your men have come at my solicitation—I shall share their dangers, and, if it be so willed, go beneath the waves with them."

"Bravely spoken: and right soothing words to hear," said the admiral. "I would our expedition had been more successful, and I can and do sympathise with your disappointed hopes and with your struggling land. As it is we can only fight and die together."

"Bravely spoken—because Tone spoke," said Eugene, coming from behind. "Who would have expected him to have said otherwise? And *mon admiral*, you are losing precious time to but little purpose. The fleet are bearing straight for us. Every moment is necessary for preparation. Let the Roise cut her cables and put on all press of sail whilst there is yet time. We shall delay, I hope, any vessel that attempts to follow. We have the power to cripple, if not to conquer, left us yet at any rate."

"Very well; give the necessary orders, then, for her to make sail," answered the admiral.

In a few moments after the Roise had slipped her cable, and with flowing sheets was standing out to sea; whilst the clangour and din proceeding with greater energy than ever on board the Hoche, showed the unmistakable intention of her men and officers.

It was a moment of supreme excitement.

About to be surrounded by several vessels, some of them more powerful, and all equal in strength and armament, there lay before her the chances of being sunk or captured. Hope there was none. Yet no one on board—and Tone watched their movements eagerly—showed the slightest symptom of despondency, not to say fear. Their whole anxiety seemed to be to make a bold fight of it, and either to let the vessel go down with the tricolor still flying from her top-mast or leave her shattered hulk for the enemy to capture. With death staring them palpably and unavoidably in the face, and for a cause not their own, he marvelled to see how from the lowest to the highest all worked with lighthearted energy and gaiety. Had they been preparing their ship for the welcome of some important visitor more pleasant words and more laughing faces could not be heard or seen on board.

Meantime the English fleet, emerging from the entrance to Lough Swilly, steadily advanced.

And truly an imposing sight they looked, as, everything having been got ready, the guns loaded and protruded through the port-holes, the shot and shell and powder ready to hand, the officers of the *Hoche* had time to take survey of them. One of them, the Valiant, was a considerable distance in advance of the others, and had reached to within a mile or less, when a flag ran up to her top-mast.

"A summons to surrender!" burst from many indignant voices.

"It is, indeed," said Bompart. "She shall get a fitting answer."

He walked over to where, beside a sixty-four pounder, the gunners stood with lighted torches. The *Hoche* stood broadside to the coming fleet, and the admiral carefully trained with his own hands the cannon on the summoner.

Taking the torch from the cannonier, he applied it to the touch-hole. A blinding explosion followed, a volume of white smoke rolled upwards, and the missile went speeding on its way. All eyes were immediately turned on the approaching vessel.

A cheer went up as they saw it strike the bulwarks, scattering the men around and throwing up a cloud of splinters. It had evidently done considerable harm, and, as they could see through their glasses, created great commotion on board.

In a moment after the colour just hoisted glided down the rope to the deck and the Valiant held on her way.

"That puts an end to all courtesies for the present," said Eugene laughingly, as the officers quickly departed to take up their different positions, leaving himself, the admiral, and Tone alone.

"It is pretty clear from their movements they did not expect that," said Bompart, still gazing through his glass.

"They are preparing to reply to it pretty energetically," said Eugene, as the huge vessel swept to leeward of them, bringing her long broadside of guns fairly abreast.

"They must have the first salute, then," said the admiral, as placing his trumpet to his mouth, he shouted, "Ready, men! Train your guns on her! Fire!"

Save the cries of the officers repeating the order, the tugging of ropes, and the noise of the shifting guns, there was no response for a minute or two.

The torches along the vast decks of the *Hoche*, burning dimly in the garish light of day, seemed, as they moved uneasily, weird and uncanny.

"How long they are getting ready!" thought Tone, his impatience making the seconds seem hours. "Will they never have done preparing? The enemy will be ready before them."

While he was yet considering, a sudden burst of thunder made him start from where he stood!

The red light, paling even the daylight, made him close his eyes involuntarily. The white mantle of smoke came in rolling gusts from the deck and from every port-hole in the long length of the vessel's side, until, floating upwards, it formed a vapoury canopy above them, through which the sun shone redly as in a fog. Unheeding of this, however, his first glance when the shock had passed and before yet the enveloping smoke had come, was at the foe.

The full force of the storm of heavy shot had told. The round bullets had struck her, making gaps in her sides, or splintering their massive planking.

Others, aimed higher, had struck the bulwarks or swept the deck, and one striking the second mast had smashed it, and it was, even while he looked, swaying unsteadily, merely sustained in its position by the ropes that connected it with the others and with the deck.

The whole thing had taking place in almost the twinkling of an eye, but the havoc wrought was indescribable The vessel, a moment before as trim and neat as if just turned from the builder's yard, so clean and new and ordered it looked, had in that short space of time become a scene of almost inextricable wreck and confusion!

A shot struck the carriage of one of the deck guns, overturning it and crushing several of the cannoniers that stood beside. A rush of sailors to the relief of their comrades; a loosening and disorderly falling about of the ropes that held the broken mast; a scattering of broken timbers around, in the air, and on the deck and the sea, and a crowd of forms tugging at the guns, were the last sights that Tone saw as the blinding smoke gathered over him, shutting the Valiant from his view.

"That broadside told," said Eugene in his ear, whilst yet the *Hoche* trembled with the recoil of her guns.

Tone was about to answer with an earnest affirmative, when a tremendous blow, as of a hundred huge iron mallets, struck the side of their vessel; and at the same moment a hissing whirlwind swept the deck, tearing through sails, splintering bulwarks, and rattling with sodden sound off their own guns.

It was the answering broadside from the enemy!

And a disastrous one it was. The flash of light, piercing even the sulphurous smoke that canopied them, had scarcely vanished when Tone, looking along the deck as far as it was visible, saw forms prone on it, or sailors staggering to their death. The officer in charge of the gun nearest him lay on his face under the trunnion, his cutlass still held firmly in his hand. Several of the men thereat had been also swept down in the rush of grape!

While Tone was watching with eager eyes, wholly oblivious of his own danger, the effects of the enemy's first broadside, and unconsciously wondering at the swiftness with which men are hurled into eternity—how ruthlessly the golden thread of life is snapped and torn by these speeding messengers of death—a rope that had been cut by a bullet fell, striking him on the face and for a moment blinding him.

At the same time a hand was laid on his shoulder and Eugene's voice was in his ears:

"That battery, Tone, has lost its officer. You must take charge of it."

He needed no further direction, but hurried to his post. The gun was not only unofficered but almost unmanned. Stripping off his gold-embroidered uniform, he aided the men to charge and load again, with his own hands ramming home the charge of canister that was to be their next offering to the foe. Thenceforward he knew but little of the work that went on beyond his own gun. Amid an entanglement of cut and fallen ropes, of patches and shreds of torn sails; amid cries from wounded men, hoarse commands from officers, and frantic cheers from the sailors as a broadside thundered at the enemy; amid whirlwinds of striking, hissing, tearing, and rending bullets, he fought on, loading and firing, as fast as hands could load and fire, at the unseen enemy—unseen in the canopy of smoke!

The continuous roar of thunder that filled the air around; the furious work that went on on deck; the hurrying swarthy forms that moved about, carrying powder and shot and shell, dimly seen in the choking cloud of sulphurous smoke—now black and grimy, save when a lurid flash from the belching cannon illumined it —rendered the scene a very Pandemonium. But he heard none of it. His whole thoughts and energies were given to the work at his hand. It was only when Eugene, laying hold of the cannon, said:

"This gun is too hot for further firing. You must let it cool," that his attention was withdrawn from the work in hand.

He turned to speak to Eugene, but the latter had vanished.

"Boarders forward! Cutlasses to the front!"

The command, shouted in Eugene's well-known voice, directed his attention to the other side of the vessel, from which the order proceeded; and turning to look there a strange sight met his eyes.

The tall masts and rigging of a huge vessel raised themselves in the air beside the *Hoche*.

Across the ribbed and torn bulwarks of the latter grappling irons had been thrown from the strange vessel; a rough passage of planks had been pushed across; and at this moment a crowd of barefooted sailors, with gleaming cutlasses in their hands, were hurrying therealong or jumping therefrom on to the deck.

So extremely quick was the movement, so little time did it occupy, that the grapples had hardly been thrown when the planks were pushed across and the English sailors were rushing along them.

The cry of "Boarders forward" brought leaping to their feet a band of Frenchmen, who, specially detailed for this purpose, had been lying on their faces, axe and cutlass in hand, along the deck beside the bulwarks. In a second they had thrown themselves on the boarders, and a furious hand-to-hand fight commenced!

The vigour of the British, or, perhaps, their number, was unequal to the determination and fury of the French, and in a brief space the deck was strewn with the dead, as the cleaving axe dealt them blow after blow. Some were forced by sheer bodily strength across the bulwarks, in deadly wrestling match, whence they fell headlong into the water between the two vessels. Others, there being no other escape from the uplifted axe, vaulted boldly across!

It was a terrible scene whilst it lasted!

Tone, standing at his gun, looked with something akin to amazement at the sudden and furious combat. The fray ended almost as soon as it had begun; the grappling irons were unhooked and thrown over; the end of the boarding plank—with the crowding sailors thereon, unable to advance, unable in the pressure from behind to retreat—was dropped into the sea.

A cheer went up from the conquerors as once more the thunders of a broadside, poured into the foe at a few feet distance, drowned all other noise and din.

It was a sorry sight—to behold, after this work of a few minutes, the mangled and cloven forms of the men lately vigorous and full of life, strewing that portion of the deck in every conceivable attitude and position. But the wreathing smoke, with kindly effect, gathered over and veiled the sight—hiding from men's gaze the cruel work of their hands.

"Bind this up, Tone. That was quick work—was it not?"

Eugene was standing beside him, whilst yet Tone was vaguely gazing through the smoke for him. There was an ugly gash in his right arm where an English cutlass point had gone through it, and it was bleeding fast.

"Hurry, Tone. The admiral is badly wounded, and I must get his directions whilst he is able to give them. Bind it up with a strip of linen. There! There, that will do."

"That was a terrible business, Eugene," said Tone, whilst he hastily bound up the wound.

"It was—short and sharp. There was not much quarter asked for or given. But not different from what has gone on elsewhere in the ship."

"The English vessels must be greatly damaged?" queried Tone, as he saw his friend departing, and longed to learn some news of the results of the last two hours' work.

"They are, but none so badly as ours. She cannot fight or float much longer. The guns are all too heated to fire much more. Scarcely a fourth of our gunners are alive at their guns, and there is five feet of water in the hold. She has been struck several times under water."

"What do you propose doing?"

"Whatever the admiral directs when I report to him. We have done all that men can do. We cannot fight much longer," said Eugene hurriedly.

"Do you suggest surrender?"

"No; I, for one, will not."

"If you cannot fight and will not surrender, what other course do you propose?"

"Blow her up! There are a hundred tons of powder yet in her magazines. That torch you hold will send her and half the enemy skyward, once I get the order."

"You are right. It is the fitting thing to do. For my part there is nothing more to be hoped for or lived for. It would be a fitting and a welcome end to my lost life and endeavours."

Eugene, his wound partially bound up, hastened away. Meantime, the lull that had accompanied and followed the attack of the boarding party was broken by a fresh outburst of cannonading; and, as if from all points of the compass, a concentration of artillery fire was poured upon the *Hoche* without intermission—now from this side, now from that, now from altogether—crashing into her sides, sweeping her decks, tearing through her portholes, killing or maiming the men and disabling the guns. Nevertheless, the unwounded of the devoted vessel stood pluckily by their guns, and, when the first fierce storm of the iron whirlwind was over, rapidly charged and shotted them: the battle went on furiously as ever—Tone's battery firing steadily at the flashing portholes of the foe, the only mark they had now to guide their aim by.

"Captain Lefebre wishes to see you," said a sailor, black and grimy enough to look negro-born, to Tone, just after a six-inch solid shot had carried away the trunnions of his gun, completely disabling it.

"It is well I am wanted somewhere, for I am wanted here no longer," thought Tone, as he turned away with the messenger.

Eugene was kneeling on the poop, beside a form lying thereon, whom, as soon as he approached, Tone recognised as the admiral. Some sand-bags piled beside him protected his wounded form from the enemy's bullets.

"I sent for you, Tone," said Eugene hurriedly and not without some embarrassment, "to acquaint you that in the present ruined and disabled condition of the *Hoche* it is necessary to surrender."

"To surrender!" said Tone.

"The admiral orders it. There are only two courses open. To blow her up, or fight until she sinks or is stormed anew by their boarders. The admiral declares both to be against the rules of war, the ship being no longer tenable or capable of defence."

"So you propose to surrender?—when?" asked Tone, with a look of pain and mortification.

"Immediately," said Eugene, as he raised himself from where he knelt receiving the wounded admiral's directions. "There is nothing else for it. As you are the one mainly concerned with the expedition, the admiral, with his usual courtesy, even in his dangerous state, desired that you should be made acquainted with the necessary and final step."

Leaving Tone to his reflections, Eugene proceeded to give the necessary directions.

The guns of the *Hoche* suddenly ceased firing; a tiny white flag ran up to the top-gallant yard-arm; and, as it did so, the great banner of the Tricolor came slowly down!

It had hung all day above the storm-cloud of battle, and as it descended from its proud position, dozens of gallant men who looked death steadily in the face closed their eyes that they should not see it. But there was never less reason for sorrow. For hours it had hung over a gallant battle against fearful odds, and it was surrendered if in defeat certainly not in dishonour.

At once, as if by magic, the firing ceased. A tremendous cheer of exultation burst from the crews of the English men-of-war, and in a few minutes a group of officers passed on board from one of the vessels.

Eugene advanced to meet them.

An officer, past middle age, whose breast was covered with stars and decorations, walked forward from the group.

"I am Sir John Borlase Warren," he said, bowing to Eugene, "admiral of the English fleet."

"In the stead of our Admiral Bompart, who lies wounded, I have to surrender the line-of-battle ship *Hoche*, of the French Republican fleet, and my sword."

"I must decline to take your sword," said the admiral, with a courteous wave of his hand. "You have fought a gallant if a reckless fight, and you shall wear it as becomes a brave and fearless officer. Where is the admiral?"

Eugene brought him to where the French admiral lay, whilst the remainder of the English officers scattered themselves through the ship—some to take curious note of the condition she was in after the fiery ordeal to which she had been subjected, others to look after the prisoners and their arms, and not a few, with quick intelligence, to the magazines, for it had been known that the *Hoche* carried an immense quantity of powder in her hold. The marvel was that in the terrific bombardment to which she had been subjected it had not been blown up long before. But, having been built into compartments surrounded with tanks of water, any opening made by a bullet only formed the entrance for an inrush of water, which speedily damping the explosive material negatived the effect of the projectile. There was still, however, the tremendous danger that some hand, full of revenge or desperation, might yet blow her as well as the surrounding fleet into mid air.

But there was no attempt of the kind made, or if any had been in preparation, the measures taken had been sufficiently swift to intercept them.

All the arrangements for the safety of their prize were carefully made; and when her gaping wounds were staunched and made water-tight, the fleet, many of the vessels of which were terribly shattered and battered, bearing their prize away, sailed up the open waters of Lough Swilly.

The mellow sun of an Autumn evening, glowing over the hills of Donegal, lit up the broad expanse of lake, and even purpled the blood-stained decks with its streaks of gold.

It fell upon the black and torn sails of the *Hoche*, and upon her sides pitted and marked from stem to stern, from bulwark to water-line, with cannon balls.

Her sails were cut into a thousand shreds; her ropes hung dangling on the deck, flapping idly in the breeze; cannon and bullet and splintered shell lay in rough profusion around; but, most awful sight of all—facing heaven, still and silent, their white teeth and white unclosed eyes looking so strange in contrast with the black and grimy appearance of their hands and faces after hours of cannonading—lay the fallen soldiers and seamen of the gallant Frenchman!

Truly against fearful odds never fought vessel more gallantly; never did Frenchmen, even in the early wars, of the Revolution, show such marvellous bravery and contempt for death. Each individual sailor and seaman fought with the same reckless bravery and dauntlessness as if the honour of the tricolor and the safety of France depended on himself alone.

"The last hope of Ireland, Eugene," said Tone, with swelling heart, as, having been taken on board the English vessel, they met among the crowd of officers.

"The last in our time," said the late captain of the *Hoche*, "but a man's life is short, whilst that of a nation is long. The years to come will bring it around again."

"But for us the day is over," said Tone.

"I fear it is," said Eugene sympathisingly.

"Then my future is void. I lived for this and this only."

"You have the consolation, my dear Tone, that you have done all that man may do. You have done better than command success—you have deserved it. But we cannot control the Fates. God holds all things in the palm of His hands, and has His own wise reasons for what happens. You have still your delightful wife and young children left you. By-the-by, lest the English might recognise you, would it not be well to disguise yourself in some way?"

Tone was but an inattentive listener. His mind, whilst yet his friend spoke, was otherwise employed; and the far-away-look in his eyes indicated that his thoughts were upon things and objects very distant.

"Take this cloak, Tone, and wrap yourself up in it. The evening is growing chilly. It will serve a double purpose."

While speaking, Eugene took from the broken trunnion of a cannon an English officer's cloak. At that moment the bugle sounded, and a number of officers came hurrying through the group, making arrangements for the landing of the prisoners, and in the confusion separating the two friends.

A tender came alongside, and Eugene was hurried on board.

But he saw Tone no more. The breeze from the hills came thin and cold, and he had had nothing to eat since morning. Moreover, his wound was painful, and the loss of blood was making him feel weak. He wrapped the cloak—the cloak he had proffered Tone—around him, and sitting down on a box of ammunition, laid his arms on the breech of a cannon, his head thereon, and in a few seconds was fast asleep.

CHAPTER XLI.

THE CLIFFS OF LOUGH SWILLY.

"Eugene! Eugene!—waken up!—what are you sleeping for? Waken, I say."

The words, whispered energetically into his ear, combined with the touch of a hand on his shoulder, woke him a little. There was a dim feeling palpable to him that he was being called, but it came so vaguely to his torpid senses that it passed away and he again relapsed into slumber.

"Confound you, Eugene! Waken! Do you know where you are?"

The person speaking this time made certain that there should be some result from his words, for he took the half unconscious sleeper, and lifting him in his arms, placed him standing upright on his feet. This had the desired effect. The necessity for physical action drove the torpor and lethargy from his brain, and he was quickly alive to what was going on around him.

His awakener was muffled up in the long cloak of an English artillery officer.

"Give me your arm, Eugene, and walk with me."

A dim perception seemed to come on his thoughts that he had heard the voice before, and that the speaker was quite familiar to him. He was about in some vague way to ask a question thereanent, but the unknown appeared to divine his intention, and said hurriedly:

"No, not now. Don't open your lips. Keep your cloak well wrapped about you and follow me."

In the crowd of men and officers passing out they passed out too. But instead of following the crowd that poured along the narrow streets of the fishing village where they landed, Eugene's companion, with a quick turn, deflected into a lane where a fisherman was standing, thence into another at right angles thereto, and, before any notice was taken of their departure, were quite out of sight and hearing.

"Now, Eugene, jump up here," he said, as a car was standing ready yoked. "We must put some miles between us and this without delay. You will not be missed for some time in the confusion, but as soon as you will, sharp search will be made for you. So there's no time to be lost. Don't stay to ask questions. I'm François—and that's enough for the present. I shall tell you all later on. We shall be on the highway to France to-morrow afternoon. Come! jump up!"

A thrill of delight, even with all his weariness and weakness, passed through Eugene at the prospect of being again free. The delight was compounded with wonderment as to how François had come there so opportunely— apparently off the enemy's vessel, too.

But both sensations were effervescent; chill and cold and deadly sense of weariness rapidly supervened; and it was almost mechanically that he allowed himself to be helped to his seat by the vigorous arm of his young friend.

A world of vague dreams grew about him as the words of the latter fell on his ear.

"Drive rapidly. There is no time for delay."

The car, with the semi-unconscious occupant encircled in the arms of his young friend, drove quickly out of the village. Fortunately along this side of the lough, and bordering the road along which they passed, thick bushes grew, hiding them from observation—if indeed observation were to be thought of by anyone after the exciting incidents of the day.

The sun was low down in the skies. The thick bank of clouds in the West had turned to purple and gold as the descending orb poured his flood of glory upwards, when they reached the pass of Cranmore.

It lay along the side of a cliff overhanging the lough Far in the distance they could see the fleet lying at anchor dimly, for the darkening eve was beginning to close. But of other sign of living presence or habitation there was none. Save the tall, half-barren cliff that lifted its summit overhead, and the scrubby mass of stunted brushwood that grew beneath, sloping to the water's edge, there was nothing else to disturb or attract the attention. The road was a narrow ledge cut by unskilled hands along the side of the cliff, and allowed passage but for one vehicle at a time. It was, therefore, necessary to proceed with the greatest care and caution up its steep ascent.

At this moment a faint noise like unto the tread of hoofs fell on the ear of the young Frenchman.

Descending from his seat and placing his hand on the horse's bridle, he listened for a moment.

"Do you hear anything?" the driver asked, in a whisper.

"Yes. I have been hearing it for some seconds. It is the tramp of cavalry. They are coming in this direction. Drive on quicker—drive as quickly as you can," said François with excitement.

"We cannot go faster in this road unless we go over the cliffs," said the driver; "and the tramping seems to be coming nearer very fast."

They had ascended the sharp acclivity of a hill whose height, elevating itself over minor obstacles, looked down on the road by which they had come. There was no intervening thing to break the noise arising from below, and therefore the tramp of the advancing horsemen came on their ears with fresh distinctness.

"They will overtake us in twenty minutes," said the driver decisively.

"And we cannot stir from this road."

"With the car, not an inch."

"What can we do?"

"Shelter in the rocks until they pass."

"But the car will betray us."

"We must get rid of it."

"But how?"

The driver shrugged his shoulders. There was, however, a look of intelligence in his eye which François read at once.

"I believe you are right; t is the only thing possible,"

said the latter with a quick smile. "Eugene! Eugene! I say, awake! There is not a moment to be lost."

A hurried and unceremonious shake quickly aroused the slumberer, who—the rest and sleep having much refreshed him—was more ready to attend to outward circumstances.

"Eh! Where am I? Is this you, François? I was dreaming of Seamore."

"Never mind Seamore—wherever that is," said François hurriedly, "and only remember that you are an escaping prisoner, with English cavalry coming swiftly after you."

"Yes. I remember now," said the late captain of the *Hoche*, shaking himself free from his stupor and dreams. "Cavalry, did you say—where?"

"Listen."

For a moment they listened; the hoof-beats on the stony road coming with greater and nearer resonance.

"We shall be taken, François," said Eugene with a shudder. "Is there no means of hurrying forward?"

"To go even a yard faster in every half hour would send us over the precipice. We must go along at a snail's pace."

"What shall we do? We cannot suffer ourselves to be retaken."

"Then I'll tell you what we must do. Take to these rocks overhead. They will afford us shelter for a time. It would be quite impossible for them to find us out in the dusk of the evening or in the night."

"But the vehicle will point out our hiding-place to them at once."

"We shall hurl it over the cliff, Eugene. It is our only chance. As Augereau hurled his cannon over the precipice of Monterey. It is a good augur in our retreat," said François, with a ray of his old gaiety beaming through his smile.

"Precisely what I thought myself," said Eugene with a faint smile.

After a short conversation with the driver the horse was unyoked, and, while yet on their ears the tramp of the pursuing horses was growing perilously near, the car and its accompaniments were by their united aid hurled down the steep embankment. It was a work of little trouble, for no wall or protection bordered the road from the cliff, and the vehicle went tumbling down, carrying with it an avalanche of stones and shingle, until it reached the bottom and plunged into the coarse brushwood that grew around the base, burying itself therein.

The driver, that operation effected, mounted the shaggy pony and galloped forward along the cliff road, whilst Eugene and François, the former helped by the latter, crept up the hill side and sought shelter behind some rocks.

"This is a queer outcome to the expedition for the freedom of Ireland—is it not?" said François as, after recovering themselves from their hurried climb, and having gathered their breath, they were free to watch for the coming of their pursuers, and talk in whispered sentences.

"It *is* unfortunate," replied Eugene.

"Unfortunate! It is miserable—disgraceful," said François emphatically. "I do not mind my own share in the business, if any honour had resulted from it, or indeed any success at all; but think of it, Eugene! to give up the chance of captain of hussars in D'Auvergne's command—and on active service, too—for this business!"

"It was unfortunate undoubtedly," said Eugene, not unamused at his companion's self-deprecation and disappointment.

"Unfortunate!" exclaimed the other. "Only think of it again! Look on me hiding here, a fugitive outcast, behind a rock on the side of a barren mountain, in—I might almost call it—a desert island. And hiding from whom? from what? A handful of cavalry that a Centieme hussar would charge single-handed!"

"You may thank your stars, François, if you can continue hiding, and safely continue. There is no dishonour when men have done their best in a good cause. And as to these cavalry pursuing us—they may be few, but, they are as powerful under the circumstances as if they numbered thousands. You may be, and have often proved yourself, daring enough when two armies were engaged—but, François, the only glory we need hope for now is the glory of escape. You don't know," added he with a shudder, "what a supreme glory that is."

"I have no knowledge of it," said François somewhat ironically.

"None, François, none whatever. No language can paint the horrors of the hulks—no imagination conceive the sickening terrors of imprisonment therein. But hush! here they come!"

They ceased speaking as the clatter of hoofs above the stony surface of the road came sharply on their ears. In a moment or two a party of dragoons—some nine or ten —came around a corner into view. The dusk had fallen on the hillside, but the bright sheen of the scabbards and the steel trappings of the horses shone clearly enough for all that.

In single file, for the road was too narrow and dangerous to admit of aught else, they passed on Their tread could be heard for some short distance, but a projection of the hill suddenly shut them out from view, and the sounds almost as suddenly ceased.

"They have passed, François. Shall we remain here?" asked Eugene, after a space of time during which their ears were strained trying to catch further token of the soldiers' movements.

"No, I think not. We had better move up higher. They must have seen the car on the cliff from the valley, and will wonder what has become of it. Trust me they will make further search."

"Well, we had better place ourselves in a position of more safety. The higher up the better. It would be a sorrowful thing after such a chance to see ourselves prisoners again."

"It would. I have not had such experience as you have had, but I am quite as unwilling to go to one of their prisons. The world is far too beautiful for that, and has, I trust, better things in store for me. Is it painful?" asked François, referring to the wound.

"It is—very. The cold and the exhaustion have not tended to make it better."

"Yes, and I completely forgot to provide some refreshments for you. In my hurry to get away I completely forgot them."

"If our friends the enemy were gone back we should probably meet hospitality here," said Eugene.

"You may rely upon it we should. Would you be able to climb the hill a little?"

"I think so—with your aid. But hush, François—did you hear anything?"

"Only the moving of a curlew through the heath. If you had been as long on the tramp through the mountains as I have been you would know their movement."

"Perhaps it is. But somehow the least thing startles me this evening. I suppose my nerves are high strung because of my weakness—which puts me in mind to ask you—curiously enough I had forgotten it before," said Eugene, as, leaning on his friend's arm, he left his hiding place and essayed to climb the steep hill, "how it came to pass that you were on the British fleet."

"It is a long story to tell, Eugene, but for the present it is enough to say that Humbert's small detachment——"

"Ay Humbert, what of him? I had forgotten him too," remarked Eugene, as he paused for a moment.

"What of him? Why, what should have been expected if we were not all most inconsiderate and enthusiastic fools. He landed with his two thousand men in a country where the insurrection had been weeks before drowned out in blood. We won a battle at a place—Castlebar, I think, they call it—where we sent ten times our number of British forces flying. But we had no time to drill the raw levies that flocked to our standard; they had neither arms nor ammunition, nor had we any to give them. We could not with two thousand French soldiers fight the whole British nation, and so we surrendered. I say we as a unit of the invading force, but not having any special reason to love the British prisons more than yourself, I took leave, when we surrendered, to escape. Guided by friendly hands through many perils and dangers, I gained these Northern regions only to be made a prisoner and brought on board their fleet. However, they treated me well—the officers were not bad fellows—but I am glad to be once more free and ——"

"Which you shall not long be!" cried a voice behind them. "Yield yourselves up prisoners, in the King's name!"

The startling words had scarcely come on their ears when they were seized; and almost before they were aware of it their hands were securely bound behind them.

"You have given us rather a long ride in search of you, gentlemen," said an officer, stepping forward; "but your escape was badly managed, after all. You had better come with us, and next time you may have safer chance of success."

Very little of this half-ironical address fell on the ears of François. This sudden seizure when he believed himself quite secure, paralysed him. Eugene, more hardened to the vicissitudes of warfare, at once accepted the situation.

The latter simply asked:
"Where do you take us?"

"Back to your friends. It was scarcely fair of you after the trouble you gave us in your first capture, to put us to the necessity of a second. Bring the prisoners down, men."

They descended the hill, and reached the road without a further word passing. The sensation of surprise had hardly time to abate with François when the sound of horses approaching fell on his ears. Looking in the direction from whence they came, he could see a number of cavalry chargers, most of them without riders, trotting towards them. A sense of dismay fell on his heart, as he thought of his beloved France, and the weary months, if not years, he must pass before he could see it again.

"It is all the fortune of war, my friend," said the officer, with no unkindness in his tones, as he noticed the passing depression in the young fellow's countenance, "but for the present it is necessary to boot and saddle. There is a long ride from here to Letterkenny, whither your comrades have been sent. We must follow."

Eugene and François were provided with separate horses, the soldiers mounting behind two of their comrades. In this manner they retraced the road they had so recently come.

"Poor Eugene," thought François to himself.

"Poor François," thought Eugene.

Each felt not for himself, but for his friend.

The road widening when they had passed into the valley, the troop quickened into a trot, the two prisoners in the centre and the soldiers before and behind.

François for a moment thought to escape, but, glancing at the bound condition of his friend, and his own equally helpless position, he abandoned the idea almost as soon as it was formed.

With thoroughly French lightness of heart under difficulties, he dispelled the annoyance that at first pressed on him, and rode gaily along. At worst he thought it would be only a question of time until he should see *La Belle France* again, and in the meantime there was no use in wearing one's self out with hopeless repining.

It was otherwise, however, with Eugene. There were many reasons why a prison life, even for a short time, would be insufferable to him. If it were nothing else, it was the thought of Seamore—the thought of Helen Barrington, and of his sister Alice.

Two years had passed over since he had heard of them, and what changes these two years might have brought about! What had become of the former? Could she have been married to the baronet—the husband and would-be murderer of his sister! But the thought in itself was torture. He would banish it from his mind. It were ill brooding to think over it.

To banish the gloomy foreboding that his position gave rise to, he sought to divert his attention by taking note of the surrounding objects. In the bay he tried to make out in the moonlight—now beginning to throw dimly a misty brightness over the waters—the forms of the ships lying silently thereon.

Turning his eyes from that vague search to the front—a blinding flash met his eyes, and simultaneously a quick sharp report—or rather reports, for they came not all together—smote on his ears!

A confused uprearing of the horses in front, a swaying unsteadily of their riders, a loosening of the reins, a hoarse cry of startled angry voices, followed by another flash of light and another burst of sound!—all occurring in such rapid succession and so unexpectedly that for the moment the whole business was quite incomprehensible to him. Not, indeed, that he had power or time to form any opinion on the matter, for, in the backward rush of the horses and the little power of control he had over his own with his manacled hands, he was thrown down in the confusion. He was only cognizant for a moment of a sense of deadly peril from the trampling and rushing steeds, and then a darkness closed over his eyes, and the world of reality vanished from his brain.

CHAPTER XLII.

TO DUBLIN.

WHEN Sir Trevor Mortimer communicated the intelligence to the soldiers, quartered in the barracks at Wexford, as to where the two fugitives were likely to be found, he wandered about in the narrow streets of which that town is composed until it was time for the mail coach to start.

There were no superstitious fears now at his heart; no despairing cry came, borne on the night air, to make him start in terror; no thought of the precipice on the island with the moaning sea beneath it, came into his brain. It was of Moya's information he thought—of her hurried breathless words.

Redmond! Could he really have been there? Could the mud of the Liffey have given up its dead? Of Eugene Lefebre, it was possible enough. But him! It was impossible. Surely, Moya must have been mistaken! And yet—could she? She knew him too well; knew him so intimately that that, too, was impossible. Unless, indeed, her own fears or her disordered imagination deceived her. And that other——

"Psha! the thing was wholly impossible. Old Moya was deceived." With a shudder he turned his thoughts away from the subject.

But control his thoughts as he might, and turn them
in what direction he would, he could not banish the sensations of coming danger that pressed at his heart. They
lay there like the touch of an icy hand, with the strange
effect that they sent a burning feel along his veins to his
extremities. And force as he might his attention to the
surroundings—to the sleeping streets around him—they
clung closer to him, sending now and then a thrill into
his very brain that promptly recalled his attention to
them.

How long that rift in the sky that betokened dawn was
a-coming! How long even after it had faintly showed, it
was until the people in the mail coach-office were up and
stirring—how long after that until the mail itself was got
ready. A dozen times he visited it, and as often took a
circuitous route through the streets until he came to it
again—thinking each turn that it must have surely started
by this time, so long and leaden the minutes seemed to
him; but coming to a fresh surprise each visit to find that
but a short time had elapsed since his last, and that there
was still no sign of its being got ready.

But Time, heedless alike of the impatient and the indolent, passes along on its unvarying career, and the hour
came at last when the coach was ready to start for the
metropolis.

He entered, and seated himself in a corner, wrapped
his overcoat around him, buried his face in its upturned
collar, and prepared to sleep. He had slept none for the
past twenty-four hours; he had had a long and distressing
walk into Wexford along the shore and across the fields;
and he would now take the rest of which he stood so
much in need.

But he found himself unable to do so. Perhaps it was
the confusion and bustle attending the crowding of the
coach with luggage for the long journey, and the settling
of the passengers into their places. Perhaps it was that
he was overwearied, and the sleep had gone astray upon
him. Whatever it was, slumber was not for his eyelids;
the more he shut his face in from the garish light of the
morning, the more wide-awake he became—the more the
horrid thoughts of the night went flying through his

brain. He pulled aside the collar that concealed his face, and sought to interest himself in the bustle around.

Passengers were getting in and seating themselves beside him—trampling the fresh straw under their feet to make it warm and cosy for themselves. Passengers were climbing up on the roof grumbling audibly at the inconvenience caused by the luggage. The yard in which the mail-coach stood was filled with the employes of the hotel in every kind and description of dress and undress, waiting to see the mail start. All of these things gave him for the moment some distraction from the rankling uneasiness that filled him; but an occasional ugly throb at his breast recalled him to himself and to his perplexing forebodements.

At last everything was ready, and the mail was off.

Past narrow streets, where there was only room for the conveyance to pass, and in which the closed curtains showed that the sleepers therein had no notion as yet of disturbing themselves from their repose. Past the suburbs, where working men lived, and where the inmates having to be at their work betimes were already astir, as was clearly indicated by the open half-doors and the smoke beginning to arise in spiral wreaths of blue from the chimney-tops. And so out into the country road, where the hedges were commencing to show in the gray light, and to make palpable the webs that the dew of the summer night, just expired, had woven over them—in such delicate tracery as girls' hands in Limerick or Valenciennes had never learned to weave.

Sir Trevor Mortimer drew the collar of his overcoat over his face once more, and sank back into the corner which he occupied. The air of the interior of the lumbering vehicle was growing hot and drowsy—the jolting of the machine was favorable to slumber. Insensibly, as the miles passed over, he fell asleep. And to dream.

Such dreams!

All sorts of wandering and perplexing ideas passed incoherently through his head.

Finally: he was standing with Helen Barrington on a cliff—oh! that cliff! What a shudder it sent through him even in his dream!—looking over the sea, which washed up to, and under, the base of the rock on which he stood. He feared to look down from the dizzy height on the thin green reach of water beneath which seemed in the great distance to be only a few inches deep, so clear and palpable the shining pebbles gleamed from under it. But he did look—mustered up his courage to look! And what a depth it was down there! How sheerly the black face of the rock descended, leaving nothing whatever to break the fall! What a length of time it would be before one falling could touch rock or water beneath! Would the life be in one, all the time? Would the terrific passage through the air frighten the spirit or life out of the falling form long before the descent was accomplished? He felt dizzy, and the soles of his feet, and the palms of his hands tingled. Helen's hand lay in his, and he was about— —feeling so giddy and terrified—to withdraw a few paces back; when, suddenly, he felt a hand on his shoulder, and —he was pushed over the beetling precipice! He felt his feet leave the solid earth; he found himself launched into pure space with nothing but the air beneath him—and destruction. A cry of unutterable agony—a screech begotten of overwhelming dread and despair—burst from his lips!

And he awoke!

Awoke to find the unreality of his dream; but also to find that every eye in the coach was fixed upon him. For in the paroxysms of his dream, he had struggled violently, and had thrown the covering from his face, exposing to public view the contortion of the one and the other. Abashed by the crowd of faces turned towards him, and alarmed by the dread that he might have said something that attracted such attention, he quickly muffled himself up again.

"Are you ill, sir?" a compassionate woman opposite asked.

He gruffly answered, "No," and shut himself up from further gaze.

But his rest was broken, and all the old mistrusts and perplexities that had slept whilst he slumbered seemed to have sprung again into renewed vigor with his awakening—like summer flies when the hot dawn comes—and harrassed him unceasingly.

What, if Helen should have changed her mind, and not have come? What, if in her halting and indecision she had again vaccillated and remained at Inch? The very doubt was terror to him—it meant ruin. Any delay at all—any postponement whatever—meant ruin.

She had arranged to have started early in the morning. He glanced outwards at the sunlight. He must have slept some considerable time, for the sun was long over the horizon, and the people were all in the fields busily at work at the harvest. She must be on the way now, if— the blood rushed back in affright at the thought—she had not altered her mind.

The more he let his mind dwell upon all the contingencies connected with it the more the possibility of her having done so grew upon him. Grew, indeed, so great that he resolved to get out at the next posting station, and await the coming of her carriage—if come it would at all. Accordingly, when the mail stopped, which it did many miles beyond Inch, and the passengers descended to stretch their legs, and refresh themselves, Sir Trevor Mortimer got down also.

But he did not enter the posting establishment. He was far too restless and uneasy for that. With an intimation to the conductor that he had altered his mind, and would not proceed further for the present, he walked back over the mail coach road by which they had just travelled.

What a torturing walk it was! How often his eyes glanced eagerly along the road when it lay straight before him—which it rarely did—for sign of approaching carriage. But there was none. Had Helen then heard of— heard any evil news concerning him? If she had not, why was she not on the road? If she had——

He felt so ill—so tired and jaded, that he was fain to rest on the grassy slope of a hedge by the way. So weak and ill, indeed, was he that for a time his eyes became obscured, and a mist seemed to grow before them. Also, his sense of hearing became deadened. He was in that position when, if he had been a weaker man, or the spirit within him was less potent, he would have swooned.

As it was he sat in stupor.

Out of which he was roused by the noise of carriage wheels beside him, and a musical voice, not without a strain of wonderment in it, fell on his ears.

"Trevor!—Sir Trevor Mortimer!"

He looked up. The carriage had stopped, and two girls' faces appeared at the window. They were those of Helen Barrington and Kate Howard.

"You here, Sir Trevor!" said the latter in considerable surprise.

"Yes," said he brightly, as the unexpected presence of the carriage renewed at once his hopes and his courage, "the mail was so hot and—so crowded and uncomfortable—that I could not proceed further in it. And I resolved to wait for you. I felt very ill for a time."

He did not look ill now. On the contrary, he looked blithe and vigorous. He stepped into the carriage, which whirled them all three on the way to Dublin. And whatever powers of pleasing Sir Trevor Mortimer had, or whatever powers of conversation, he certainly did not spare them on the way.

What with stoppages, changes of horses, and the needful rest, it was the following morning when they reached the metropolis.

As had been arranged between them, Sir Trevor descended from the carriage when they entered the city, and proceeded to his quarters in the Castle to prepare himself for the approaching ceremony. There being no one in Seamore to whom Helen could address herself on this momentous occasion, she determined to proceed to Leinster House to place herself under the protection of the Fitzgerald family who were closely related to hers. It was an unusual way of doing matters, she felt, but Sir Trevor's impatience and importunity were not to be denied.

CHAPTER XLIII.

THE WEDDING BREAKFAST.

To the man under sentence of death, reprieve comes with overwhelming sensation; to the soldier, badly wounded on the battle-field, the intimation that the wound is not mortal brings joy exceeding; but it is doubtful if either of these can compare with the exultation, the radiant sense of success, that filled the breast of Trevor Mortimer as he stood up at the little breakfast party in Leinster House, when they had returned from the church, to respond to the toast of his health.

There was a feeling of success—that he had overcome all the thousand nameless perils and dangers that encompassed him by the sheer force of his own strength of will and resolution. He was like the storm-tossed mariner, who after a long disastrous voyage, and in the teeth of a hurricane, sees his good ship sweeping into the haven-mouth and to safe anchorage.

He was safe now. Despite all that man could do, he was safe. And it was, therefore, with an exultant heart, and with a radiant countenance, that he stood before the little family group returning thanks.

"It is the proudest moment of my life," he said—and well he might. "Wedded to one who was my sole and only love ——"

But at this moment a light phaeton drove hurriedly up to the door, and a gentleman, tossing the reins to his servant, descended quickly from it and ascended the steps.

In a moment more a knock came to the door of the drawing-room. Lord Edward himself went to open it— not caring to have their happiness disturbed by the intrusion of strangers. But it was only one of the servants

"Well?" said the young nobleman rather angrily.

"A gentleman wants to see your lordship."

"I cannot see him. Tell him I am most particularly engaged. Who is he?"

"Sir George Ponsonby, my lord."

"Oh! Sir George—eh? Where is he?"

"In the Yellow Room. He is most anxious to see your lordship for a second."

"I shall see him for a second," said his lordship, closing the door after him carefully, and descended to the apartment mentioned.

"Well, Sir George," said he, shaking hands warmly with the new arrival. "I am glad to see you. You must excuse me if I cannot spare you much time. There is a wedding, at which some friends of yours ——"

"It is about that wedding I called to see you, my lord ——"

"It is quite a private and hurried affair, else you, Sir George, being, I believe, like myself, a relative of the fair bride, should have been present; but as I said ——"

"Present! my lord! Then I should have been present at one of the greatest acts of scoundrelism that ever —— Do you know that Mortimer is married already, and that his wife is living?"

"Hush! Sir George," said Lord Edward, as he glanced at the excited face of his friend, "these are wild words— and at such a time, too!"

"But they are true, Lord Edward," said Ponsonby passionately. "Perfectly true! There never was a baser or more scoundrelly act perpetrated than this ceremony just concluded. It is an outrage upon all that is innocent and ——"

"This is too absurd," said the nobleman quietly, attributing these vehement expressions to some cause other than the right one. "I must ask you—I must, indeed—not to make use of such expressions."

"Do you think I am speaking what is not true, my lord?" said the impetuous baronet, rapidly hastening to that state of temper in which it made little matter to him with whom he quarrelled.

"Peace, George, peace! Remember the place and the occasion."

"But I do remember them. It is because I remember

them that I am here. But, my lord!" said he pausing, "I see there is no use in further addressing you on the subject. I must see Helen Barrington myself."

"You must be aware," said Lord Edward coldly, for his sense of what was decorous and becoming had been grievously outraged, "that Lady Mortimer is not to be disturbed now."

"Lady Mortimer!" said Ponsonby, with great contempt —the name seeming to call up every sensation of loathing and repugnance he was capable of—"I tell you she is no more Lady Mortimer—though all the clergymen in Dublin assisted at the ceremony—than she is Lady Fitzgerald or Lady Ponsonby. But I must see her. I shall not leave this house, except by force, until I do. If there be no one else to protect this poor girl, by the Heavens above me!—I will!"

The young nobleman looked at him steadily for a few seconds. Then, impressed by the firmness, the determination, and the passionate resolve thereon, he said: "I think I had better call in Sir Trevor. He has a right to hear this!"

"Do so, my lord. Bring him here."

Lord Edward rang the bell. The same servant appeared. Desiring him to whisper Sir Trevor out, he disappeared, and, in a second or two after, the baronet entered the apartment.

"Sir Trevor," said Lord Edward, carefully closing the door, "I sent for you because I thought it fitting that you should hear what Sir George Ponsonby has to say. Before it goes further, I may say that I am convinced he is mistaken; but still it is right that you should hear him, and relieve his mind——"

"About that note of hand," said Sir Trevor. "I may acquaint Sir George," said he with ill-concealed haughtiness and exultance, "that but for my unavoidable absence in the country it would have been paid long since. Tomorrow I shall ——"

"You quite mistake, sir," said the baronet, "I did not come here to speak of money matters or gambling debts. I came here, as an Irish gentleman should, to extend the hand of friendship and protection to a young girl who is being cruelly deceived."

"And who may that be?"

"The young girl whom you went through the mock ceremony of marriage with this morning."

"I think there is no need to listen further to the gentleman's rhapsodies," said Sir Trevor, moving away contemptuously towards the door.

"Nay," said Sir George, intercepting him, and placing his back to it, "no one shall leave the room until I have said what I have to say."

Sir Trevor Mortimer's face reddened, and the moment after grew very white. It would be difficult to say which hue exhibited the deadlier state of passion or anger. A rapid movement of his hand to his breast pocket, as if he searched for something there—a pistol or a dagger; but he was in his wedding suit, and there was nothing in it. So he stood still, and—still with singularly white face—listened to the intruder.

"My lord," said the latter, "it was only last night I learned—how I cannot say now, nor have I time to tell—that this gentleman was already married. It came to me from one who had somehow heard that he was about to wed Helen Barrington, and who knew the whole circumstances and placed the proofs in my hands. Yes, married. To a young French girl, a former visitor of the Barrington's, and a friend. Aided by the ministrations of an old hag, that once ——"

Sir George Ponsonby had let his rage get so far the better of him that his voice failed him at this point. Taking advantage of the pause, Trevor Mortimer said with a sneer to which his manner and white face lent an indescribable tone of insult:

"It is false. This gentleman has been up all night and is dreaming!"

"It is true, every word of it. True as God is in Heaven!"

"It is false!" said Sir Trevor, "false as a vile and lying tongue can make it."

Ponsonby lost all control of himself, perhaps made to do so the more by the coolness and calm demeanour of the other. It was a case of cool villainy against honest indignation.

"Villain and scoundrel, it is true!" he shouted, at the same time as, elevating his arm, he brought the back of his extended hand down with great force on the face of his opponent.

The blow was strong and scalding, and for a moment stars shone in clusters before Sir Trevor Mortimer's eyes.

"See this, Lord Edward! Bear witness to this!" he cried savagely, all his previous coolness totally gone. "He has struck me!—He has struck me, I say! I call you to witness he has struck me!"

"Ponsonby, Ponsonby!" Lord Edward could only say in dire amazement.

"I have to apologise to your lordship for my hastiness, and for taking such liberty in your house, my lord," said Ponsonby, who now recovered his coolness.

"There must be satisfaction for this," said Mortimer, hoarsely.

"You must have it at any moment," said Sir George. "Where shall it be?—and when?"

"This forenoon," said Sir Trevor whilst a gleam of malignant satisfaction shot through his eyes. His face seemed to have grown paler and white, save where Ponsonby's blow had left it heated and flushed. "By the yew tree in the Park. In an hour's time."

"I shall be there," said Ponsonby, as he opened the door. "Excuse me, my lord, I did not intend this scene when coming. *Au revoir.*"

And walking gravely down the broad marble stairs, Sir George stepped into his phæton and was whirled away.

"This is an extraordinary business," said Lord Edward, when their visitor had left. "Of course there is no foundation for ——"

"My lord, I have no time, as you can understand, for much talking now. Send Sir Laurence Parsons to me, and make apologies to the ladies for my absence. Say Government business, or something of that kind. I shall be back in two hours."

Sir Laurence Parsons, who was best man on the occasion, was speedily by his side, and they were soon driving rapidly towards the Park. On the way they stopped for a few minutes at Mortimer's quarters at the Castle, whence the latter shortly emerged with a small mahogany case under his arm.

"Parsons," said he, after they had resumed their rapid journey. "Feel my hand."

Parsons took his hand in his.

"Is it cold?"

"Yes, quite cold."

"Is it firm?"

"As iron."

"Does it tremble any?"

"No, none at all."

"That's right," said Sir Trevor, whilst the hurt part of his face grew more flushed, and the other more yellow-white.

"You will only pink him," said Parsons with a shudder, as he noticed this expression. "In the shoulder or the hip. You will not kill him?"

But Sir Trevor, clutching the case as if he would drive thumb and fingers through its mahogany sides, bent over his face to the other, put his white firm lips to his ear, and hissingly whispered:

"I will. Perdition seize my soul if I don't!"

There was no other word spoken, they were driving too fast for that, until they reached the yew tree in the Park. There they found Ponsonby and his friend awaiting them. Unlike the usual formalities in cases of the kind, there were no bows interchanged or words spoken. In an atmosphere so charged with malignant intention and deadly hate as almost to be felt, the preliminaries were arranged, and the two took their places.

"Parsons," said Sir Mortimer in a whisper, before he stepped to his place, "watch where I shall send the ball. Straight in the centre of his forehead. Keep your eye on it."

The signal was given, and both parties fired. Parsons' fascinated eyes were upon the spot indicated. As he looked it seemed to him that a shadow had passed—an instantaneous shadow—across it.

He shut his eyes involuntarily, and as if under a dreadful spell; but opened them as quickly before the wreathing smoke had time to ascend and shut out his gaze. There was no mark on Ponsonby's forehead : he stood upright ; but a thick rush of blood from his side temple showed where the bullet had skimmed it.

Parsons turned towards his friend. He, too, was upright; but the ascending smoke shut out view of his features.

"Both unhurt," he thought. "I hope it is over now."

He was about to move towards Sir Trevor, who stood stock still where he stood, when, suddenly, he placed his left hand hurriedly on his side ; the smoking pistol fell from his right hand, and after a spasmodic step backwards he fell, with heavy leaden thud, on the broad of his back.

Parsons hastily tore open his dress. There was a small blue wound under the nipple of the left breast.

He then looked at his face—at his eyes.

"It is all over," he said. "Mortimer is dead."

It was even so. It was all over. Out through the blue mark Mortimer's life—or soul—or whatever it was — had sped forth : who knew whither ?

CHAPTER XLIV.

IN THE CAVES OF DONEGAL.

"WHY, Eugene, I thought you would never come to ?" was the exclamation that fell on his awakening ears.

"I—where am I ?" was his first astonished question.

"Here—in very comfortable quarters, and among friends."

"Thank God!" was his reply. The incidents of his capture were quite fresh in his memory.

"It is rather an odd place—is it not François?" was his next query.

"It is. There is no doubt of it. But," said his young friend sententiously, "there might be worse. But we shall have time enough to discuss that. Tell me how do you feel ? You do not feel seriously hurt ?"

"No. I do not feel hurt at all. I have been stunned

—nothing more. I shall feel quite well presently. That rescue—how did it take place, François?"

"Why, our friend the driver—whom by the way you will see presently, and who happens to be a very influential personage in the neighbourhood—knowing with better sense than we seemed to have had that we should be captured, rode swiftly on, called to his aid some friends in the surrounding glens, and hurrying back by the other side of the hill, intercepted our captors successfully—and here we are!"

"And where is *here*, François?" inquired Eugene.

"Upon my word, further than what you see around you," said François laughingly, "I am able to give you very little information."

"We are underground, seemingly," said Eugene, glancing at the aperture overhead, through which the light came in a sort of trellis work owing to the long ferns and heath bushes that shaded it.

"We are;—you are quite right there. So much, and little more, I know myself."

"Is it a cave, or prison, or what?" asked Eugene again, taking in with a curious glance the surroundings.

"It is a cave—a factory."

"A factory" repeated Eugene, who only understood the expression in its application to the extensive establishments in France with which he was acquainted, wherein powder and cannon and shot and shell were manufactured for the use of the revolutionary armies.

"Yes, a factory. That is, Eugene, probably about the most imposing—if not appropriate—name to give it."

"And what," inquired Eugene, glancing around him at the rough clay walls apparently dug out of the mountain-side, and the numerous casks which filled its many crevices—diffusing a hot though not unpleasant aroma through the place—"what may be the article they manufacture here?"

"Medicine," said François, with a gravity that but thinly veiled his light airy pleasantry.

"Medicine!" echoed Eugene, taking his statement for truth. "Medicine! what kind of medicine?"

"Medicine, my dear Eugene, that would carry the life back into your heart if you were dying; that would restore your spirits though you were in the deepest dejection ever mortal man sank to; that would make you fight the *Hoche* once more against the whole British forces?"

"Ah! the *Hoche. La pauvre Hoche!* Our unhappy expedition!" said Eugene, sinking back into dejected reflection. Quickly recovering himself, however, he asked, with a smile which had some of his old airiness in it: "And what, François, may be the name of this most potent medicine? I feel as if I needed some of its aid just now."

"It is called *poteen*, Eugene."

"*Poteen!*" said the latter. "What a queer name."

"It *is* a queer name; but everything seems to me to be strange and queer in this ill-fated land."

"And here is some of it to taste," said a strange voice, emerging from the gloom of a subterranean archway, and bearing in his hand a small measure.

Eugene looked up at the words, and a smile crossed his pallid face as he recognised the friendly features of the quondam driver.

"Take this," said the latter. "You will find it do you good after your mishaps. You have need of something to refresh you."

"It would be difficult to refuse anything from your loyal and true hand, my friend," said Eugene gratefully and frankly; and he took the measure from him.

He had swallowed but a little of it when a heavy fit of coughing supervened—so heavy that for a moment François believed he was choking.

"Don't be afraid," said the driver. "He will recover presently. It has proved a little too strong for him."

"Why, François," said Eugene, when the fit had subsided, "that is brandy."

"No, not brandy, but a twin brother of it. Drink such as this was never grown in Charente, nor floated down the Garonne. This is the ancient Ambrosia—the nectar of the gods. So, at least, they say here. How do you like it?"

"It is very fine."

"You will find nothing better in Ireland—in the world indeed, I may say—save one place only," said his entertainer, replenishing the tiny measure.

"And where may that be?" asked Eugene, as a sense of reviving strength and health flushed through his veins.

"In Dublin!"

"In Dublin! Why I have been there for weeks and have not known of it."

"You were too much occupied with other matters probably. But it is there. In the west of the city—Marrowbone Lane they call it—is the temple of the gods—distillery, they profanely term it—where they distil spirit to which this, fine as it is, is but as water to sparkling Champagne. Talk of ambrosia or nectar when once you taste that! It is liquor fit for Paradise."

"I shall certainly call there, if ever I live to see Dublin again. How long is it in existence?"

"Since 1750. It was established shortly after the battle of Culloden—where the Scottish chivalry died so gallantly. A gentleman named Jameson, who had been an officer in the King's service there, obtained the knowledge somehow, started this famous concern, and ——"

"—— Did better work I fancy," said Eugene laughing indolently, "than in putting the gallant Prince Charlie off the Throne of Scotland. I wonder he has not rivals?"

"So he has, but none can evoke the potent spirit that lies hidden in the waving grain, so well or readily as he; and ——"

"Upon my word," said Ronald impatiently, "it is a very profane discussion we are carrying on, considering that one has only just wakened from the confines of the other world. How do you find yourself, Eugene?"

"Well. The little of this I have taken seems warming every vein in my body and strengthening every nerve. I feel quite revived."

"Take a little more, and I warrant you you will have appetite and strength for a slice of the haunch of deer that is roasting inside. Do you think you could stand up?"

"With help I could."

"Then the help is near you. Place your arm under him, Ronald, opposite mine. There, lift him now. Why, you are quite strong already," cried François gaily, as

Eugene, lifted from his couch of rushes and heath, stood unsteadily on his feet. "A day or two of rest and we shall be ready to seek the friendly shelter of the French colours again."

"I feel quite refreshed," said Eugene. "I shall be quite well in a short time. How long have I been here?"

"Since yester-night. You slept soundly, whether your sleep was refreshing or not. That's the mark of a horse's hoof on your temple. It was well it was no worse. You must forgive the good steed, however, for his master's hand was unable to guide him. He had a bullet through his brain."

"What became of the soldiers?" asked Eugene in a whisper.

"We did not stop to inquire," said François carelessly, as he directed his friend's footsteps towards an inner cavity, from which the pleasant aroma of roasted venison was now emerging. "Some of them leaped the barrier and escaped; others lie to this moment, if they have not been removed, in front of it. But, what is more to the purpose, we were carried here by trusty hands, and here we are now."

"We are under infinite obligations to you," said Eugene, turning to the quondam driver, whose appearance—now that Eugene was able to see him in the light of the lamp burning in the inner apartment of the cave—was quite altered, his dress rich and costly, and his features grave and aristocratic.

"Obligations!" cried François enthusiastically. "The truth and loyalty shown to us in our need would redeem the dangers of the most unfortunate expedition that ever sailed the seas, and brighten the darkest tide of misfortunes that ever encompassed man. We owe our lives to Ronald. Allow me to introduce you: Ronald MacDonald, Captain Eugene Lefebre."

"You forget, gentlemen," said the stranger thus introduced, laughing, "what *you* have perilled by coming to aid *us*. I am sorry some gleam of success did not shine on your banners, but that was not your fault."

"Well, a brighter day may come," said Eugene, with a cheerfulness that he was far from feeling

"I fear not. Indeed I know it will not," said the Irishman sadly—"know it so well that I intend leaving this country for ever. There is no home for true Irishmen in Ireland now."

"You should come to France with us," said François eagerly. "That is the home for freemen."

"Precisely what I mean to do," said Ronald, as they took their seats at the dinner-table, which groaned, if not with dainty fare, at least with appetising viands.

"Then you have decided aright," said François delightedly. "We shall all sail together. I know what you are thinking of, Eugene," said he, turning from the subject, as he saw his friend's eyes fixed on a fourth seat at present unoccupied. "You are wondering whom that is for?"

"I am."

"It is for an old friend, whom you will be glad to see."

"An old friend, François?" said Eugene, whose thoughts immediately referred to Redmond Barrington.

"Yes, an old friend who ——"

"Who is here to answer for himself," said a well-known voice behind Eugene's chair.

"What! M'Nevin!" said the latter, as that gentleman advanced gaily and shook hands with the invalid. "This is astonishment, truly. How did *you* manage to come?"

"Why, if I might speak in hyperbole, I came on the wings of misfortune. Nothing else would bring a man to this woful land at present."

"But, hyperbole aside, how did you come? We left you behind in France."

"I could not bear the agony of suspense—I could not be away from Ireland when her need was sorest, so I sailed from France some days after Bompart started. Finding on my arrival in Ireland that the revolution was crushed out and that Humbert had surrendered, I made my way here with the intention of warning your fleet that the expedition had been already rendered useless, and that you should turn your helm again for France. But I was too late to be of use—I arrived only to hear the thunders of the bombardment borne in from the sea."

"Not of no use, certainly," said MacDonald, as he proceeded to carve the dinner, "for if it had not been for your good advice and strategy we should not have been able to bring our friends away from their captors."

"So that I am again obliged to you for my freedom," said Eugene, appreciating the information conveyed by the last speaker.

"Well, it is a long lane that has no turning. Some day," said M'Nevin, anxious to avoid the subject, "you can repay the favour. And now to dinner. These Irish hills, if good for nothing else, are capital for giving an appetite."

The dinner passed over pleasantly, although Eugene's weakness prevented his doing justice to the excellent haunch of venison and capital grouse set before him. But when it was over, and hot water and tumblers were placed on the table, the disappointing fortunes of war were forgotten, mirth and gaiety reigned around, light-hearted pleasure beamed on every face, and the conversation was cheerful and animated—as, indeed, might be expected among a quartette whose lives and fortunes had been so changeful and adventurous.

"You have not yet told me how you came here, François," said Eugene.

"I briefly sketched it out for you, if you remember," said the former. "I told you, I think, that Humbert's force landed safely in Killala Bay; that we beat the English at Castlebar, where they ran from us at such a rate that not even our cavalry could come up with them; that the people flocked in thousands to our standard, but that we had no time to drill recruits; and with all the available forces in Ireland—some thirty or forty thousand—marching on us, resistance, not to say success, had become hopeless. Surrounded on all sides, our little column had to surrender. We beat some ten thousand at Castlebar, but we could not hope to fight the entire British army. I did not choose to become prisoner of war. I had heard enough to make me dislike that. I separated from the officers on the eve of the surrender and took my way towards the North of Ireland—in hopes, like M'Nevin— to save your force from a like disaster. I took all the unfrequented ways, rode across mountains, over rivers, through green valleys, everywhere sheltered by the grateful and kindly people. My French accent opened a way at once to their hearts; I never had occasion to tell who or what I was—they seemed to know it instinctively; and, truly, fugitive soldier in invaded country, flying from its defenders, never met such welcome before. There was no kindness, no hospitality, that they did not lavish upon me. I think I must have been a week or more on my journey northward—guided in this land—to me so strange!—by the directions of the people, who spared no pains to put me on the right track—when I fell in with a body of men, retainers and friends of—and under command of—Ronald here, who were hurrying southward at the news of the landing. My unlooked-for information made them retrace their steps—probably saved them from useless slaughter—and safe among friends and guides we travelled unceasingly night and day. How much I owe to his good offices I cannot now say."

" But I thought you were on board the fleet. How ——"

" So I was. That adventure was in store for me, too. Wherever there is trouble I am generally into it. Having occasion to pass through the streets of the town—Letter—Letter——"

" Letterkenny," suggested Ronald.

" Yes, Letterkenny—that is it—through Letterkenny one night, I heard a gentleman speaking in French—in French, Eugene! Think of the delight of that, after days and weeks of fugitive wandering! I could hardly believe my ears! I took an opportunity of speaking to him alone—beyond measure glad to meet a countryman here. Who do you think he was, Eugene?"

" I could not say."

" Well, guess."

" How could I guess?"

" You might well say that. Nor could I. Well—he was the officer in command of the British troops here—one General Levau."

" In command of the British troops, François—nonsense!"

" If it be nonsense I did not find it so; for, having heard my story, he had me promptly arrested."

"Who was he?"

"One of these *emigres*—the curse of France in every country. However, I should not blame him too much. To gratify his hatred of his native land, he had me brought on board the fleet, on their return, to be witness of the defeat of our vessel, and the debarkation of French prisoners. It was that gave me the opportunity of seeing you. Ronald here did the remainder. But I see you are looking weak and pale. It is time to retire to rest. A sleep will restore you. And now to dream of home and beautiful France."

CHAPTER XLV.

THE ESCAPE.

THERE was much searching after the fugitive officers, a circumstance that the peasantry kept them acquainted with. Often the military parties passed within short distance of their hiding-place; but the loyalty of their humble friends stood them in good stead, and the secret of their concealment was kept inviolate. Neither were their wants unattended to. The deer from the hillsides, the grouse from the heather, the mutton from the fertile valleys—all were brought by Ronald's friends and tenants at night to their hiding place; and what with the pure spring water of the hill, mixed with the *poteen*, their time was passing in an ease and abundance that was strikingly at variance with their late experiences.

But, as the days rolled by and Eugene's strength gathered and grew, a restlessness to be away again and mingling with the busy world outside came upon all. In especial it came upon him, who, now that his foot was on Irish soil, was tenfold anxious to see Seamore. He spent many an hour of reverie wondering what changes had come thereover since he last saw it, and how its inmates had fared. To get away, therefore, had become the leading thought of all. But how?

The answer to this question was a difficult one.

The country was covered with troops, and was carefully watched. Strangers would be sure to be detected, and the accents of the Frenchmen would be quite certain to betray them. Even if otherwise, conveyances in these remote places were not to be had easily, and on the whole any chance of reaching Dublin overland, which they had proposed to themselves, was as hopeless as that of reaching the moon.

With the difficulties, however, grew greater their yearning to get away. MacNevin and François, finding all hopes of active service in Ireland dead, were panting to leave the country and betake themselves again to France, where great enterprises were in course of preparation. Once there, in the bustle of life and in the excitement of military glory they could afford to forget their fruitless efforts in this unfortunate land. Eugene, as we have seen, was most intent on reaching Dublin.

There remained, therefore, only one practicable way— that of escaping by sea.

But that seemed nearly as impossible as the other. The fleet and its captured vessels lay at anchor on the Lough. A guardship watched the entrance thereof, and man-of-war's boats were busily cruising about both by day and by night.

"I protest I shall go mad if I remain here longer," said François one afternoon, after returning from a stolen reconnaisance through the heather, and a view of the fleet that lay so stately on the unruffled waters of the Lough.

"And I, too," said MacNevin wearily.

"I must say I share your feelings," said Eugene. "Has no one a mode of getting away to propose?"

"I saw a boat drawn up on the beach some distance yonder," said François meditatively.

"A boat?" said the captain of the *Hoche* quickly.

"Yes; she lies there at present—a four-oared boat, with a lug and foresail furled. One would think she was placed there for us."

"He should have a strong imagination that would think that under present circumstances," said MacNevin drily.

"We had better find out something about it, at any

rate. I should run any risk to get away at present?" said Eugene. "Do you know anything of her, Ronald?"

"She comes in each night with a searching party—and occasionally in the daylight," answered Ronald.

"Do they leave her unprotected?"

"They do, for a while—at least whilst they are searching the cabins on the hill, where they believe you to be hidden."

"There is a chance for us, gentlemen!" said Eugene, a new hope arising in his breast.

"It's but a small one—if you mean of escaping by that means," said Ronald gravely.

"It is precisely of escaping I am thinking," said Eugene brightly, "and by that means."

"I am afraid there is but little hope of that. The boat would soon be missed; and, even if you escaped the other boats in the Lough, the guardship at the mouth of the bay would capture or sink you."

"I wish we were once in her, that's all," said François, breaking in delightedly. "I should be glad to run the chances of escape."

"And I, too," said MacNevin. "We cannot remain here for ever, and escape seems as feasible now as at any other time. Besides, every day adds to the danger of detection"

"I say, Ronald," said Eugene, after a moment's thinking, "what do you think would be our best plan of securing her? How could we find out when the searching party leave her?"

"I could not say, her time of coming is so uncertain."

"I shall tell you what we can do," said MacNevin, after a long pause, during which each was occupied in devising plans. "We should have intimation conveyed to them that we are sheltering in this neighbourhood. If a trusty friend conveyed to them the information, and appointed a certain time—say, at dark to-morrow evening—to reveal our whereabouts, we could take advantage of their absence and seize the boat, and be far off before they returned."

"It is not a bad idea at all," said François.

"What do you say, Eugene?"

"If it were well worked, I agree with you. But how is it to be done? Could you assist us, Ronald?"

"I shall do anything in my power," answered the latter; "but have you considered the danger? It is rushing on certain capture or death—one or other—probably the latter."

"For my part, I am willing to risk it," said Eugene.

"And I," said François.

"And I," said MacNevin.

"If," said Eugene, resuming the subject, "we could have a message conveyed them——"

"If you have made up your minds," said Ronald, "to face the danger, I shall have the matter arranged. You need not trouble yourselves as to that."

"To-morrow evening, then!" said François eagerly. "And hey for *la belle France* again!"

"I think it would be better to wait," said Ronald, "for a few weeks, until the fleet moves away and search dies out. We shall be ready to run you across to France in one of our boats. It is not the first time we have run from here to Bordeaux."

"A few weeks, Ronald!" cried François impatiently. "As well say a few years. Great events are hastening forward in France whilst we lie hiding here. Every day spent is lost and wasted time. For heaven's sake let us have the chance—whatever comes of it."

"Very well," said Ronald reluctantly; "to-morrow night be it. And, as this night is to be your last here, I do not think we can do better than enjoy it. So I move we proceed to dinner."

A smoking salmon was on the table, flanked with a brace of grouse. A haunch of venison smoked on a side table. The prospect of escape added a new zest to the meal, and three happier guests or with lighter hearts seldom dined amid the heath of the Donegal headlands. The sconces affixed to the clay walls gave a quaint light to the apartment, that made the place feel cozy and pleasant; and when justice had been done to the rough but appetising meal, and their cigars were lit, all four prepared to enjoy their last night amid the heather of Lough Swilly.

Anecdote and incident were related. Two of the party, at least, had seen much of the world—much of that portion of it that lay amid battle scenes—amid the tumult of contending armies; and the stories once heard beside the bivouac fire were retold again.

The morning rays were beginning to come in through the aperture overhead and to dim the light of the candles when they threw themselves on their beds of dried heath and grass, after a night spent in most interesting and unflagging conversation. They were soon sound asleep, and noon had long passed before they opened their eyes.

When they did, a storm was raging on the hillside.

Ronald, with the active habits of the country, was awake and out long before the slumbers of the others had been dispelled.

He returned some time after they had arisen.

"Well, gentlemen," he said as he entered, "that matter has been arranged. Their searching party, guided by one of our men, will land below us when darkness sets in, and the venture can be made. They feel certain of success this time."

"It seems to be blowing strongly," said François, as the storm of wind and rain blew down the opening.

"It is blowing a hurricane on the Lough," said Ronald. "A dangerous night, if it does not abate, to put to sea."

"So much the better," said Eugene cheerfully. "The worse the storm the better for us."

"Then, if you think so, you had better prepare for the occasion. You will need some arms. Here are some for your use."

He opened a rough press in the earthen wall, from which he brought some very handsomely-finished silver-mounted pistols and some cutlasses.

"Why these are some of our own," said Eugene in surprise, as he glanced at the latter. "Where did you get them?"

"That is a question hardly fair to ask," said Ronald, laughing. "You don't suppose we have no friends on board the fleet?"

"I trust you have. They were never more wanted than now. And so that is how you got the weapons?"

"Yes. How do you like them? Will they answer your purpose?"

"They are the very things to suit us. Why, Ronald, you are a magician?"

"I am glad you think so. But I shall be still more glad if you have no occasion to need them. And the next thing I should fancy you will want is your dinner. When that is finished, it will be time to start."

Dinner was soon ready, and the four friends sat down to partake of it. The preparation for the expedition occupied most of their conversation, in the course of which Ronald informed them of his intentions.

They were to climb down the hill in the dusk, hide behind the shrubbery that covers its shores, and, when the searching party in company with their guide had passed up the hill, they were to seize the boat, put out into the bay, hoist their sails, and trust to heaven for the future.

Accordingly when the dinner was over, and that they had exhausted a cigar or two, the time had come for essaying the attempt. It was a bold and dangerous effort; there were many enemies and dangers to be passed; but in the minds of all it was better to run whatever risks might come than encounter another week's *ennui* and enforced imprisonment. The chance of adventure, in the mind of more than one, added to the charm of escape rather than subtracted from it.

Dusk closed in, the shadows of night crept down the hillsides, when, bidding a warm farewell to the humble friends who attended them during their fortnight's rest, the party of four emerged from the cave, and proceeded to descend cautiously the hillside.

Arrived at the lake-shore, they ensconced themselves under Ronald's direction, in a thick brake hard by the shingly strand in which the boat from the fleet generally pulled up.

Here they waited, with no little anxiety, the sound of oars on the water.

An hour and a half of anxious suspense passed over, in which they scarcely dared to whisper to one another. The danger that looked so trifling when they were com fortably situated in the shelter of the cave began by degrees to look vastly greater as the moments grew on.

Finally their ears were gladdened with the noise of voices over the water; the sound of oars was distinctly heard gradually growing nearer; and, whilst they listened with suppressed breathing, the boat grated on the shingly shore, the searching party stepped out, the skiff was drawn a little out of the water, and the soldiers commenced climbing the hillside.

It was blowing hard from the land—from the direction where the party disembarked—and the sounds came with greater distinctness on their listening ears.

"Have you a light, sergeant?" The query fell on their ears. "It is so long since I had a smoke that I think a cigar would be of no harm?"

"It is the officer who speaks," whispered Ronald.

"You would find it difficult to get a light in this storm," said the party addressed.

"If you have your flint and touch-paper I shall be able to manage it. Have you? For I have forgotten my own."

"Yes, here they are. But they will be useless. The wind is too strong."

"Never mind. I shall try it whilst you are ascending the hill. I shall overtake you. There is a brake yonder a good deal sheltered, in which I fancy I shall manage to light it."

"All right, captain. You will follow us?"

"Yes; I shall shortly overtake you."

The short conversation carried on in a loud voice was clearly enough heard by the anxious listeners. The brake referred to was that wherein they were hidden, and a sudden dread of discovery fell on them.

"He is coming this way," whispered Ronald, whose ears, more accustomed to the buffetting of storms, could distinguish the steps more accurately. The only sounds that came to the ears of the others were the noise caused by the clambering of the soldiers up the rocky sides of the mountain, and the displacing of loose stones that gradually rolled down the declivity behind.

Meanwhile, the officer in charge came in their direction,

where the tangle of the scrub and bushes would give him greater shelter for striking a light,—came, indeed, so near that, as they lay close together, his foot nearly touched him nearest. It was with difficulty they could restrain their breathing. Escape was so near; and yet so little might effectually preclude its possibility.

The boat lay almost within hand's reach. A minute or so would, if all things went well, see its sails set, and in the force of the gale blowing send them sweeping up th stormy waters of the Lough. They hey for freedom, and perchance for France! But now what an awkward *contretemps!* The slightest movement would betray them, and the slightest call bring their enemies rushing back upon them. No wonder they lay with stifled breath, and that they tried even to check the beating of their hearts!

The officer, wholly unconscious of the presence of anyone, essayed several times to strike a light with the flint and tinder. But the wind prevented his efforts. The sparks, before they took light on the touch, were rudely blown out by the storm.

Every effort calmly essayed by him added hours to the lingering anxiety of the fugitives.

Finally, he succeeded, but at that moment, just as the torch began to take light and burn, an unconscious movement on the part of Eugene begotten of his impatience and his high-wrought tension of mind, drew the attention of the officer! Indeed it could scarcely do otherwise—occurring at his very feet!

He stooped down with the lighted touch in his hand to see what occasioned the noise. The light gleaming on the ground disclosed the forms of the fugitives!

In a sudden outburst of surprise the officer uplifted himself, the touch dropping from his hands as he did so—uplifted himself to cry aloud to his men now far up the hill!

It was a moment of dreadful danger. The slightest cry or noise would have brought his men hurrying back down the cliff side.

Alive to the tremendous necessities of the occasion, Eugene leaped to his feet and placed his hand on the mouth of the surprised officer. In a second after the others were beside him, and without a word being spoken or a cry uttered, the officer was gagged with a handkerchief which prevented him from either stirring or speaking.

François presented a pistol to his ear, the cold muzzle of which gave significant intimation of what was meant, and made the operation less troublesome.

"Stir hand or foot, utter but the faintest cry, and you are a dead man," whispered Eugene in breathless accents in his ear. "We are escaping prisoners. We shall die before we are taken. Your death is assured if you but breathe a word."

The manner in which he spoke was sufficient token of his earnestness—as it is always where a man feels and means what he says—and the officer taken aback by the suddenness and surprise of the movement, stood still. He had no intention of speaking under the circumstances even if the handkerchief thrust rudely into his mouth permitted him.

At that moment the whistle of the sergeant on the hill, impatient at the unexpected delay of the officer, was heard.

"The boat, gentlemen—the boat," whispered Ronald to his comrades.

The hint was speedily taken. The danger was urgent to all. The slightest sound or alarm would have brought their enemies tumbling back. They hurried the prisoner to where the boat lay, their footsteps on the broken brambles and brushwood making but slight noise. A few vigorous pushes sent the boat into the waters; and, bringing their prisoner with them, they were speedily launched into the Lough!

"Who meddles with the boat? That is the king's boat! Who dares touch it?"—called from the hill above them in loud tones—assailed their ears.

Then in a moment after came the call for the officer—
"Captain Melville! Captain Melville!"

But the officer, fast bound and gagged, made no reply, nor even was he disposed to, with the touch of the cold muzzle of a pistol at his cheek. That they were desperate men on a desperate errand there was no need to tell him, and that they carried their lives in their hands. Wherefore no answer came to the call from the cliffs.

The oars were swiftly fixed in the rowlocks, whilst the surf driven by the storm threatened to overturn the boat, and beat painfully about the ears of the escaping party. A few strokes, uncomfortably noisy as the irons grated in their sockets, sent them out to deeper water!

The searching party high above, uneasy at the departure of the boat, and hearing no response from their leader, grew alarmed. A suspicion of treachery fastened on their minds, which was not lessened by the non-appearance of their leader.

Before the boat had gone many perches through the water a rocket shot from the hillside, racing up aloft into the stormy night and bursting into a thousand fragments.

"That is a signal to the fleet," said Eugene hurriedly, after they had for a moment watched its picturesque ascent and extinguishment.

"And there goes the response," said Ronald, as another, in answer, ascended from the deck of one of the vessels. "We are discovered."

"Hoist the sail. We must run for it now," said François energetically. "Unship the oars. Spread enough sail, and the storm will carry us half way into the Atlantic before they can get ready!"

Almost as he said it, the oars were removed, placed inside the boat, and whilst the signal roll-call from the fleet came, borne shrilly on their ears on the breast of the wind, the sails were run up and spread. Ronald, best acquainted with the inland waters in which they were sailing, took the rudder; and they were immediately driving with headlong speed towards the mouth of the Lough, towards the broad waters that formed their ocean pathway to freedom and France.

It was pitch dark.

The wind veering blew with hurricane force down from the mountain valleys, and swept as with a tornado the surface of the Lough. The masts creaked and bent as the storm, pressing on their sails, nearly buried the prow of the vessel in the water. A long streak of phosphorescent foam behind them alone showed a ray of brightness in the thick blackness.

Save where and alone a slight faint thread of light ascending from the fleet, now rapidly distancing itself from them, showed where a signal was given forth, no light broke on their vision!

"This is tremendous going, Eugene," shouted François in his friend's ear, for the rushing of the vessel, the howling of the storm, and the straining and the groaning of the masts, made spoken words unheard. The boat with the force of the wind and speed sometimes ran on her side until the water surged over.

"It is. We shall be at sea presently," said Eugene. "This is the mouth of the Lough we are passing through. Somewhere yonder, if we could only make it out through the darkness, the *Hoche* fought her brave battle."

"Where is that guardship we were told that hung about here? I see no light in the black waste of waters," asked MacNevin.

"Sheltering probably from this storm," said Eugene. "I wish we could do similarly. We shall never stand this wind at sea. This gale comes from the South, and the cliffs by keeping near them might shelter us. Don't you think so?" added he, turning round and shouting his query into Ronald's ear, where he crouched at the tiller.

"It is dangerous in this pitch blackness. The coast abounds with rocky islands," returned the latter.

"But we shall be swept to sea otherwise—blown right out of our course," argued Eugene, "even if we can live through it."

"Yes," commented MacNevin, "if this hurricane holds, I fancy we shall be half way to the North Pole before the morning."

"I think we had better tack round, and run in for shelter under these cliffs, if the boat can wear round in such a storm as this. Do you think she can, Ronald?"

"She may."

"I shall try at any rate."

"It will need be quick work, then," said Ronald, shouting in his ear. "I have never seen such a storm blow from the South before. Watch me when I shift the helm and let the mainsail go, else we are lost."

They had left the region of black and swelling waves, and emerged into a sea of broken, white, and tossing surf. Far as the eye could reach the hissing foam upheaved—forming a striking contrast with the leaden darkness around and above. The wind descending from the high headlands struck the water here, and with great violence tore its surface into spray.

"We shall never be able to tack round here. We shall capsize first," was Eugene's thought as he stood by the mainsail, and a gust of wind nearly swept him overboard.

The mainsail was so taut with the force of the storm that it stood against his hand as if made of steel. At the moment the prow of the boat plunging forward tore through a surf-laden wave, completely burying herself therein and well nigh filling with water.

"Another like that, Eugene, and we are lost! The boat is already half full. See how she staggers more than sails through the water."

"I see that, François. We must go round at all hazards. Tell Ronald I am standing by the sail. Let him shift the rudder next lull, and I shall let go."

There was not much distance wherein to carry the order, yet François, what with the difficulty of crossing the seats in the dark and the danger of being blown overboard while standing up, was some time in moving to where Ronald sat at the helm.

"Ronald, we are in great danger."

Ronald with a motion of his head assented.

"Eugene intends letting go at the next lull. Can you shift the helm at the same time? We must get into still water."

"Unless done at the same time we shall drown," said Ronald, as a huge wave struck against the side of the boat; but a motion of the helm rapid as lightning placed her so that the wave skimmed by, its white crest gleaming strangely against the dark background.

"Now!" shouted Ronald, and at the moment shifted the helm.

Instantaneously Eugene let go the sail, which cracked with the force of a thousand whips; a huge wave burst over the vessel; all held their breaths for a moment of dreadful suspense; the boat swept around on her side, and almost immediately was gliding peacefully in quiet waters. Save and except the quantity of sea she had shipped, the dangerous movement was swiftly and safely performed.

"Thank God!" burst with one accord from all hearts. A moment's hesitation in the breast of the steerer or him who stood at the sail would have plunged them into the drowning waters—into eternity!

"Well, François," said Eugene, "I think we shall long remember our parting from Lough Swilly."

"I fancy so; though we can be scarcely said to have got quite clear away yet."

"You are wet, I suppose?" said Ronald.

"Wet!" said François. "I am thoroughly drenched."

"For the matter of that, so are we all," said Mac-Nevin.

"Then I suppose this will be acceptable. It was fortunate I thought of bringing it," said Ronald, producing a flask.

"It was never more needed," said MacNevin emphatically, as Ronald handed it around. "You might be called the beneficent genii of the Donegal cave."

The grateful liquor seemed to create a new spirit within the breast of all; and even the imprisoned officer, who had run all the dangers of their perilous trip without the attendant excitement of escape, felt that the generous drink had given him new heart and life.

"Hallo," cried François, who was looking ahead through the blackness as the boat glided smoothly along in the shelter of the high cliffs, "we appear to be perilously near land. There is a something rising up here to the right which seems to me to be like it!"

"I wish it were," said Ronald, "and that we could have an hour's rest ashore if only to stretch one's legs. I am perfectly crippled with sitting here."

"Where is the land, François? I cannot see it," said Eugene, who had gained his side, and was peering with him through the darkness.

"Yonder it is; and, lo! there seems a light on it, too," cried François, indicating the position of the supposed cliff.

Eugene looked for a moment in the direction, then suddenly left his side with an exclamation of surprise which startled François, and hurried to the tiller.

"Ronald," said he, "shift the helm. Quick, man! put her head to the North or we are lost!"

"What! to the North?—to the open sea again?"

"Yes, at once—or we are undone?"

"Why, what is the matter?" cried Ronald, who believed that his companion had lost his senses, or that the small quantity of poteen he had taken had had some effect on his brain.

"The guardship is ahead of us! We are running directly under her bows. See!"

Looking, Ronald saw the huge hulk of the ship looming vaguely upon them from the darkness, and right in their front. She was sheltering under bare poles in the security of the beetling headlands, and, save her swaying and tossing on the troubled surface of the water, was perfectly noiseless and quiet. The movements of their own boat through the water and the conversation that had been carried on had attracted the attention of the watch on her deck; and whilst Ronald looked, a second light made its appearance, defining clearly enough her previously vague form.

A muttered malediction came from Ronald, who was far from expecting this incident. The next moment a movement of the tiller sent the little boat at a strong angle to her former course, and not a moment too soon, for they were almost running against the huge sides of the guardship, the contact with which would inevitably have capsized them, and the suction of the water have drawn them under her keel.

A breathless silence fell on all on board, as the sails, fluttering with the altered course of the boat, speedily filled again with the wind. All eyes were cast on the vague form above them and the lights moving high up as in some solitary watch tower. A bugle came on their ears.

"That is a signal for us to come around to them," said Ronald, bending forward to his companions.

"They will wait for us a while," whispered François gaily. "This is an unreasonable time for visiting"

THE ESCAPE.

"Yes, I think they will have to travel pretty far to converse with us," said MacNevin.

"I fancy they are going to speak to us in another way. There is a porthole thrown open."

"So there is!" said François.

A porthole did indeed disclose through the darkness its ominous light—which was quickly shaded, however, as a gun was run out and depressed in their direction.

"Hush!—not a word!" said Eugene impressively. "They are guided only by the noise of our voices, and are going to fire at random in this direction."

The noise of the boat rushing through the water was the only sound save the roaring of the storm, as they held their breath in suspense for the first shot.

It was not long in coming. A sudden violent flash of red light, that died out as suddenly as it appeared, a thud as of several substances striking the surface of the water near, and a shower of spray was dashed over them! Following came the boom of the gun, and the cloud of white smoke lifted itself spirally through the darkness and lazily disappeared.

"That was a narrow escape!" whispered Eugene. "A little more elevation and there was an end of our attempt."

"We are not quite done with them yet—hush!" said François, as the lights once more glimmered in the little window-like port-hole. A second time the sharp lightning flash pierced the darkness, the howl of the wind gave way to the heavy, dull boom of the big gun, and a shower of grape sweeping overhead—some even piercing the sails —struck the water in advance of them.

"This is coming too close," said Ronald from his place at the helm. "I shall run her Nor'-East to get out of reach of that gun. Stand by to answer the helm!"

"I am ready. Call when!" said Eugene, taking his stand at his place, sail-rope in hand.

"Now!"

"Now, be it!" cried the former, loosing his hold; and immediately the boat was spinning along on her new course. A third discharge of grape struck the sea a long way behind

"We are out of range of *that* gun," said MacNevin. 'Let us hope they may not send a boat after us."

"They will scarcely tempt this night of storm. The chances are they have taken us for a smuggling vessel, taking advantage of this gale to make a favourable venture, and will not think us worthy of the trouble. Meanwhile we had better creep along the coast until morning breaks, when the gale out at sea may moderate."

Thus Ronald.

Through the darkness of the night they kept their silent way until in the distant east there appeared a cold, grey breadth of daylight. As it grew stronger and the hills along the shore began to have their sides tipped with brightness, a singular scene presented itself. The sea, inshore in the shelter of the cliffs, was still as a mill-pond; but further out, where the headlands failed to protect it, and where the wind had power to strike it, it was, far as the eye could reach, one sheet of surf and foam.

A marvellous sight! and seemed as if the surface of the tossing sea had been suddenly overlaid with a mantle of snow. On the edge of the horizon, a vessel caught in the storm of the night, could be seen heavily labouring and helplessly tumbling in the trough of the foaming sea.

"Well, gentlemen," said MacNevin, as the high cliffs of the Giant's Causeway came on their sight, "it is pretty nearly time for us to shape our course. Which way shall we steer?"

"For the coast of Scotland, I suggest," said Ronald. "We shall find friends there who will aid us to escape."

"And run a further chance of capture, or at least of detention from France," exclaimed François, whose breast was glowing with the hope of shortly reaching his native country. "Certainly not. What say you, Eugene?"

"Why, as for me," said Eugene, "I should wish to remain in Ireland some time longer. I have pressing business to arrange."

"It would be perfectly impossible for you to do so at present," said Ronald. "We could not land you any place where you would not be certain of capture."

"Why not proceed down the Channel, and make straight for France?" suggested François.

"Because you would be certain to be captured before you could reach mid-Channel," returned Ronald. "I vote that we steer for Scotland. I have friends in every harbour along the coast. We can then suit our own different purposes, and choose our own modes of departure."

"I think that is the best plan," said MacNevin. "I don't see how escape is practicable any other way."

Eugene thought so, too, particularly as once there he was within easy reach of the Irish coast. François being in a hopeless minority, was obliged to consent, though with manifest reluctance; and, having put their prisoner ashore, they turned the boat's head to the North-east, intending to reach the coast of Scotland by rounding Rathlin Island.

In a short time the shores of the Northern coast were fast receding from them.

"Good-bye, Ireland!" said MacNevin, as the tall bluffs of the Giant's Causeway, with its wondrous architecture —Nature's own handiwork—began to grow cloud-like. "Your hills appear to me for the last time. I would I left you under happier circumstances."

"Good-bye, Ireland!" cried François gaily. "I had hoped to win my marshal's baton on your green plains, but Fate has willed it otherwise."

"All hopes are not lost yet," broke in Eugene cheerfully.

"They are—completely," said MacNevin emphatically.

"The Directory may ——"

"The Directory will never do anything more—and if they did it would come too late. They could not galvanize this broken, dispirited, and defeated land into fresh life. No; I shall never look on Irish shore, or stream, or hillside again. I feel that with the strength of prophecy. The gates of eternity shall unroll themselves to me, and the wonderful land that is beyond them appear, before I shall see this land again. Good-bye, dear Ireland! And now for the hills of Scotland!"

He spoke with deep feeling; and a sense of dejection and disappointment was palpable in his words.

As he concluded, all eyes turned in the direction in which they were steering, when suddenly an exclamation burst from them!

For—tossing and tumbling in the water, so close to them that every pulley and block in her rigging could be distinctly seen, was a large three-masted vessel. Their exclamations were caused by the suddenness with which she had appeared to their gaze.

If she had risen out of the water the effect could not have been more startling.

"Where has she come from?" asked François in amazement. "She was certainly not here the last time when I looked."

"It seems to me," said Ronald, "that she has suddenly started out of the water. But stay! this must be the vessel we saw earlier. The mist had hidden her."

"She is in a bad way, at any rate," said Eugene, scanning her intently. "There seems to be no one working her. Her sails hang loosely, as you see, and her rudder is untended. She is abandoned."

"Strange she should be abandoned," said Ronald, "for she seems to be all right. Her masts are standing, and she is too high out of the sea to be water-logged. It seems extraordinary. Let us board her."

"And possibly fall into the danger we are flying from," said MacNevin.

"There is no fear of that," said Eugene decisively; "that is not an English-rigged vessel. She is more of the American style."

"Yes," broke in Ronald, "and look yonder, there is a remnant of a flag flying. That flag is American. She must have been beating up the Channel all night. Unless some aid is given her she will bear down on the rocks around Rathlin and be smashed to pieces in an hour or less."

While they were thus discussing the derelict, the vessel still continued to pitch and flounder, lifting herself unsteadily on the top of a wave and lumberingly descending again into the trough of the sea, whilst the sails, or rather the remnants of them, flew out in every direction as the wind, catching in the folds, got power over them. But there was no sign of human beings on board, nor anything to indicate their presence.

It was a weird sight to see the vessel uninjured, yet thus derelict and abandoned, driving along helplessly at the mercy of wind and wave, no one knowing whence she had come, or what strange story she had brought out of the night and storm.

"I agree with you, Ronald. I think we should board her. There is something curious about her. What say you gentlemen?"

"I think so," said Ronald.

"And I," said François.

"Very well, gentlemen. I have no objection," said MacNevin, rather reluctantly.

They turned the prow of their boat in her direction, and ran under her side to leeward. A rope descending from her bulwarks was swinging unsteadily, anon high in the air and again descending into the water.

Eugene caught it, and, with the dexterity of an active sailor, swung himself on deck.

After the lapse of some moments, during which those in the boat awaited with some anxiety his coming, he reappeared over the bulwarks and let down a rope-ladder.

His face was very white, and there was a strange look on it which they did not fail to notice.

"There is something curious within this vessel," said François, as, catching hold of the ladder, he rapidly mounted on deck, whither, after fastening the boat, he was quickly followed by the others.

"What is it, Eugene?" asked MacNevin. "What's amiss? What's wrong with the vessel?"

"Come below," said Eugene, with, as he turned to descend the companion ladder, something like affright in his voice.

His friends followed him, wondering at his manner. They entered the cabin, and a strange sight met their eyes.

A number of bodies lay around dead, and dead for some time, for the senses of the spectators gave sufficient evidence that decomposition had set in.

The blood scarcely yet dried on the floor, and the gashed faces and arms of the fallen, showed that a terrible struggle

Y

had taken place. The pistols and cutlasses that had fallen from the hands of the combatants lay in disorder around, where the tossing and pitching of the ship had flung them.

"There has been terrible work here," was the commentary of MacNevin as he looked in surprised silence on the evidences around.

"What could it have been?" whispered François, as the four in the gloom of the cabin stood for a moment surveying the scene before them.

"A mutiny, I fancy," said Eugene.

"Robbed and plundered by pirates," suggested Ronald.

"Nay, I think not. She is an American vessel; look here!" and pointing to the name over the hatchment he showed her Boston origin. "Besides, if it were an attack by pirates it is not here but on deck the dead would be found."

"What shall we do? The vessel is driving forward towards the rocks dangerously fast," said Ronald.

"We must explore a little more, and see what it all comes to. A few minutes will suffice."

"Eugene! Ronald! come here!" cried François, in a second after, from one of the sleeping berths leading off the cabin, to which he had gained entrance. "Come here!—quickly!"

Entering where the call came from, they were some time before, in the darkness, they could plainly see around them. Then they noticed that two men lay bound securely, and tied in a sitting posture to the bunk. A gag was in the mouth of each, and as they lay back, their shoulders against the partition, they appeared to be dead.

"They are not dead—there's life in them still!" said Eugene, in reply to a whisper from François, as he felt their pulses. "Find a light some one, until we unbind them. And some one also see if there be any stimulant in the cabin. Their lives may depend upon instant attention."

François was fortunate enough to find a light. There was not much difficulty in obtaining stimulants either, for the place was but little disturbed. Whatever was the origin or cause of the quarrel it seemed clear that ordinary robbery or plunder had nothing to do with it.

In a moment the cords that bound the two insensible forms were cut, and carefully a few drops of brandy were poured between their lips. Little by little the quantity was increased until the action of the pulse gave Eugene token of a movement towards strength and recovery.

"François," whispered Eugene, "have you ever seen that face before?"

"Let me see. Hold the light a little nearer. Let it fall over his face. Why, Eugene, it is ——"

"Who?"

"Our old captain."

"The very same. I could not for a moment remember Your recognition confirms my own impression."

"I thought he was on board the British fleet?"

"What could have brought him here?"

"Heaven alone knows."

"If he recovers we shall soon know. Meantime, François, we shall leave you to take care of them. The ship needs minding, too, and it will take us all our time to fix the helm and shift the sails. Thank Heaven, the storm is abating a little."

It was fortunate that two men so skilful as Eugene and Ronald had come on board, for the vessel had got into the race of waters that with swift current bear down from the North Channel on the iron rocks of Rathlin. What with the treacherous current, added to the storm of the night, and the heavy gale still blowing from the South, she was driving with blind speed towards the pitiless rocks.

An hour, or even half an hour would place her where human aid would be unavailing.

"There is no time to be lost here, Ronald," said Eugene, as they reached the deck and took in the surroundings.

"None," said the other emphatically.

"Shall we be able to wear her round?"

"We must try. Some of the sails are still good. Unless we can—and immediately—we shall never set foot on French or Irish soil again. We are among the breakers."

"We must wear her round. We cannot abandon her."

"You could not even if you would. No small boat would last a minute in this boiling surge."

"Very well, Ronald. Help me to tie this helm; the villains have let it sway loose. Stretch the mainsail whilst I run aloft and clew up the top yards. You had better stand at the helm, MacNevin, and see that it does not shift. Keep it hard a port. We may weather the terrible danger yet. But it will need all our efforts."

Whilst Ronald braced up the mainsail that had been fluttering about with every movement of the ship, Eugene mounted swiftly aloft, and spreading out some sails, and making them taut, clewed and fastened up others.

It was wonderfully quick action, but the hands at work were gifted with the skill derived from long experience; and precisely as a horse, galloping loose with trailing reins, finding himself caught and with a hard hand in command, goes steadily forward in a fixed direction, so in space of a few minutes under the guidance of the two active hands at work, the ship ceased her tossing and tumbling, and plunged steadily forward over the waves that had so lately made her their sport. Nothing to MacNevin's unpractised eye showed more the marvellous power of men's hands and intelligence than the suddenness with which the huge ship obeyed their will, and, abandoning her former helplessness, sprang forward as if gifted with new life and energy.

But the danger was still imminent! Before the vessel's head could be brought around, what with the engulphing whirlpool and the driving wind, she was forced to make a curve that brought her perilously near to the iron rocks over which they could see the surf beating—the white foam in striking contrast with their black and jagged peaks. Eugene remained aloft to make the necessary changes of sail, occasionally motioning his directions to Ronald, who stood lower down; and the helmsman looking at the white faces and active forms of both ready to let go or clew-up as the instant demanded, could see by their nervous movements that the danger was imminent and deadly.

After a time the ship curved round her head to the open sea, and leaving the black rocks to her left—so near that the rush of the surf over them came distinctly on their ears—headed like a panting steed forward. There was no tossing in the trough of the waves now, as, with sails taut to the hardness of sheet-iron, she rode buoyantly over them.

Once safe, Eugene and MacNevin, leaving Ronald at the helm, proceeded downwards to where the captain lay. The stimulant had produced its effect, and the latter was not only sufficiently recovered to be able to recognise François, but to speak.

The greeting between himself and Eugene was most cordial.

"Of all the places in the world the last I should expect to see you in—and the last of all circumstances. How did it come about? I am impatient to hear it," asked the latter.

"It is easily enough told," said the captain when his strength had sufficiently recovered. "The Thunderer when refitted was sent to cruise off the coast of Canada. I deserted at Quebec and came to Boston. There I met some Irishmen whom I knew years before—men who loved their old land, and were ready to make sacrifices for her. They raised funds—they were all of high position and opulence—to purchase this vessel, and to load her with firearms and ammunition for the cause of Ireland."

"With firearms and ammunition?"

"Yes, the hold is stored from keel to underdeck with them at present. But she carried something as good or better—large funds for the support of the Irish cause—for the army in the field."

The captain paused, partly with emotion and partly with regret.

"But what has happened—what means this terrible scene outside?" asked Eugene, impatient for an explanation.

"The gold was too much temptation for some of our crew. We shipped at Boston—for we found it difficult to get hands—part of the crew of an English slaver which had been seized there."

"And they attempted to rob you?"

"They did—more than attempted. They succeeded. Decoying the rest of the crew into the cabin with a false cry of fire, they fell upon them unexpectedly with cutlasses and pistol-shots until they overpowered them."

"That explains the sight outside?"

"That explains it," said the captain.

"And they bore off the gold?"

"They took all the treasure with them."

"I wonder that they did not kill you also."

"They intended worse; they left us to die, to bear all the agonies of knowing that the vessel was driving to destruction without power to alter or guide her course, and to die a living death, as we have been during the past eight and forty hours."

"Where did this take place?"

"At the entrance to the Channel."

"And you have been beating up the Channel in this manner all the time?"

"We have been pitching and tossing—driving hither and thither—in all the fury of last night's storm. And what a hurricane it was! It seemed to me before I grew unconscious, as if the spirits of all that ever were drowned at sea were whistling and shrieking in the rigging and on deck."

"It was the wind tearing through the ropes and sails."

"Perhaps it was; but the sounds were not like that. I should know the shrieking of the wind after twenty years at sea, but the cries and wails that were around us all night were not like that. Where are we now?"

"North of Antrim—off the North coast of Ireland."

"We must have been driven with great speed."

"The gale of last night was not likely to let a ship rest on the waters," said Eugene.

"That is true. Singular how we steered clear of the shore on either side, to reach this far safely. Which puts me in mind to ask what brings you here—what good luck brought you on board?"

"The extraordinary chances of war. But I shall tell you again. We have other more pressing matters now on hands."

"One word—how goes the insurrection in Ireland?"

"Over—over for our lifetime. Crushed out—drowned out in blood."

"And Tone?"

"A prisoner."

" And—the rest ?"

" Dead—or in prison. Some on the gibbet, some in the jail. Don't ask me further about them. It is the cruellest story of brave hearts crushed and bright hopes disappointed that ever dimmed the page of history. The very fates seemed to fight against this hapless land."

" And that is the end ?"

" That is the end—in our time."

" I can hardly believe it," said the captain, lying back wearily and disappointedly. " A nation's life and liberties cannot be trampled out so summarily. A further effort will be made."

" I wish I could hope with you, but I cannot. We shall talk these matters over again. Meantime it is necessary something should be done with the ship. Where do you propose going ?"

" Under the circumstances, now, I do not know."

" Then we had better sail for France."

" Are you going there ?"

" Yes, I think so. At least some of us are."

" Then I suppose it is the best thing to do."

" We had better run up the American flag. The one flying is tattered to pieces. Have you another ?"

" You will find one in the locker to the right," said the captain. " I shall be able to go about myself presently."

" There is no need until you grow stronger. But," said Eugene, as he stepped to the door and the sight outside presented itself again to his view, " it will be necessary to get rid of these bodies. They had better be hove overboard as soon as possible. Who were they."

" Irish-Americans. Poor fellows ! it was not here, nor in that way, they expected to die."

" Coming over in the cause ? "

" Aye; with high hopes, poor fellows, for Ireland and themselves."

" Well, they will never set foot on its shores now. But for their cause we shall give them fitting burial. It is not the first time I made the shroud for dead messmates —killed in gallant action, however, and not by an assassin's cutlass. Have you got canvas ?"

You will find all the necessary matters in the locker."

The sun was high in the sky, brightening the troubled surface of the sea with a flood of glorious light, and the three-master, with all the sails they could muster set, was bearing gallantly down the Channel over the course where she had been tossed and tumbled by the hurricane, when, over the side, shrouded in canvas, a cannon ball sewn in at the feet, the bodies of the dead men were committed to the deep!

It was a sad sight.

The senseless forms, rendered more gloomy from being completely shrouded, let down feet foremost, with tender and reverent hands, sank swiftly out of sight—the weight of iron attached bringing them down. It was weird to see them disappear in the dark waters for evermore from the sunlight overhead.

Where they had been born, on what Irish hillside or valley their cradles had been rocked, why they had left Ireland, and what their varying fortunes had been in the far-off land, were things wholly unknown. Possibly eyes wept and hearts mourned for their absence; but even of this no one knew. They had come hoping to strike a blow for the freedom of the land that bore them; they had come, as the captain said, with high hopes; but the end was thus. Till the day when the sea gives up its dead, and the history of each one is written in words of fire that all gathered mankind shall read, their names and the story of their lives were blotted out with the waters that closed over them as they sank swiftly out of sight!

CHAPTER XLVI.

AN OLD STORY RE-TOLD.

There was a gloom over the faces of all as the last of the forms sank in the waves. But there was little time for sorrow. They were short-handed in the vessel, and it required all their attention to repair the sails and to supply new ones from the ship's stores for those that the storm had torn to shreds.

"If we keep on at this rate," said François exultingly, "we shall not be long until we see France."

"I am not going to France, François—at least not directly," replied Eugene, as they both looked over the bulwarks towards the Irish shores.

"What!" cried the astonished youth. "Not coming to France! What do you mean to do?"

"To land on Irish soil again, François," said Eugene, amused at his young friend's surprise.

"What for? A soldier's sword is needed there no more."

"I am going to pay a visit, François—a long-promised visit, and a long deferred one."

"But your friends—those gentlemen we met that night—they are all dead or in prison, you have told me."

"So they are, François; but there are other friends whom I wish to see—indeed, whom I must see. You remember the night we drove to the boat?"

"Well. Capital reason I have to remember it."

"And the visit I paid?"

"Yes."

"François, I mean to visit there to-night again if God gives me strength and life."

"But you will be arrested, Eugene. MacNevin tells us that a reign of terror exists in Dublin—that the jails are full, and the battlements of the bridges decked with rebels' heads. Is not that so, MacNevin?"

"Yes, I have seen them myself," said MacNevin, who had joined them.

"Hear that, Eugene! See the dangers you run."

"It does not matter. It is my destiny to go there—and I shall. Not all the terrors of an English prison could dissuade me."

"It is an unwise intention, M. Lefebre," said MacNevin gravely. "I am an Irishman myself, and yet I never intend to place my foot on the soil of that land again, dearly as I love it. It is no place now for a free man. And why you with your high command in the French service, with your youth and the brilliant prospect opening before you ——"

"Why I should choose to do so you cannot understand?" broke in Eugene. "Well, I cannot fully explain, but go I must. Do you know what day this is, François?"

"A curious question to ask. It is the last day of October."

"So it is, François. It is a night when spirits are abroad and the dead leave their graves, and they call it in Ireland, Hallowe'en. Twenty-five years ago on this night a French man-of-war was wrecked in a storm on this coast. Not a French soldier or sailor lived to tell the tale but one—her captain. He held a name remarkable in France; but fate brought him to the Irish shore that Hallowe'en night, a quarter of a century ago. He presented himself—a waif that destiny bore from the wave and storm—at a gentleman's mansion, and whilst—as the story was told me—the family were enjoying themselves. It was a night of storm and wind—something like last night—and the appearance of the half-drowned sailor washed ashore from the vanished ship was not a little calculated to alarm them. It was, however, a dear, fair girl who was the most terrified and frightened at his unbidden appearance, and who afterwards became his wife—and—and my mother."

The speaker's voice trembled with emotion, and for a time he ceased whilst his eyes sought out the ranges of cloudlike tints on the rim of the horizon—the faint far off hills of Ireland.

"I never knew before," said François, in low, serious tones, "that you had Irish blood in your veins. I do not wonder now you were so fond of Ireland."

"Nor should I have told you now, François, but that an unwonted softness is in my heart. Perhaps it is the poor fellows who have gone to their low bed in the deep waters—forgotten and unknown—that have caused it. But for the last hour or so I have been thinking—of what do you think?"

"Heaven knows, Eugene—in your adventurous life there must be so many events to think of!"

"Not of any of them. I was thinking of my mother's grave."

"But that, my dear Eugene," said François, the tears

welling sympathetically into his eyes, "should be rather the reason why you should visit France."

"She is buried in Ireland, François—her grave is in Irish soil."

"Ah! How sad—away from dear France," said François, with a feeling of deep regret in his voice—for to him absence from his own country, living or dead, seemed the acme of all grief and sorrow.

"Well, perhaps, not sad after all," said Eugene, an airy smile breaking through his previously grave and serious, if not depressed, face, as the enthusiastic love of his young friend for France exhibited itself somewhat irrationally in this remark. "Her rest may be as peaceful under Irish grass and under Irish sunlight as elsewhere. I hope to see it, however, before I see France."

"After all, if you will permit me to urge it," said MacNevin gently, "that is not a reason strong enough to make you peril your safety and freedom by landing now on Irish soil."

"Quite right, MacNevin," urged François earnestly; "there is no feeling of reverence for the dead that can justify danger to the living. I myself should like to see ——"

"I am sure you would, François—anyone that was dear to you; and I shall be sworn, considerations of danger would not deter you. But I did not finish my story. As twenty-five years ago a half-drowned sailor presented himself before the merry group in the mansion I spoke of, so two years ago on this very evening, I myself, heaven knows without any intention of following, or even knowledge of the precedent, presented myself there, with equally alarming effects."

"Ah! Citizen Lefebre, I see!" said François gaily. "There is a fair girl in this story, too. Well, in that case, sorry as I am and shall be for your absence, I cannot have the heart to urge you to remain with us."

The news of Eugene's intention spread quickly among the little party, to whom it came with infinite regret, but there was no altering his decision.

Indeed, he felt himself powerless to do so. The yearning within him to see Seamore again—to see even the lights burning in its windows, much less those so dear to him within walls—was too powerful for him to control. Dangers, imprisonment, death itself would not stay him in his intention.

The ship's head was altered, and as the dusk was closing and the lamps began to appear on the distant coast, Eugene put out from the ship's side in a small punt belonging to her.

"Good-bye, François," cried Eugene. "We shall meet again. Good-bye, all!"

"Good-bye, Eugene," responded François.

"Good-bye, M. Lefebre! Farewell, Ireland! I shall see your fair shores never-more!" said MacNevin. "Trampled and crushed, but fair and thrice beloved land, farewell—for ever farewell!"

The vessel's prow was turned seaward, and in a short time a tiny speck on the distant waters showed where their gallant friend was pursuing his solitary way to that land which the others were, indeed, destined never more to see.

CHAPTER XLVII.

THE DEATH OF TONE.

EUGENE landed at the basin at Ringsend, and, mooring his little skiff to one of the rings that depended from the granite blocks that formed it, leaped lightly to the quay, and took his way along the South wall to the city.

The dusk had fallen, and the lamps began to appear by ones and twos; lights grew in the shops as he walked swiftly along; and here and there a flickering gleam showed where, on the black surface of the river, vessels were anchored.

There was no vehicle to be had in this half-abandoned fishing village where he had landed, and he could not expect to find a jingle nearer than the heart of the metropolis.

This was in no sense a disappointment to him; rather he was glad of the opportunity of a walk; it was a novelty, and a refreshing one, to him who had been so long cooped up within the narrow limits of a man-of-war or the still more confined boundaries of a cave on the Donegal highlands; and so he stepped out briskly and faced for Sackville-street.

His heart was light and his spirits high. True, the dreams of fame and honour to be won on Irish soil were over; the bright visions that danced before his eyes for years past had vanished suddenly into the gloomy land where the ghosts of things that might have been, but are not, wander in grim and uncouth shape. The high hopes of the day when, amid the thunders of French cannon, the flashing of French sabres, the charges of French cuirassiers, and the rolling volleys of French musketeers, the banner of a liberated Ireland should be unfurled amid the smoke of victory, were gone like last year's snow, never to return.

But what of all that? He had done his best; he had laboured zealously to change his dreams into realities, to turn his hopes into assured prophecies; he had done all that his right hand found to do to aid in the good cause; but the fates had been against him. The fortunes of war lay doggedly with the enemy. Chivalrous impulse, gallant effort, high-hearted enterprise, all had been enlisted in the grand cause of freedom, but with non-success. What brave hearts could do had been done. Where, therefore, was the use of repining?

> "No chains so unworthy to bind thee
>   As those of a vain regret."

Eugene may not have thought these things in this order, as with swift pace he proceeded on his way, but they alternated in his mind with other matters. He was too much of a Frenchman to burthen himself with unavailing regrets; he had fought the good fight and had been worsted; and he began to look upon the past as if it had never existed—as if it were but the hateful memory of a fevered and disordered dream.

In doing this he had—besides his light-hearted mercurial nature—a powerful aid. And that was the bright eyes and fair face of Helen Barrington. In the happiness of soon seeing her, of having his soul gladdened with a glance at the glory of her rare handsomeness, of hearing her musical voice come in welcoming tones to his ears, like angel sounds from Paradise, disappointment and sorrow, imprisonment, exile, the prison-hulk, and the storm-tossed ship, all the memories of the past, faded from his mind—vanished as the dark things of the night vanish before the first gleams of the rising sun.

Curiously enough, no thought of Sir Trevor Mortimer obtruded itself to disturb his delighted anticipations.

His mind was filled with radiant visions of her. How would she look? Was her face as fair, her eyes as bright as when last he saw her? Had she ever thought of him in all his time of imprisonment, his escape, and his stay in France? Did a remembrance of him cross her mind what time the *Hoche* tossed and tumbled on the stormy waste of waters, with the warring sea beneath, the hurricane around, and the black sky streaked with lurid lightning above? Did a prayer for him come from her lips, mayhap, what time the thunders of the British fleet were turned on the gallant ship, and the red line of fire from her guns dauntlessly replied to the foe? Did that invisible spell that connects loving hearts, though miles of land and sea lie between, that carries the sudden throb of danger or the soft thrill of joy—mysterious but certain current!—bear to her sudden sinking of heart during the long hours when the overmatched *Hoche* fought her foes, until her decks were strewn with her gallant dead and her scuppers ran with blood, and the smoke of their guns ascended until it arched the Donegal hills, ten miles away?

Ah, the *Hoche*! And Tone?

He had somehow forgotten Tone of late, and he paused in wonderment at himself and his forgetfulness. What had become of him? Brave and enthusiastic Irishman! How did his true and faithful heart bear the——

A hand was quietly laid on his shoulder—not so quietly, however, but that it made him start in its suddenness and unexpectedness. His mind was so occupied with its train of thoughts—so high-wrought—that this interruption came upon him with startling effect.

He was passing by an inn, whose lighted window flung the glare of its lamps full on his face.

"Lefebre!"

"Yes, I am he," said Eugene quickly, turning around to see his accoster, and for the moment believing it was Tone himself who spoke; but a glance undeceived him.

"I knew your face, though I saw it but once."

"I don't remember," said Eugene disconcertedly, "having seen you before."

"You have, nevertheless."

"Pardon me, but where?"

"You remember the meeting in ———"

"The night I left for France?"

"Yes."

"Perfectly."

"I was one of those present that night."

"I am glad to meet you again," said Eugene with ready courtesy extending his hand, though, indeed, now that the cause was lost beyond hope of recovery or recall, he would have preferred not meeting any of his former acquaintances. It could no good, it interfered with his present intentions, and every moment was valuable to him. He had ventured on Irish ground again for a special business, and that carried out or otherwise, the colours of France beckoned to him from afar.

Perhaps something of this shone in his face a second after his greeting, for the stranger apologetically said:

"Excuse me for addressing and delaying you. I know your mission and your anxiety as well as if you told me, and respect both. Nor would I stay your course, but that I know you would be glad to know something of your former companion—Tone."

"Tone!" cried Eugene quickly. "What of him? I was thinking of him when you interrupted me. Where is he? What of him?"

"Come with me," said the stranger softly; and forthwith he led the way into the house, followed by Eugene.

The latter was quite surprised to see the number of men that were gathered at the bar drinking; and still more surprised when the sudden opening of a door at the end disclosed a large room crowded with people.

The stranger passed into a little apartment shut off from the rest of the shop by a small door and a red curtain hung from a brass bar at the top.

"About Tone?" said Eugene anxiously, as the stranger stood still for a second or two after entering, apparently revolving some thought in his mind.

"Tone, M. Lefebre, is in prison in the city."

"In this city—in Dublin?"

"Yes; he was brought here from the North—where he was taken prisoner."

"But he will be liberated?"

"I fear not."

"He is a prisoner of war."

"I fear not."

"He is a commissioned officer in the French service."

"Even so, it will not avail."

"Not avail!" cried Eugene perplexedly.

"No."

"Why not?"

"The English Government won't recognise that. They look upon him as a rebel, taken with arms in his hands, as hundreds and thousands have been within the last four months. The fate meted out to them they will mete out to him."

"What is that?"

"Death—death on the scaffold."

"No! It cannot be possible! Dishonouring death on the scaffold! It is impossible!"

"It may be a dishonouring death in your land," said the stranger; "it is not here. It is the shrine at which for many a year the bravest and most gallant of Irish hearts have offered up their lives for the freedom of their country. But that is not to the point. Honouring or dishonouring, that is the doom intended for him."

"Bonaparte will interfere—the First Consul will prevent it."

"He *has* interfered. He has threatened to take summary vengeance on the English officers in his prisons if Tone's life be sacrificed. But to no use. He may shoot them by the dozen, the score, the hundred if he likes. A stroke of the pen at the War Office can create successors

THE DEATH OF TONE. 337

to them. But Tone's life will not be the more safe. They would rather lose a general battle than spare *his* life. Well they might."

"Are you certain of this? Do you speak with certain knowledge?" asked Eugene, in great anxiety and perplexity.

"With certainty itself. He has been tried by court-martial and sentenced. The workmen are engaged for the past few days erecting the scaffold outside his cell window. Every stroke of the hammer falls on his ear as distinctly as my words do on yours."

"My God! Can nothing be done? Can no effort be made to save him? Is there no way that ——"

"An effort," said the stranger, sinking his voice to the lowest whisper, "will be made—to-night! The gates will be forced in a few hours from hence, and he shall walk forth a free man, or he shall be buried in the ruins of the prison."

"Good," said Eugene heartily, and his heaving breast and quickened breathing showed his anxiety and his interest. "How is it to be done?"

"You saw all these men here?"

"Yes, I saw them."

"They are a portion of the men deputed for the purpose. Resolute men and true, every one of them. Each carries a dagger and a pistol. They are only one of several groups detailed for the purpose."

"How do you propose to effect it?" asked Eugene, who listened with an eager and throbbing heart to the statement.

"A barrel of powder, or two, or three—or more if the need be—will be exploded under the walls. We shall rush in through the breach made and overpower the guards. We shall force the prison and free him, though every man here piled his dead body under its battlements."

"Good!" said the young Frenchman, in high approval. "I shall be one of the party. Unfortunately I am unarmed."

"I knew you would," said the stranger, grasping his hand enthusiastically. "From the moment I saw you, I

z

knew you were destined for his liberation. I saw you passing along the quays. I thought it was you. I followed you until, in the light, I made belief a certainty. You shall take command."

"I? Nay; I am unknown here."

"It matters not. Our men will have more confidence if they know a French officer leads them. It will be a second taking of the Bastile. Do you accept?"

"If you wish it, certainly. I shall never risk my life in a worthier cause."

"Very well. In an hour or less the news will be known at every meeting-centre in the city. Don't fear defeat. As I said before, our men will pile their dead bodies under the wall of the prison or he walks a free man. Newgate will be a heap of smoking ruins or he sleeps in safety to-night."

"Reckon on me. I have perilled my life often enough for France and freedom. I may now give it for my friend—and such a friend! So brave, so noble, so self-sacrificing, and so chivalrous! Yes; I shall willingly take the command; prouder no man need pine to have."

"Settled, then. Nothing further need be said."

"When do you propose to attack?"

"At midnight. The men will gather silently from all quarters. The signal—the explosion of the powder and the breaching of the wall. After that, pistol-bullet, cold steel, and resolute hearts."

"Three good aids," said the Frenchman approvingly, "before which prison-walls and barred gates are as things of nought."

"So your people found it at any rate," said the stranger gaily. "But you must be weary and tired. I am displaying but poor hospitality. Will you permit me? Unpretending as the place looks, you can be well catered for. Not even in the city by the Garonne will you find brandy to match that these cellars can produce. Come up stairs. We shall be alone there."

The repast provided for the hungry traveller did not belie the encomiums passed upon the hostelry by the stranger. Eugene did it ample justice, listening intently meanwhile to the information conveyed to him by his companion as to the course events had taken in the metropolis and Leinster during the past six months. He was surprised to learn that most of the men whom he met the night he left for France—whose hearts beat high then with the golden hope of liberty and freedom—had perished in the prison or on the scaffold. The light of their lives had gone out as the hopes of the nation flickered and died —drowned in blood.

There was a pause at the conclusion of the information —each being engaged with his own sad thoughts.

Finally Eugene said :

" You know Seamore ?—the Barringtons of Seamore ?"

The stranger nodded assent.

" Redmond Barrington ?"

The stranger again assented.

" Perhaps you could tell me—I may not have the opportunity of hearing again—in this world at least ——"

A hurried rap came to the door.

The stranger went softly and opened it.

" Oh! is that you, Luke ?" said he. " Come in; none here but friends."

The new comer entered, a curious look on his face.

And as he did—a curious look grew also into Eugene's eyes—but not of the same character. For, whereas the expression on the new comer's face was that of horror and surprise, that on Lefebre's was compounded of recognition and pleasure.

" What is it, Luke ?" said Eugene's companion, as he took notice of this expression. " There must be some bad news. What is it ?"

The new comer muttered some words which Eugene failed to hear.

" What!" cried his companion, in great astonishment. " Dead! Who said so ? When did you hear it ?"

The reply was again lost on Eugene's ears.

" My God! It is murder—pure murder! It is the fate of Oliver Bond over again. Done to death by a cowardly hand in the silence and solitude of the prison cell. Oh, me! that such deeds should be permitted by Heaven!"

" What is the news ?" asked Eugene, advancing towards

them, struck by the look of dismay and horror that covered his companion's face. "Any news from France?"

"Oh, M. Lefebre! such news—such shocking news!"

"From France?" cried Eugene, whose mind reverted there at once.

"Oh, no! From ——"

"Seamore?" cried Eugene again, filled with fresh apprehensions of he knew not what. In truth, the look of trouble and horror on his companion's face had now reflected itself in his own heart, and a hundred evil forebodings were crowding therein.

"The news is from—Tone!" said his companion huskily.

"Tone!" ejaculated Eugene. "What of him—what of him? Has he escaped?"

"He has," said his companion in a broken voice— "escaped from further troubles in this world. They have murdered him!"

"What!" cried Eugene, who scarcely believed he heard aright.

"It is true enough, M. Lefebre. Tone will never see the sun rise above the hills of Ireland again. He is dead."

"Dead! How did it happen? of his wound?"

"Of wounds surely—but of wounds the assassin gave him in the darkness and silence of the prison cell. They have put out the report that he has caused his own death. It is the old, old story—old as Irish history and Saxon conquest—the poison cup and the midnight dagger for those they fear."

"But is it really true?" asked Eugene doubtingly.

"True enough," said the new comer; "see here!"

Looking at the official bulletin which he produced, published in an extra issue of the evening paper, Eugene saw that it announced the death of Theobald Wolf Tone in the prison cell by his own hand.

"By his own hand!" said Eugene's companion in a burst of rage and sorrow. "By the hand of the midnight assassin in the silence of the dungeon! That is how it was! They have compassed his death and avoided the vengeance of Bonaparte at one and the same time. Oh, robbers and assassins! From the days of Mullaghmast to the present, the race is the same. The poisoned wine bowl and the secret skien for those whom they fear. As it is now, so it will be in future when a foe arises ever whom England fears—really fears! O Ireland! Ireland! will thy day-star never rise!"

This news, corroborated as it was subsequently by other reliable visitors and friends, put an end to the efforts intended for his liberation, and the assembled men secretly and silently departed for their various homes.

With a heart heavy with sorrow for his friend's untimely ending, Eugene prepared to depart too. There was no further need for his service. The patriotic soul of the gallant and chivalrous Irishman was where nor Saxon guile nor treachery could reach it, and there was nothing further to be done.

"You do not remember me, I suppose?" asked he of the new comer.

The latter, filled with deep dejection and astonishment at the news whereof he was the bearer, had never once looked at the third party in the apartment. He lifted his eyes to his face now at the question addressed him, and, as he did so, the gleam of recognition that shone in his questioner's eyes flashed out from his own, and he fell back a pace or two.

"Eugene Lefebre!" he exclaimed.

"It is I, indeed, Luke, and delighted to see you. How are all in Seamore?"

"Oh, M. Lefebre!" said Luke, in his astonishment unheeding the latter's question, "where have you been through all these troubled times in Ireland? Where did you come from? Or, can I believe my eyes that it is you that's in it."

"It is I, indeed, Luke. And where I have been it would be too long to tell. How is Helen Barrington, and all in Seamore?"

"I am going there now," said Luke. "I have not been there for months."

"So am I," said Eugene. "We shall be together."

"You had better disguise yourselves a little then," said Eugene's entertainer, "these are not times when strangers can pass through Dublin without danger or without detection."

So saying, he produced for them two large overcoats, similar to those worn by the yeomen, and which, he assured them, would be a sufficien disguise.

"I am sorry," he said, as they prepared to depart, "you do not carry more cheering news with you. The stars have fought against us—the fates have been on the side of the Saxon again. I can only wish you a happier and a more successful career in France than you have had in this crushed and bleeding land. Good bye."

"I should wish to know your name," said Eugene, as he put forth his hand to his late companion. "One who was prepared to risk his life for his friend as you were— —his name and memory is worth preserving."

"My name," said his companion, as he warmly shook the proffered hand, "is Dwyer—Michael Dwyer of the Wicklow hills!"

CHAPTER XLVIII.

RETURNED!

We pass over the incidents that succeeded the return of Redmond. Full of interest or otherwise, the years move by with slow and steady succession. Old Time takes little heed of human passions, loves, or sufferings, and turns his wheel with perfect indifference as to what fate his annual circle may have for the dwellers upon earth. To some it may bring happy hearts, love, pleasure, and delight; to others it may bring wrinkled faces, whitening hair, corroding cares, and dim eyes. It is all one to him, however; he turns with ceaseless and unvarying monotony, and the years pass on by slow and steady succession into the depths of the vanished past.

Wherefore it was that two years passed over Seamore since our last presence there, and Hallow Eve night of the year 1798 had come. Much changes had come over the land in the interim, and Seamore showed palpably enough that changes had come to it likewise.

For the old gathering had departed. The spacious

kitchen that we have seen full of pleasant faces in the opening chapters of our story was nearly empty. The logs burned, no doubt, with undiminished brightness on the hearth; but they shone on no row of laughing faces, an' the shadows they threw on the walls were weird, gr ,cesque, and mocking in their very grotesqueness.

"An', Grannie honey," said Norah, for they alone sat at the fire, the others having departed to their beds, leaving the two to continue their conversation in whispers, "wasn't it quare that he never turned up? Who would have thought that goin' out for a walk, after parting with Redmond, we should never lay eyes upon him again. What could have happened him?"

"I don't know, Norah," said the old woman, crying feebly, as she pursued her wonted task of knitting, the tears falling on her ball of worsted as she did so. "Maybe the waves swept him away an' drowned him. Who knows? Who can tell?"

"I'll engage they didn't," said Norah. "Eugene Lefebre was not likely to lose himself that way. But I'll tell you what happened him. The sojers caught him, and they aither shot or hung the poor young fellow. That's what happened. An' faix it was no wan or two or three that was there to do it—for it's little his brave heart and strong arm would care for half a dozen ov 'em—no more nor Luke, poor fellow!"

The sudden twist in Norah's thoughts from the young gentleman of whom she was first speaking to Luke had the effect of bringing the tears into her eyes also.

"Ay, Luke, poor fellow! I wonder where is he now," said the old housekeeper, whose sympathetic heart beat strongly for Norah's troubles.

"Wherever he is, there is not many like him," said Norah, throwing a fresh log on the fire to shadow its brightness and hide her tears. "The heart in his body was sound an' thrue, an' wherever he goes there's no wan need be ashamed of him."

"An' why did he go, Norah asthore?—you never told me that."

"He was hiding in Wicklow," said Norah, now giving full vent to her sorrow, "after the battle of Arklow—

he got a bullet in the breast there, Grannie honey, an' a thrust from a sojer's sword; but he was gettin' all right, an' I was mindin' him, an' he was in safe hidin', until that unlucky ring turned up again."

"Anan, honey?" queried the old woman, not understanding.

"Ay, Grannie, the ring Eugene gave me the night he went away. I don't know what was the reason of id, but I never could bring myself to tell him how I came by it. I am sorry now I didn't; but I thought then he had no right to be inquirin' or misdoubtin' me, and it pleased me to keep the mysthery over him But, Grannie dear, who would have thought it? Because I wouldn't tell him, he left the house, wounded and ill as he was, athout sayin' a word to anyone, one mornin', and sailed from Arklow to France—just when all danger was over to him."

The girl's tears fell bitterly now, and without restraint.

"Norah, *aroon*, machree," said the old woman, "Eugene brought throuble to you, as well as to everyone else. It was the sad an' sorrowful time this night two years that he came to Seamore. He brought the curse with him, my dear—he brought the curse with him."

"I don't know, now, why you should say that, Grannie," said Norah, with a girl's chivalrousness, taking the part of the absent one. In truth, when Norah bethought her of the handsome foreigner, his courteous ways, his frank smile, and his airy good humour, the old housekeeper's words grated on her, and her kindly heart yearned to the lost visitor. "I don't know why you should say that. There couldn't be bad luck around or near him; for, if all we're told is true, it's the very height of good luck should be where his light step, handsome eyes, and merry laugh were. An', Grannie," continued she, drying her eyes and sinking her voice, "wasn't it well for Miss Helen —God forgive me!—I never can call her the other name! —that he came, or how would she be now? The wife of another's husband. And how would that dear girl his sister be, if he hadn't come? There are two—an' between you an' me, Grannie, you'll find it hard to match them for handsome and winning girls—that his coming saved.

Think you, would they be as happy as they are now at Seamore if he hadn't come? An'," said Norah, the tears growing into her eyes again. "if he was the means of putting between Luke and myself, it was not his fault but my own. I could have aisily explained an' settled it all if I had sense—but I hadn't. An' the young misthress, I'm sure an' certain she'll never forget the handsome ——"

"Norah, aroon," said the old woman, finishing her knitting and tying stocking-needles and all up in a roll, as she prepared to raise her bent form from her seat, "there's the clock striking twelve. Everyone in the house has the first sleep over now. We ought to be in bed long ago."

"They're not all in bed," said Norah, unwilling to dry up the flood of gentle reminiscence and regrets that were welling up into her affectionate breast. "Miss Helen nor the young ladies haven't gone to bed yet, for I can hear them talkin' in ——"

"Hush!" said the old woman interruptingly, "there's someone near the door! There's some people in the orchard!" She held up the stocking in her extended hand as a warning for silence.

"There's nobody," said Norah. "It's the ladies up-stairs you hear talking in their bedroom You can hear them down the chimney wall."

"There's somebody comin' through the orchard, Norah."

"No. It's Miss Helen that's comin' down. She has not gone to bed yet. I hear her footstep. Here she is!" continued Norah, as the young lady entered the kitchen.

"I was wondering if you remembered, Grannie dear," said Helen, as she glided softly in, and seated herself between them, "this night two years; and I came down to talk with you for a few minutes, my dear old ——"

The old woman with a motion of her stocking beckoned back the embrace about to be bestowed on her.

But her warning of silence was quickly broken in upon as the wicket gate into the orchard was suddenly slammed to, the latch of the kitchen door lifted, and two men heavily muffled up entered.

It was the time when midnight visits were the law of the land, and no family, however respectable, was safe from military intruders.

Before the sudden shudder of alarm that seized the girl had time to take effect in a scream or otherwise, one of the strangers had dropped his outer covering and stood revealed in his true presence.

"Eugene!" was the astonished cry that came to Helen's lips as her eyes fell on his face, and her cheeks grew ashy white.

If Norah were inclined to cry aloud—which, judging from her trembling lips and eyes, it is more than probable she was—any efforts in that direction were completely rendered abortive by the overwhelming squeeze which Luke Mahon gave her when he caught her, which he quickly did, in his arms.

CHAPTER XLIX.

CONCLUSION.

WE shall not weary our readers over the joyousness of the meeting in Seamore that night, nor of the narrative which Eugene gave of his adventures for the past two years.

Neither shall we attempt to tell the resumption of old loves that took place.

Nor anything further.

Only this: That shortly after, in the drawing-room of Seamore there stood one Sunday morning quite a number of people. The priest had finished saying Mass, and seemed about to perform a further office. A quiet family group apparently, but none the less one impressed with the unmistakeable signs of high standing and worth

The priest says—his Spanish accent betrayed him as having studied in Valladollid or Coimbra :—

"'I, Eugene Lefebre'—say the words after me—'I Eugene Lefebre'"—

"Nay, nay, good father," said the young Frenchman courteously, bowing most respectfully. "Not Eugene Lefebre, but—Henri Prince de Joinville."

"Prince de Joinville!" said the priest in amazement.

CONCLUSION.

He had learned the extraordinary reverence paid to that august name in the Peninsula and in France. Who had not?

"It is even so, reverend father. The proofs are here—have lain here"—pointing to the cabinet—"undisturbed for twenty years. I am indeed, as was my unhappy father before me, Prince de Joinville. That title has been in abeyance for years, but I am here to offer it, with my heart, to her who is to share its perils with me If I have brought trouble and sorrow, if my father brought trouble and sorrow before me, the fault was not his and is not mine—it is fate. It is the unhappy fortune that has always attached itself to the Bourbons. In that fortune, however, I am quite prepared to take my part. Nor shall the beautiful girl that stands beside me as my bride regret to share it with me."

What further might have been said I don't know, but a gentle touch on Eugene's arm from Norah recalled him to the fact that there were other ceremonies than that in which he took part to be performed that morning. "I suppose," said Norah in her pleasant way afterwards, "Eugene thought there was nobody but Helen and himself in the world, but Luke an' I had a notion to the differ, and so had Redmond and Kate Howard."

*　　　*　　　*　　　*　　　*

High up in the roll of famous French dignitaries, on that proud escutcheon whereon kingly hands have graven their names, may be seen inscribed the name of Helen Barrington. There are people, no doubt, who will disbelieve this story; but there are stranger things in heaven and on earth than are dreamt of in philosophy: and it is true in history and in fact that in the veins of the legitimate kings of France runs, with all the freshness of latter times, the blood of an Irish girl—the heiress of the Barringtons of Seamore.

THE END.

www.ingramcontent.com/pod-product-compliance
Lightning Source LLC
Chambersburg PA
CBHW030310240426
43673CB00040B/1117